DATE DUE

~~MY 24 '02~~			
~~DE 17 '02~~			

DEMCO 38-296

The Failure of Antitrust and Regulation to Establish Competition in Long-Distance Telephone Services

AEI Studies in Telecommunications Deregulation
J. Gregory Sidak and Paul W. MacAvoy, series editors

The Failure of Antitrust and Regulation to Establish Competition in Long-Distance Telephone Services

Paul W. MacAvoy

The MIT Press
Cambridge, Massachusetts
London, England

and

The AEI Press
Washington, D.C.

1996

London, England

and

The AEI Press
Washington, D.C.

Library of Congress Cataloging-in-Publication Data

MacAvoy, Paul W.
    The failure of antitrust and regulation to establish competition in long-distance telephone services / Paul W. MacAvoy
        p.   cm. — (AEI studies in telecommunications deregulation)
    Includes bibliographical references and index.
    ISBN 0-262-13332-6 (alk. paper)
    1. Telephone—United States—Long distance. 2. Telephone—Deregulation—United States. 3. Corporate divestiture—United States. 4. Competition—United States.   I. Title.
    HE8815.M33   1996
    384.6'4—dc20   96-21011
                                                                CIP

Printed in the United States of America

Contents

Foreword

Dramatic advances in communications and information technologies have been imposing severe strains on a government regulatory apparatus devised in the pioneer days of radio and are raising policy questions with large implications for American economic performance and social welfare. Before the passage of the Telecommunications Act of 1996, one was compelled to ask, Is federal and state telecommunications regulation impeding competition and innovation, and has that indeed become its principal if unstated function? Is regulation inhibiting the dissemination of ideas and information through electronic media? Does the licensing regime for the electromagnetic spectrum allocate that resource to less than its most productive uses? Now that the 1996 act is in place, is it likely to correct any of those ill effects?

Paul MacAvoy assesses the competitiveness of long-distance telephone service markets after the divestiture of the Bell System in 1984. The study is one of a series of research volumes addressing those questions commissioned by the American Enterprise Institute's Telecommunications Deregulation Project. The AEI project is intended to produce new empirical research on the entire range of telecommunications policy issues, with particular emphasis on identifying reforms to federal and state regulatory policies that will advance rather than inhibit innovation and consumer welfare. We hope this research will be useful to legislators and public officials at all levels of government and to the business executives and, most of all, the consumers who must live with their policies. The volumes have been written and edited to be accessible to readers with no specialized knowledge of communication technologies or economics; we hope they will find a place in courses on regulated industries and communications policy in economics and communications departments and in business, law, and public policy schools.

Each volume in the Telecommunications Deregulation Project has been discussed and criticized in draft form at an AEI seminar involving federal and state regulators, jurists, business executives, professionals, and academic experts with a wide range of interests and viewpoints and has been reviewed and favorably reported by anonymous academic referees selected by the MIT Press. I wish to thank all of them for their contributions, noting, however, that the final exposition and conclusions are entirely the responsibility of the author of each volume.

I am particularly grateful to Paul W. MacAvoy, Williams Brothers Professor of Management Studies at the Yale School of Management, and J. Gregory Sidak, F. K. Weyerhaeuser Chair in Law and Economics at AEI, for conceiving and overseeing the project's research and seminars, and to Frank Urbanowski, Terry Vaughn, and Victoria Richardson of the MIT Press, for their support and steady counsel in seeing the research to publication.

CHRISTOPHER C. DEMUTH
President, American Enterprise Institute
for Public Policy Research

Preface

THE TWO THEMATIC ELEMENTS in this book were developed in the course of research undertaken as a cooperative effort in the period just before the 1984 antitrust divestiture of AT&T from its local service operations. In collaboration, Kenneth Robinson and I produced two articles,[1] which raised three questions. What was the purpose of the largest antitrust proceeding in history? Could it be achieved by divestiture? How would antitrust and public utility regulation interact to produce the intended results? Our answers were that antitrust action was intended with the assistance of regulation to lead to competition that would displace regulation and would lead to tangible long-distance consumer benefits. Antitrust action occurred; the rest has not been obvious but rather has remained open to analysis and interpretation. I became concerned with whether those results were being achieved in the early 1990s while I was writing a book review of Robert Crandall's *After the Breakup: U.S. Telecommunications in a More Competitive Era* and Barry Cole's *After the Breakup: Assessing the New Post-AT&T Divestiture Era* for *Regulation* magazine.[2] Both volumes expected competitive bene-

---

1. Paul W. MacAvoy & Kenneth Robinson, *Winning by Losing: The AT&T Settlement and Its Impact on Telecommunications*, 1 YALE J. ON REG. 1, 14 (1983); *Losing by Judicial Policymaking: The First Year of the AT&T Divestiture*, 2 YALE J. ON REG. 225, 228–32 (1985).

2. ROBERT W. CRANDALL, AFTER THE BREAKUP: U.S. TELECOMMUNICATIONS

fits from the divestiture, but neither pronounced that goal achieved.

In the 1990s further work proved to be difficult because of lack of data on which competition could be judged. The main obstacle was an inability to test for competitiveness with the price behavior of the large long-distance carriers. But in 1993 extensive data on tariff prices became available from HTL Telecommunications Incorporated. On the basis of that data source, in preparation for an affidavit submitted to the antitrust divestiture court, I developed software and a database that produced time series of representative prices for long-distance calls. That database development was undertaken with Michael Doane and Michael Williams of AG Economics, an Analysis Group Company, and was financed by a consortium of local Bell operating companies for whom the affidavit was submitted to the court. The price series, combined with then-newly public data of AT&T on the cost structure of long-distance services, enabled me to analyze the competitiveness of long-distance markets by using tests of price-cost margins offered up by the theoretical literature in industrial organization.

The second thematic element has come from the legal-regulatory literature. Numerous studies have focused on the telecommunications industry, generally to arrive at a judgment of the efficacy of regulation. But by conflating the performance of the local and long-distance segments, their findings have been limited. Moreover, as a result of divestiture, there are now three governmental institutions wielding power over the long-distance carriers: the Federal Communications Commission, the antitrust divestiture court, and Congress. The commission after 1984 found itself sharing decisions with the divestiture court in administering entry and pricing of AT&T's services. The antitrust court built its own regulatory process in administering requests of the divested companies for waivers from the decree. Congress has weighed in with the Telecommunications Act of 1996. The result has been that after divestiture, regulation intensified, in effect by institutionalizing pricing procedures that

IN A MORE COMPETITIVE ERA (Brookings Institution 1991); AFTER THE BREAKUP: ASSESSING THE NEW POST-AT&T DIVESTITURE ERA (Barry G. Cole ed., Columbia University Press 1991). *See* Paul W. MacAvoy, *Deregulation by Means of Antitrust Divestiture: How Well Has It Worked?* 15 REGULATION 88 (Winter 1992).

affected competition as much as had antitrust policy.)

That second thematic element—the implementation of antitrust policy by regulation—has been developed over recent years with the collegial assistance of J. Gregory Sidak of the American Enterprise Institute, with whom I have taught telecommunications policy, with Solveig Bernstein of the Cato Institute, and with Cara Lombardi, a private legal practitioner.

An economics journal article on pricing competition was published in the *Journal of Economics and Management Strategy* in 1995.[3] A Yale Working Paper with Michael Williams and Michael Doane has focused on the California long-distance market.[4] The second stage of that research resulted in Yale Working Paper No. 44, which was used as the basis for seminars at the Yale School of Management and the American Enterprise Institute in 1995 and 1996.[5]

This work was undertaken with the generous support of the John M. Olin Foundation Research Program for the Study of Markets and Regulatory Behavior at the Yale School of Management. The Olin Foundation program provided funding for the price data sets, for the assistance of Kathleen Thompson on the manuscript, and for the research assistance of Sharon Winer. Her able assistance in the analysis of institutional and intercarrier interactions is deeply appreciated.

The book manuscript was given over to three anonymous reviewers at the MIT Press, who provided numerous suggestions for more research, which by and large were accepted. In addition, participants in the AEI Telecommunications Policy Project provided helpful comments and suggestions for improvements. Their assistance is more than noteworthy, as is indicated by acknowledgments and references to their work throughout these chapters.

3. Paul W. MacAvoy, *Tacit Collusion Under Regulation in the Pricing of Long-Distance Telephone Services*, 4 J. ECON. & MGMT. STRAT. 147–86.

4. PAUL W. MACAVOY, MICHAEL DOANE & MICHAEL WILLIAMS, POLICY VS. REALITY IN ESTABLISHING COMPETITION IN CALIFORNIA LONG-DISTANCE TELEPHONE SERVICE MARKETS (Yale School of Management Working Paper, 1995).

5. PAUL W. MACAVOY, THE FAILURE OF ANTITRUST AND REGULATION TO ESTABLISH COMPETITION IN MARKETS FOR LONG-DISTANCE TELEPHONE SERVICES (Yale School of Management Working Paper No. 44, 1995).

Substantive criticism and suggestions have come from Michael Doane and Michael Williams of AG Economics, J. Gregory Sidak and Christopher DeMuth of the American Enterprise Institute, Robert Crandall of the Brookings Institution, William Jentes of Kirkland & Ellis, Alfred Mamlet of Steptoe & Johnson, Sharon Oster of the Yale School of Management, David E. M. Sappington of the University of Florida, David Sibley of the University of Texas, Daniel Spulber of Northwestern University, Dennis L. Weisman of the University of Kansas, and John C. Wohlstetter of GTE Service Corporation. Editorial assistance and database production assistance are gratefully acknowledged from Colleen Connolly, Amanda Riepe, and Marshall Smith. Thanks are also due to Alex Mandl and John Sumpter of AT&T, who under oath in regulatory proceedings cited in the text provided the data that formed the basis of the cost estimates. I am most grateful for the assistance of all those mentioned but do not ask them to share responsibility for the results.

Lastly, my research is dedicated to the memory of Professor George J. Stigler of the University of Chicago, with whom I had the honor and pleasure of working in my formative years as an assistant professor. The quotation from his work on the facing page may explain why.

PAUL W. MACAVOY

"Regulation and competition are rhetorical friends and deadly enemies: over the doorway of every regulatory agency . . . should be carved: Competition Not Admitted."

—George J. Stigler, "First Lecture," in Manuel F. Cohen and G. J. Stigler, *Can Regulatory Agencies Protect Consumers?* (Washington, D.C.: American Enterprise Institute, 1971).

About the Author

PAUL W. MACAVOY holds the Williams Brothers Professorship in Management Studies at the Yale School of Management. He was formerly dean of the Yale School of Management, and dean as well as John M. Olin Professor at the University of Rochester's William E. Simon Graduate School of Business Administration. At the Massachusetts Institute of Technology in the 1970s, Professor MacAvoy was the Luce Professor of Public Policy, and at Yale in the early 1980s he was the Steinbach Professor of Organization and Management and the Beinecke Professor of Economics.

Professor MacAvoy's professional work has centered on regulation of and strategic decision making by firms in the energy, transportation, and telecommunications industries. He has authored numerous journal articles and sixteen books, including most recently *Industry Regulation and the Performance of the American Economy* (W.W. Norton & Co. 1992). Professor MacAvoy has served on the editorial boards of several journals and was the founding editor of the *Bell Journal of Economics and Management Science*. His writings on regulation have been referenced by the Supreme Court in four cases and by lower federal courts in more than twenty cases.

A considerable part of Professor MacAvoy's career has been devoted to public service. In 1965 and 1966, he served as staff economist on the Council of Economic Advisers and in 1966 was a member of President Johnson's Task Force on the Antitrust Laws. During the Ford administration, he was a member of the Council of

Economic Advisers and cochairman of the President's Task Force on Regulatory Reform. President Carter appointed Professor MacAvoy to the Council of the Administrative Conference of the United States, and President Reagan appointed him to the National Productivity Advisory Committee. Professor MacAvoy's work in Washington has also included fellowships at both the Brookings Institution and the American Enterprise Institute.

Professor MacAvoy is a member of the board of directors for several corporations, including the Alumax Corporation, the Chase Manhattan Bank Corporation, the LaFarge Corporation, and the Open Environment Corporation. His previous directorships include the American Cyanamid Corporation, Colt Industries, Inc., Combustion Engineering, Inc., the Columbia Gas Corporation, and the United States Synthetic Fuels Corporation. He has consulted and testified in numerous antitrust and regulatory proceedings.

Professor MacAvoy's M.A. and Ph.D. degrees in economics are from Yale University, and his A.B. degree as well as an honorary doctorate are from Bates College. In 1981 he was elected to the American Academy of Arts and Sciences.

1

The Importance of Competitiveness in Long-Distance Markets

WITH THE 1982 settlement of the antitrust suit against the American Telephone and Telegraph Company, there began what has been the most fundamental change in structure ever required of a single corporation and a single industry. Previously franchised by regulation with a near monopoly in telephone "end-to-end" service through its "universal network," AT&T was required by the federal court to scale back to becoming only an equipment and long-distance telephone service provider, while its former operating companies were required to specialize in local exchange and long-distance service within local calling areas. And AT&T was no longer alone, even in its long-distance service markets. By virtue of the settlement, two other large long-distance carriers, MCI and Sprint, emerged to reshape the structure of long-distance service markets.

That restructuring took place in a dynamic public policy framework. The Department of Justice, and the federal district court with jurisdiction over the settlement, undertook a process of regulating long-distance providers to develop the forces of market competition in those long-distance service markets. The Federal Communications Commission intended to use its control of the long-distance franchise to constrain prices and specify service offerings in ways that would enhance the growth of the smaller long-distance carriers.

Competition was to be the goal, and regulation of the restructured AT&T organization was the chosen instrument to be used to achieve the goal. The justification—with some validity—was that public utility regulation of monopoly service providers had for decades generated results with limited impact on consumer welfare. Further pursuit of such consumer gains as lower prices and higher rates of technical change required different policies from those embedded in the utility regulatory process. While prices for local residential services had been kept down by state regulation, prices of long-distance services were at higher levels under federal utility regulation than would have prevailed in unregulated markets. The goal was to bring long-distance prices down by introducing competition into long-distance services, given that divestiture had unbundled the long-distance provider, now without a monopoly franchise, from the local service provider, still with the single line to the household.

Would competition in long-distance markets make a difference? In theory, the stakes in competitive price reductions for business and home subscribers could be quite large, indeed. Spending on interstate long-distance services was in excess of $80 billion per year at the time of the settlement and was expected to increase significantly after restructuring. By 1989 spending had grown to $101 billion and in 1994 to $124 billion (see table 1–1). If competition emerged in the first ten years after divestiture, and, assuming that prices were reduced as a result, by no more than even 10 percent, toll service subscribers would spend $10 billion less per year.

That is so since, as competitors entered, market prices would decline as they have in other network industries after deregulation.[1] But it might be argued that, since long-distance service prices have fallen, in fact competition has emerged. Long-distance rates have indeed fallen, by as much as 50 percent, so that the argument would be that because of the outbreak of competition, since 1984 subscribers have avoided having to pay as much as $60 billion for current levels of service.

---

1. Paul W. MacAvoy, *Prices After Deregulation: The United States Experience*, 1 HUME PAPERS ON PUB. POL'Y 42 (1993).

TABLE 1–1
LONG-DISTANCE SALES REVENUES
AND ACCESS CHARGES, 1984–1994
($ BILLION)

Year	InterLATA	Local Toll	Total Toll	Access Charges
1984	51.2	30.6	81.7	20.4
1989	66.0	35.3	101.3	25.6
1994	80.7	43.2	123.9	28.5

Note: Discrepancies due to rounding.
Sources: STATISTICS OF COMMUNICATIONS COMMON CARRIERS 1994, tables 6.1, 6.2, 6.3; LONG-DISTANCE MARKET SHARES, FCC INDUSTRY ANALYSIS DIVISION (Oct. 1995); LONG DISTANCE MARKET SHARES (Oct. 1995); FCC INDUSTRY ANALYSIS DIVISION, table 5; PRELIMINARY STATISTICS OF COMMUNICATIONS COMMON CARRIER, table 2.9; FCC INDUSTRY ANALYSIS DIVISION.

\ The alternative argument is that competitive forces have not determined the observed price behavior from 1984 to 1994. To the contrary, state and federal regulatory agencies have set in place requirements that have reduced rates. Regulation, not competition, is to be "credited." The agencies have reduced the charges levied on the long-distance carriers by the local operating companies for access to local exchange services. Those access rates have constituted the major element of operating costs for the long-distance carriers; as they have fallen, so have prices, as they should have, whether they were competitive or otherwise.[2]

It is at least hypothetical that more competition would have reduced prices to much lower levels than consumers realized from the pass-through of cost reductions from 1984 to 1994. Those ef-

2. Whether prices have fallen as much as access charges is an issue in analysis of the "competitiveness" of long-distance markets. Table 1–1 indicates that they have not—the margin of interstate revenues over access costs has increased from 60.1 percent of revenues in 1984 to 64.6 percent of revenues in 1994 (equal to (col. 1 − col. 4) divided by col. 1).

fects from competition would be evident not in price levels but definitively in lower price-cost margins. The sequence of events would be that, as entrants and the smaller incumbent carriers expand, the contest for shares generates discounts on AT&T's standard tariff rates. Whether or not costs at the margin decline, the difference between prices and costs per call decline.

As is evident in their financial returns, the three large carriers have had considerable capacity for reductions in margins. Consider the recent performance of those interexchange carriers, as shown in table 1-2. The difference between their long-distance revenues and total direct costs of operations is economic rent or surplus over the level necessary to bring into the market the competitive level of long-run supply. In the short run, without capacity replacement, that equals revenues minus operating, advertising, and access costs equal to $30 billion. In the long run, the cost of replacement capacity equals $12 billion, so that rents reach an amount less than $18 billion.[3] Monopoly rents are generated from prices that are above competitive levels. The prospect would be that competition would eliminate a substantial part of those rents in the process of reducing prices toward unit costs. Conservatively, a 20 percent price decrease could by the instigation of extensive competition generate gains for business and home consumers of more than $15 billion per year in interstate telephone service charges.[4]

The stakes are high in public policy formation. Basic changes in rules on entry and pricing in the regulatory agencies, in the divestiture court, and in congressional legislation could create more competition. The most important source of new competition is entry of new carriers at the scale of AT&T, MCI, or Sprint; the candidates are the Bell operating companies, in their specific service ter-

3. There remains an accounting for selling, general, and administrative expenses (SG&A), the infrastructure costs of the three carriers. That is by and large an expenditure of rents, as is indicated by recent actions on the part of all three firms to reduce management costs in the anticipation of more competitive market conditions. But revised estimates of rents can be constructed by adding one-half of those, or two-thirds, to costs.

4. That price reduction would generate gains equal to the percentage price change multiplied by existing revenues plus a surplus of one-half the change in price times the induced change in demands. The second amount is not estimated here.

TABLE 1–2
REVENUES AND COSTS OF MAJOR
LONG-DISTANCE CARRIERS AS REPORTED, 1994
($ BILLION)

	AT&T	MCI	Sprint[1]	Total
Cost of Network Operations	4.7	1.5	2.5	8.7
Access Charges	17.8	5.4	3.0	26.2
Advertising Outlays[2]	2.8	0.5	0.5	3.8
SG&A (net of advertising)	8.5	3.3	2.1	13.9
Interest Cost	0.8	0.2	0.4	1.3
Implicit Equity Opportunity Cost[3]	1.9	2.5	1.0	5.4
Total Costs	31.2	14.6	10.9	64.7
Average Price-Cost Margin (percentage)	48.1	51.8	53.8	
Average Long-Term Price-Cost Margin (percentage)	29.3	21.8	26.1	

[1] Sprint data are for long-distance, wireless, and local operations. MCI's access charge expense is calculated as 20 percent of 95 percent of total 1994 access charges.
[2] MCI advertising from 1993 annual report is adjusted for 1994 sales growth rate. Sprint advertising expense is author's estimate.
[3] The equity opportunity cost is estimated on the assumption that the capital market requires an equity rate of return on investment of 15 percent after taxes.

Sources: FCC, INDUSTRY ANALYSIS DIVISION, PRELIMINARY STATISTICS OF COMMUNICATIONS COMMON CARRIERS, tables 2.8, 2.9 (July 1995); MCI, AT&T, and Sprint 1994 annual reports.

ritories, but their entry had been prevented by the divestiture court's prohibition of operating company operations in long-distance markets across local service areas. The Bell companies' established telephony infrastructure gives them the potential to become full-scale competitors in interstate long-distance markets. A reversal of the policy of vertical separation of local and long-distance providers that was at the core of the AT&T divestiture is all that is required.

The policy question is, then, If the operating companies were allowed to extend their service networks into the important interstate long-distance markets, how much more competitive would those markets become? Given the size of long-distance service markets, and the hypothesized effects on prices and service offerings of a full-scale entrant in each market at each location, the answer is clearly of great importance to the future performance of telecommunications. Any new policy agenda would seek to establish a regime that would generate lower prices, more service, and a higher level of nationwide economic activity. It is widely recognized that, as a matter of course, prices will decrease whether or not markets become competitive. But long-distance service has become marked by significant regulatory constraints since divestiture that have controlled entry of carriers and technologies. The alternative is to add new sources of supply into those markets that force the large established interexchange carriers to move toward more competitive pricing.

The analysis of long-distance competitiveness in the following chapters is based on the hypothesis that regulation and antitrust policies have determined the behavior of prices, market shares, and price-cost margins of the large carriers through the ten years after the divestiture. The regulators have made many attempts to influence the competitiveness of pricing in long-distance markets. But analysis here of actual price behavior of the large carriers does not lead to the conclusion that markets have been transformed by that policy process. Those attempts to increase the competitiveness of long-distance markets have had opposite results. The policy agenda, as implemented, has constrained, not furthered, the development of competition.

2

Intentions of Antitrust and Regulatory Policies as to Competitiveness

IN 1974 THE DEPARTMENT OF JUSTICE filed suit under the Sherman Act charging AT&T with monopolizing pricing and service offerings in both local-exchange and long-distance telephone service markets throughout the country. That extraordinary antitrust litigation against a regulated public utility company advanced inexorably, spanning four Congresses, three presidents, and two U.S. district court judges.[1] The end came on January 8, 1982, when Assistant Attorney General William F. Baxter and Charles L. Brown, chairman of AT&T, announced settlement of the government's suit.[2] The consent decree, as approved by Judge Harold Greene, required, among other structural changes, that AT&T divest itself of its local Bell operating companies.[3]

The principal authors of the decree—AT&T, the Justice Department, and later Judge Greene—expected that divestiture would unleash competition in markets for long-distance telephone

1. *See* Paul W. MacAvoy & Kenneth Robinson, *Winning by Losing: The AT&T Settlement and Its Impact on Telecommunications*, 1 YALE J. ON REG. 1, 14 (1983) [hereinafter *Winning by Losing*].

2. Ernest Holsendolph, *U.S. Settles Phone Suit, Drops IBM Case; AT&T to Split up, Transforming Industry*, N.Y. TIMES, Jan. 9, 1982, at A1, col. 1.

3. United States *v.* American Tel. & Tel. Co., 552 F. Supp. 131 (D.D.C. 1982) (text of the decree), *aff'd sub nom.* Maryland *v.* United States, 460 U.S. 1001 (1983); United States *v.* Western Elec. Co., 569 F. Supp. 1057 (D.D.C. 1983) (approving the plan of reorganization).

services. That, they also expected, would cause the Federal Communications Commission to deregulate rates and entry in long-distance telephone service markets. The authors of the decree expected that the discipline imposed by the operation of competitive markets eventually would replace regulatory oversight of both the FCC and the state regulatory agencies.

But the decade following divestiture saw the commission and the state agencies take only partial steps toward deregulation of long-distance markets. The analysis in chapters 4 and 5 concludes that competition among AT&T and other long-distance service providers has not emerged. Tacit collusion among the three large incumbent providers of long-distance services developed instead, principally because of the methods the commission used to regulate tariff rates and because the judgment court had forestalled the entry of other potentially competitive carriers.

It is necessary, therefore, to reexamine the central premises and purposes of the consent decree. To facilitate that reexamination, this chapter first describes long-distance markets and regulation before divestiture. Next, the chapter analyzes the divestiture decree itself and what it was expected to accomplish and contrasts those expectations with the reality of today's long-distance markets. Finally, we see how the current result has served the interests of various parties to the divestiture.

LONG-DISTANCE SERVICE BEFORE DIVESTITURE

Before divestiture, AT&T supplied, through some twenty-three fully or partly owned "operating companies," approximately 85 percent of local telephone service and, through its Long Lines department, from 80 to 90 percent of all U.S. domestic and international outbound long-distance service.[4] AT&T's subsidiary, Western Electric, was the largest producer of telephone equipment and supplied al-

---

4. STAFF OF HOUSE SUBCOMM. ON TELECOMMUNICATIONS, CONSUMER PROTECTION, AND FINANCE, 97TH CONG., 1ST SESS., TELECOMMUNICATIONS IN TRANSITION: THE STATUS OF COMPETITION IN THE TELECOMMUNICATIONS INDUSTRY 124 (Comm. Print 1981) (estimating AT&T share at 90 percent) [hereinafter HOUSE STAFF REPORT]; United States *v.* American Tel. & Tel. Co., 552 F. Supp. at 171 (AT&T concedes share of 77 percent in 1981).

most all installations for the entire Bell System.[5] Western Electric and AT&T jointly owned Bell Laboratories, a research facility that developed most of the new technology in the domestic telecommunications industry.[6]

Long-distance services were generally priced above message unit costs, so that earning on those services could be used to keep down monthly flat rates on local telephone services for home and small business subscribers. That scheme of earnings transfer was protected by state and federal regulatory agencies' policies on entry and pricing of all service providers—services with high profit margins were to be kept noncompetitive. Ultimately, however, new entrants' competition began to erode that arrangement. That competition threatened the subsidy and caused A&T to respond by cutting prices in its rate filings with the Federal Communications Commission.

Pricing before Divestiture

The FCC and state regulators read the Communications Act of 1934 to call for "universal service," the pursuit of which required holding rates for local services down to levels at or below the long-run marginal costs of just those services so that more low-income or rural subscribers would stay on the system. To do that required the long-distance service provider to take profits from long-distance service to pay for an inordinate share of the joint and common costs of the national network.

Beginning in the 1950s, technological innovations reduced the costs of long-distance service, while inflation began to increase the costs of providing local service.[7] State regulators, with jurisdiction over rates on intrastate local and long-distance calls, were

---

5. *See* HOUSE STAFF REPORT, *supra* note 4, at 159.

6. United States *v.* American Tel. & Tel. Co., 552 F. Supp. at 131.

7. GERALD W. BROCK, TELECOMMUNICATION POLICY FOR THE INFORMATION AGE: FROM MONOPOLY TO COMPETITION 68 (Harvard University Press 1994); *see also* Richard E. Wiley, *The End of Monopoly: Regulatory Change and the Promotion of Competition, in* DISCONNECTING BELL: THE IMPACT OF THE AT&T DIVESTITURE 23, 25 (Harry Shooshan ed., Pergamon Press 1984) [hereinafter DISCONNECTING BELL].

reluctant to allow increases in those local rates. By working together with the commission, they were able to institute a policy of keeping both local and long-distance rates relatively constant to take advantage of local exchange costs' increasing and long-distance costs' decreasing. Ultimately, that strategy of the regulators divorced rates on any set of services from the marginal costs of those services.[8] Business rates were pushed above residential rates, relative to their respective direct costs, and urban and rural users were charged similar rates even though the costs of serving rural users were higher.

In the 1960s and 1970s, the Ozark Plan for that pricing structure made for significant transfers of earnings from long-distance services to cover the costs of local services. The Ozark jurisdictional separations[9] procedure pooled earnings from local and long-distance services to recover joint system costs and resulted in what Judge Greene later described as a "subsidy from interexchange revenues to local rates."[10] Price levels for all classes of service were set to satisfy "revenue requirements" sufficient together to generate earnings to cover all assigned portions of joint costs. The revenues generated under the requirement were then paid to local companies as "divisions of revenues," if the company was a Bell affiliate, or as "settlements," if the company was an independent firm. At the time of divestiture, the Ozark Plan[11] was still in effect. It had substantially increased the proportion of joint and common costs borne by earnings on long-distance services.[12]

---

8. For a theoretical discussion of the case for rates oriented to costs, see William J. Baumol & David F. Bradford, *Optimal Departures from Marginal Cost Pricing*, 60 AM. ECON. REV. 265 (1970).

9. *See, e.g.*, Separations Procedures, FCC-NARUC Joint Board on Jurisdictional Separations, Recommended Report and Order, Dkt. No. 18866, 26 F.C.C. 2d 248 (1970) [hereinafter *Ozark Plan*].

10. United States *v.* American Tel. & Tel. Co., 552 F. Supp. at 169.

11. *Ozark Plan, supra* note 9, at 248 ¶ 1.

12. Under the Ozark Plan, the percentage of time that equipment was used for long-distance service was multiplied by 3.3 to determine the percentage of joint and common costs allocated to interstate jurisdictions. Thus, if such equipment was used for interstate calling 7 percent of the time, then 23 percent of the joint and common costs were allocated to interstate jurisdictions. *See* Testimony of Charles R. Jones at 11–12, United States *v.* American Tel. & Tel. Co., 552 F. Supp. 131 (D.D.C.

In fact, over time, that system of revenue shifting placed an intolerable burden on long-distance rate-to-cost margins. In 1955 long-distance operations bore a share of common capital costs roughly comparable to their relative minutes of use of local telephone plant. Interstate telephone calling generated earnings that then covered 3 percent of common costs, and interstate calling minutes accounted for about 3 percent of total message traffic.[13] But local service rates were kept relatively constant (so that earnings fell short of making the previous contribution), and the level of contribution from interstate services escalated. In 1981 interstate telephone calling earnings covered 26 percent of all fixed capital costs, but calling minutes accounted for only 8 percent of total message traffic.[14] The widening profit margins on long-distance service made the larger contributions to cover joint costs possible but also made long-distance markets more attractive to new entrants. The commission and state regulators, however, blocked competitive entry into long-distance service markets until 1977. As a result, competitive forces could not operate to lower toll charges.[15] Ultimately, the political pressures for more carrier choice increased so that the commission did allow new entrants into those markets. Local service subsidies in the separations process had to be reduced.[16]

The New Entrants before Divestiture

In the 1950s and 1960s the commission opened equipment sales markets to entry.[17] In the 1970s the agency permitted entrants into

1982).

13. CONGRESSIONAL BUDGET OFFICE, THE CHANGING TELEPHONE INDUSTRY: ACCESS CHARGES, UNIVERSAL SERVICE AND LOCAL RATES 10 (1984) (numbers estimated from chart).

14. *Id.* at 9.

15. *See* STEPHEN G. BREYER, REGULATION AND ITS REFORM 296–98 (Harvard University Press 1982); Gunter Knieps & Pablo T. Spiller, *Regulation by Partial Deregulation: The Case of Telecommunications*, 35 ADMIN. L. REV. 391, 395 (1983).

16. Paul W. MacAvoy & Kenneth Robinson, *Losing by Judicial Policymaking: The First Year of the AT&T Divestiture*, 2 YALE J. ON REG. 225, 228–32 (1985) [hereinafter *Losing by Judicial Policymaking*].

17. Hush-a-Phone Corp. *v.* United States, 238 F.2d 266 (D.C. Cir. 1956) (FCC

networkwide, long-distance service markets in an elaborate sequence of case decisions.[18] During those three decades, microwave technology that had been developed by Bell Laboratories during World War II could have made entry into markets for long-distance transportation services relatively straightforward for carriers of all sizes. New carriers could have used microwave relays to provide service at costs substantially below the fully embedded costs of AT&T's existing wire facilities that were accounted for in AT&T's rates. But the commission was wary of the impact that "cream-skimming" by new entrants might have on separations payments within the incumbent network.

The commission authorized certain nontelecommunications companies to provide microwave services for their own internal use in 1959.[19] By 1963, MCI applied to the agency to supply private-line communications between St. Louis and Chicago; MCI did not request interconnection with the Bell switched network connecting local users to other users or to long-distance trunk lines. But if granted access to that network, another carrier could offer telephone service across the country without constructing its own facilities except for initiating calls for its own subscribers. In 1969 the commission granted MCI's application, but on the condition that it offer only private, nonswitched services.[20] And in its 1971 *Specialized*

policy preventing customer's use of non-AT&T equipment was "unwarranted interference with the telephone subscriber's right reasonably to use his telephone in ways which are privately beneficial without being publicly detrimental"); Carterfone Device, 13 F.C.C.2d 420, 14 F.C.C.2d 571 (1968) (relaxing regulations on use of non-Bell equipment for equipment already in place). *See also* AT&T Foreign Attachment Tariff Revisions, Mem. Op. and Order, 15 F.C.C.2d 605 (1968), 18 F.C.C.2d 871 (1969).

18. Bell System Tariff Offerings of Local Distribution Facilities for Use by Other Common Carriers, 46 F.C.C.2d 413 (1974), *aff'd sub nom.* Bell Tel. Co. of Pa., 503 F.2d 1250 (3rd Cir. 1974); *see also* MCI Telecommunications Corp. *v.* FCC [hereinafter *Execunet I*], 561 F.2d 365 (D.C. Cir. 1977), *cert. denied*, 434 U.S. 1040 (1978); MCI Telecommunications Corp. *v.* FCC [hereinafter *Execunet II*], 580 F.2d 590 (D.C. Cir.), *cert. denied*, 439 U.S. 980 (1978); Specialized Common Carrier Servs., Report and Order, Dkt. No. 18920, 29 F.C.C.2d 870 (1971), *aff'd sub nom.* Washington Util. & Transp. Comm'n *v.* FCC, 513 F.2d 1142 (9th Cir.), *cert. denied*, 423 U.S. 836 (1975) [hereinafter *Specialized Common Carrier*].

19. Allocation of Frequencies in the Bands Above 890 Mc., Report and Order, Dkt. No. 11866, 27 F.C.C. Rcd. 359 (1959), *modified*, 29 F.C.C. Rcd. 825 (1960).

20. Microwave Communications, Inc., 18 F.C.C.2d 953 (1967), *recons. denied*,

Common Carrier decision, the commission adopted rules sanctioning general entry into private-line services.[21]

Because AT&T Long Lines made separations payments to cover the costs of the infrastructure to provide local services, while independent "specialized common carriers" (SCCs) did not, the latter could generate larger investor profits from such toll services. Thus, following MCI's lead, affiliates of Southern Pacific Railroad and other large companies entered long-distance markets where and when they were allowed. But when MCI proposed a new switched service, to be called Execunet, in direct competition with AT&T's Long Lines, the commission refused approval.[22] In reversing the commission's *Execunet* decision,[23] the U.S. Court of Appeals for the D.C. Circuit opened the floodgates to new carriers' buying AT&T's switching services and installing their own long lines in toll markets across the country.

The commission took steps to adapt to the new judicially imposed reality.[24] But the agency failed to change the separations process to reflect the effects of entry on the price-cost margins of the incumbent carrier. The commission required the other carriers to pay access charges to use AT&T's switching capacity, but those charges provided AT&T with margins that recovered only part of the joint and common costs of the national network and were less than the contributions required of AT&T.[25] Those differentials in the per-call earnings from access put AT&T's prices above the average total costs of the new entrants.[26] As a result of price

---

21 F.C.C.2d 190 (1970), *modifications granted*, 27 F.C.C.2d 380 (1971).

21. *Specialized Common Carrier, supra* note 18, at 870.

22. MCI Telecommunications Corp., Investigation into the Lawfulness of Tariff FCC No. 1 Insofar as It Purports to Offer Execunet Service, Dkt. No. 20640, 60 F.C.C.2d 25, 42–44 ¶¶ 61–69 (1976); Exchange Network Facilities for Interstate Access (ENFIA), Mem. Op. and Order, CC Dkt. No. 78-371, 71 F.C.C.2d 440, 441 n.4 (1979).

23. *Execunet I, supra* note 18, at 365; *Execunet II, supra* note 18, at 590.

24. Resale and Shared Use of Common Carrier Services & Facilities, Report and Order, Dkt. No. 20097, 60 F.C.C.2d 261, 263–66 ¶¶ 3–9 (1976), *aff'd sub nom.* AT&T Co. *v.* FCC, 572 F.2d 17 (2d Cir.), *cert. denied*, 439 U.S. 875 (1978); Resale & Shared Use of Common Carrier Public Switched Network Services, Report and Order, CC Dkt. No. 80-54, 83 F.C.C.2d 167, 177–85 ¶¶ 21–43 (1981).

25. ENFIA, 71 F.C.C.2d at 443 ¶ 8.

26. MacAvoy & Robinson, *Winning by Losing, supra* note 1, at 13. *See* Ex-

differences, AT&T's revenue share in long-distance services markets began to fall about two percentage points a year.[27] Either AT&T could have lowered its long-distance rates and faced the wrath of regulators who relied on long-distance revenues to subsidize universal service or it could have continued to lose market share.

AT&T resisted competitive inroads not only by seeking to cut long-distance rates,[28] but also by delaying or refusing to provide equal local-exchange interconnections to the competing carriers.[29] The Antitrust Division responded to that pattern of behavior by taking the position that pricing and interconnection problems of the new vendors were the consequence of the Bell System's monopoly position and AT&T's incentive under regulation to exclude competition to protect revenue sources necessary to cover total costs.[30] The Antitrust Division failed to recognize that such a pattern of behavior in opposition to competitive entry was not limited to the Bell System. For example, local telephone companies owned by GTE, and others, with virtually no toll operations, reluctantly provided local connections in much the same way.[31] Almost all independent tele-

change Network Facilities for Interstate Access (ENFIA), Report and Order, CC Dkt. No. 79-245, 51 Rad. Reg. 2d (P & F) 677, 677 ¶ 1 (1982); AT&T, Manual & Procedures for the Allocation of Costs, 84 F.C.C.2d 384, 412–31 (1981) (App. A, Cost Allocation Manual).

27. Southern Pac. Com. Co. *v.* AT&T Co., 556 F. Supp. 825, 884 (D.D.C. 1983).

28. *See* MacAvoy & Robinson, *Winning by Losing, supra* note 1, at 6 (chart indicating that the price charged by AT&T for a long-distance call decreased in 1975 and 1977). AT&T reacted to competition in the private-line market by seeking lower deaveraged tariffs for high-density areas. *Id.* at 15–16 (discussing AT&T's Hi/Low tariff proposal); Wiley, *The End of Monopoly, supra* note 7, at 33–34. AT&T's proposed and implemented price reductions prompted significant private antitrust litigation. *E.g.,* Southern Pacific Com. Co. *v.* AT&T, 556 F. Supp. 968, 968–69 (D.D.C.), *aff'd,* 740 F.2d 1081, 1105 (7th Cir. 1983), *cert. denied,* 440 U.S. 971 (1984) [hereinafter *Southern Pacific*].

29. *See* United States *v.* American Tel. & Tel. Co., 552 F. Supp. at 1354–57.

30. *See* MacAvoy & Robinson, *Winning by Losing, supra* note 1, at 14–15.

31. *See, e.g.,* United States *v.* GTE Corp., 1985-1 Trade Cas. (CCH) ¶ 66,354 at 64,756 n.23 (D.D.C. 1984) (alleged denial of equal access); Illinois Bell Tel. Co. *v.* FCC, 740 F.2d 465, 476 (7th Cir. 1984) (alleged hobbling of equipment competitors).

phone companies resisted long-distance competition, although they had neither equipment manufacturing nor toll operations.[32]

The separations scheme, rather than anticompetitive strategies, explains that opposition to entry.[33] Diminished contributions from long-distance market operations resulted from long-distance entry and caused the regulatory authorities to impose "access" charges on the other long-distance carriers for connection to the AT&T local exchange system. To be sure, the access charges paid by the competing carriers were a fraction of the settlements paid by AT&T Long Lines. Until 1984, the leading competitive carrier, MCI, paid $235 per local line per month; AT&T paid settlements on average of $600 per line per month.[34] Even with such charges, potential competition in long-distance service markets posed a threat to the traditional transfer of earnings in the direction of covering costs for local telephone services. New entrants, with increasing shares, did not have the same regulatory obligation to subsidize those local services. AT&T's declining market share meant that the earnings available to cover local exchange costs would decline. While the traditional regulatory apparatus remained, the transfers on which it operated were disappearing.

Antitrust Action against AT&T

The Department of Justice filed its antitrust case against AT&T on November 20, 1974, following an intensive three-year investigation of Bell System activities. The suit was brought under section 2 of

32. *See, e.g.*, Hearing Before the Subcomm. on Telecommunications, Consumer Protection, and Finance of the House Comm. on Energy and Commerce, 97th Cong., 2d Sess. 768 (1982) (testimony of Richard A. Lumpkin, U.S. Independent Telephone Association); Hearing on S.611 and S.622 Before the Subcomm. on Communications of the Sen. Comm. on Commerce, Science, and Transportation, 96th Cong., 1st Sess. 425 (1979) (statement of Carlton Appelo, Organization for the Protection and Advancement of Small Telephone Companies).

33. MacAvoy & Robinson, *Losing by Judicial Policymaking, supra* note 16, at 231–32.

34. See National Ass'n of Regulatory Util. Comm'rs *v.* FCC, 737 F.2d 1095, 1144–45 (D.C. Cir. 1984); MCI Telecommunications Corp. *v.* FCC, 712 F.2d 517, 527 (D.C. Cir. 1983). *See also* R. Davidson, *AT&T and the Access Charge* 7–8 (1984) (Harvard Bus. School Study No. 0-384-208).

the Sherman Act[35] and relied initially on a novel "triple-bottleneck" theory.[36] The Justice Department alleged that AT&T had leveraged its dominant position in three sets of markets—equipment, local exchange, and long-distance—to monopolize the entire domestic telecommunications industry. To prove liability, the government had to establish that AT&T possessed monopoly power in relevant markets and that it willfully had maintained that power by means other than through providing superior products, use of business acumen, or by historic accident.[37]

The department pointed to episodes that demonstrated that AT&T "willfully maintained that power" in both long-distance and equipment markets. But the allegation related to equipment markets went nowhere. Judge Greene dismissed claims of predatory pricing in equipment markets[38] and expressed doubts as to the strength of remaining equipment charges: "[W]here the government was able to show that AT&T's market share was high, it was generally unable to demonstrate significant anticompetitive behavior; where evidence of behavior was more damning, it had difficulty establishing market power."[39] And the Justice Department's episodes supposedly demonstrating exclusionary behavior in long-distance markets were likewise unconvincing. To begin with, Justice could not show that AT&T had monopoly power in long-distance markets. According to the Supreme Court, "[m]onopoly power is the power to control prices and to exclude competitors."[40] Courts often look to market share as the principal sign of monopoly power.[41] At the time of trial, despite Bell's allegedly exclusionary activities, entry into the long-distance market in the 1970s had become significant and sus-

35. 15 U.S.C. § 2.

36. *See* Hearing on H.R. 13015 Before the Subcomm. on Communications of the House Comm. on Interstate & Foreign Commerce, 95th Cong., 2d Sess. 748 (1978) (testimony of Assistant Attorney General for Antitrust John H. Shenefield).

37. United States *v.* Grinnell Corp., 384 U.S. 563 (1966); United States *v.* Aluminum Co. of Am., 148 F.2d 416 (2d Cir. 1945) [hereinafter *Alcoa*].

38. United States *v.* American Tel. & Tel. Co., 524 F. Supp. 1336, 1380 (D.D.C. 1981).

39. United States *v.* American Tel. & Tel. Co., 552 F. Supp. at 174.

40. United States *v.* E. I. du Pont de Nemours & Co., 351 U.S. 377, 391 (1956); American Tobacco Co. *v.* United States, 328 U.S. 781, 811 (1946).

41. *Alcoa, supra* note 37, at 424.

tained. Such entry even accelerated during the trial period. In fact, as Judge Greene noted in the decision, "[b]oth the Department of Justice and AT&T contend that competition in the interexchange market is growing and that this increase in competition demonstrates an absence of monopoly power."[42] But AT&T's strongest argument against the government's contention that the company had power to control price and exclude competitors in long-distance markets was that AT&T was comprehensively regulated by the commission and state regulatory bodies so as to prevent it from setting prices.[43]

The Justice Department also had trouble showing a monopolizing purpose on AT&T's part. In attempting to prove that AT&T's actions were purposeful, the department contended that AT&T had engaged in predatory pricing in long-distance markets—that is, that it raised rates for local service where there was no entrant so that it could lower rates and exclude entrants in contested long-distance markets.[44] In their influential article published in 1975, Phillip Areeda and Donald Turner defined predatory pricing as responsive prices below the alleged predator's average variable costs of targeted products or services.[45] But the Justice Department did not concern itself with establishing that AT&T's pricing practices met that or any other recognized predation standard. The government's chief trial attorney told the court, "Your Honor, we don't know whether they were pricing above any particular standard of cost."[46] Instead, the government alleged that AT&T had priced in its response to competitors *without regard to cost*, and that such "strategic pricing" constituted the functional equivalent of predatory pricing.[47] But as Judge Greene himself noted, there was no legal basis for the novel theory that pricing by a regulated utility without

42. United States *v.* American Tel. & Tel. Co., 552 F. Supp. at 171. Interestingly, the Justice Department took a contrary position at trial.

43. That argument was adopted in *Southern Pacific Communications Co.* v. *AT&T Co.*, in which AT&T faced a private antitrust plaintiff. *Southern Pacific, supra* note 28, at 825, 885–86.

44. United States *v.* American Tel. & Tel. Co., 524 F. Supp. at 1365 n.118.

45. Phillip Areeda & Donald F. Turner, *Predatory Pricing and Related Practices Under Section Two of the Sherman Act*, 88 HARV. L. REV. 697 (1975).

46. Transcript at 13,113, United States *v.* American Tel. & Tel. Co., 552 F. Supp. 131 (D.D.C. 1982).

47. United States *v.* American Tel. & Tel. Co., 524 F. Supp. at 1364.

regard to costs constitutes an antitrust violation.[48] And, beyond the analytical substance, AT&T had a powerful defense to the government's predation arguments: Even if it had used control over local service to maintain monopoly power in long-distance service, AT&T did so using rates set with the approval of the regulatory agencies charged with constraining the rate level to the average costs of all services.

The Justice Department also alleged that AT&T's delay in providing interconnection to its long-distance competitors showed a monopolizing purpose.[49] But those episodes were subject to ambiguous interpretation. They could have been no more than slow adaptation to rapidly changing market conditions but unchanging regulatory requirements. AT&T was caught between the market necessity of lower pricing and the regulatory requirements for rate averaging. AT&T did not have the option, as the Justice Department alleged, of responding to new entry by cutting rates for some services and then raising rates for others, because regulators controlled rate levels as well as specific rates to favored classes of subscribers. AT&T's response was to delay compliance with interconnection requests until the regulatory agencies gave measured and detailed guidance on the scope of the interconnection privileges. That took time because it put responsibility for the resulting rate structure on the federal and state regulatory agencies. In *Southern Pacific*, Judge Charles R. Richey observed, "Had the Commission not engaged in its usual regulatory lag and dealt forthrightly and properly with the problems as they arose, then few, if any, of the cases would now be before the antitrust courts, such as this one."[50]

Given those weaknesses in its case, the government would probably not have succeeded in showing that AT&T's actions were carried out with the purpose of monopolizing telecommunications. Nevertheless, in ruling on AT&T's motion to dismiss at the close

---

48. *Id.* at 1370; *see Southern Pacific, supra* note 28, at 914. Nevertheless, by denying a motion to dismiss following the close of the government's presentation, Judge Greene refused to reject the theory. United States *v.* American Tel. & Tel. Co., 524 F. Supp. at 1369.

49. United States *v.* American Tel. & Tel. Co., 524 F. Supp. at 1354, 1355–57.

50. *Southern Pacific, supra* note 28, at 1097.

of the government's case, Judge Greene declined to rule in AT&T's favor; instead, he put the burden of disproof of the monopolizing claim on the defendant.[51] And AT&T's defense was severed two-thirds of the way through the trial by a settlement agreement that it initiated. The department achieved its litigation objectives without a judicial decision on the merits of its argument that the dominant incumbent carrier foreclosed competition.[52]

THE DIVESTITURE DECREE

As negotiated, the settlement required AT&T to divest itself of its local exchange operations by setting up independent, regional Bell operating companies. The agreement eliminated restrictions on AT&T imposed by a 1956 consent decree[53] and left it free to diversify into data processing and other new fields.[54] The new operating companies were required to offer all long-distance carriers "equal interconnection"—that is, technically equivalent connection of a locally originating or terminating call from its subscribers to be transported and switched over a long-distance system.[55] The decree also restricted the operating companies to providing local exchange and certain within-state toll telephone services.[56]

Judge Greene refused to approve the proposed settlement without several changes, including a seven-year ban on AT&T's participation in "electronic publishing." He barred the operating companies from entering that field altogether.[57] The court approved a revised decree embodying those changes in August 1983. On January 1, 1984, AT&T formally divested its local Bell operating companies.

51. United States *v.* American Tel. & Tel. Co., 524 F. Supp. at 1343.

52. *Id.*

53. *See* United States *v.* Western Elec. Co., 1956 Trade Cas. (CCH) ¶ 68,246 (D.N.J. 1956).

54. United States *v.* American Tel. & Tel. Co., 552 F. Supp. at 179–80.

55. *Id.* at 188–89.

56. *Id.* at 228.

57. *Id.* at 180–86.

The Justice Department's Purpose

The premise of the decree was that competitive enterprises providing long-distance service, information services, and equipment manufacturing should be separated from those providing local exchange services. The first set of activities would be the province of a new AT&T, and the second would be that of local Bell operating companies. The first had the potential to evolve so that the activities would be provided in competitive markets, while the second would still operate in the single-carrier, public utility mode. In the words of the Justice Department in 1982:

> [T]he basic theory . . . was that . . . AT&T has had both the incentive and ability . . . to leverage the power it enjoys in its regulated monopoly markets to foreclose and impede the development of competition in related, potentially competitive markets . . . . The divestiture will separate local exchange functions, which, in today's technology, by and large have monopoly characteristics and are to be provided by the local operating companies, from those that technology has opened to competition, which will be provided by AT&T.[58]

The department's theory was that AT&T had monopolized the potentially competitive long-distance markets to generate earnings that were "lost" when it kept local rates artificially low. That monopolizing strategy depended on its control of local exchange markets. In 1994 former Assistant Attorney General William Baxter recollected:

> The pre-divestiture Bell System provided regulated monopoly local exchange service, but also competed in markets such as long distance that depended on local exchange service as an essential

---

58. Response to Public Comments on Proposed Modification of Final Judgment, 47 FED. REG. 23,320 (May 27, 1982) (statement of Department of Justice).

input. Because local exchange service was subject
to rate-of-return regulation that limited the revenue
yields of monopoly power, and because the local
exchange was a necessary input for other offerings,
the BOCs had an incentive to leverage their power
in regulated exchange service markets so as to
foreclose competition in the dependent markets.
Revenue "lost" to vigorous and politically popular
low local telephone rates could often be captured in
these associated markets where regulation was
usually either less vigorous or non-existent.[59]

Or was that the theory? As the Justice Department said in 1982,
when Baxter ran the Antitrust Division, Bell supposedly used the
monopoly rents from its local services to support predatory pricing
in long-distance markets:

[Divestiture] will remove the incentives and abili-
ties that have existed within the Bell System to
subsidize competitive activities with supra-competi-
tive earnings from monopoly activities.[60]

The Bell System, it would seem, leveraged *in both directions at the
same time* by using its local monopoly earnings to price below its
competition in long-distance markets while also using monopoly
long-distance earnings to subsidize shortfalls in local exchange
markets. Those apparently contradictory statements on strategies
can be partly reconciled if one accepts the Justice Department's
view that AT&T kept prices in some segments of the long-distance
markets high, while dropping them in high-volume markets where
entry of specialized carriers was taking place. But the department's
theory that AT&T had raised local service rates when regulators

59. Hearing Before the Subcomm. on Antitrust, Monopoly and Business Rights
of the Sen. Comm. on the Judiciary, 103d Cong., 2d Sess. (Sept. 20, 1994) (testimony of William F. Baxter) [hereinafter *1994 Senate Telecomm. Hearings*].

60. Response to Public Comments on Proposed Modification of Final Judgement,
47 FED. REG. 23,320 (May 27, 1982) (statement of Department of Justice).

had required subsidies to run from long-distance to local,[61] and that AT&T had also restricted long-distance carriers' access to local switching facilities, necessarily could not both hold. Thus, the department's "multiple bottleneck" theory was, at face value, only partly inconsistent within itself.

Yet the FCC adopted the Justice Department's view of the bottleneck sources of Bell's exclusionary strategies.[62] So also did Judge Greene, who pointed out that "the key to the Bell System's power to impede competition has been its control of local telephone service . . . . With the loss of control over the local network, AT&T will be unable to disadvantage its competitors."[63]

On the basis of its theory, the Justice Department expected the divestiture to achieve two goals. First, it would create effective competition in long-distance markets; second, as that was achieved, divestiture would permit reduced regulation of AT&T's long-distance operations.[64] In fact, the department believed that long-distance markets were on the verge of becoming competitive, a belief supported by some economists[65] and by Baxter himself.[66] Baxter

61. *See* MacAvoy & Robinson, *Winning by Losing, supra* note 1, at 2–9.

62. Competition in the Interstate Interexchange Marketplace, Notice of Proposed Rulemaking, CC Dkt. No. 90-132, 5 F.C.C. Rcd. 2627 (1990) [hereinafter *Competition in Interstate*]. The FCC stated:

> As a result of . . . divestiture, AT&T lost any ability to discriminate against its long-distance competitors through its control of bottleneck local interconnection facilities . . . . AT&T also lost any ability either to subsidize the prices of its interexchange service with revenues from local exchange services or to shift costs from competitive interexchange services.

Id. at 2631 ¶ 39 (quotations omitted).

63. United States *v.* American Tel. & Tel. Co., 552 F. Supp. at 223.

64. *See, e.g.*, Hearing Before the Sen. Comm. on Commerce, Science, and Transportation, 97th Cong., 2d Sess. 59 (1982) (testimony of William F. Baxter, Assistant Attorney General for Antitrust) [hereinafter *1982 Senate Commerce Hearings*]; Hearing Before the Sen. Comm. on the Judiciary, 97th Cong., 1st & 2d Sess. 68, 133–34 (1982) (testimony of William F. Baxter and testimony of Morris Tanenbaum, AT&T Executive Vice-President).

65. BROCK, *supra* note 7, at 303, 307.

66. *See* Hearing Before the Subcomm. on Antitrust, Monopoly and Business Rights of the Sen. Comm. on the Judiciary, and Before the Subcomm. on Telecommunications, Consumer Protection, and Finance of the House Comm. on Energy and Commerce, 97th Cong., 2d Sess. 76 (Jan. 28, 1982) (testimony of William F.

predicted that, despite AT&T's large market share in long-distance service, there would rapidly be "significant entry on trunk routes" upon divestiture.[67] Baxter said, "[W]e can have a very large market share without having a significant degree of market power,"[68] and "Long Lines will effectively be checked on many of its routes relatively soon."[69] Baxter also stated that divestiture would "substantially accelerate the development of competitive markets for interexchange services, customer premises equipment and telecommunications equipment generally."[70]

With the achievement of full and effective competition, the Justice Department expected that long-distance rates would be closely aligned with the marginal costs of providing such service.[71] Judge Greene similarly predicted, "[W]ith the removal of those barriers to competition, AT&T should be unable to engage in monopoly pricing in any market."[72] At that point in time, divestiture would bring about deregulation throughout long-distance telecommunications. Speaking after the announcement of the AT&T settlement, Baxter stated that divestiture would permit total deregulation of a very important portion of the telecommunications industry—the long-distance operations of the new AT&T.[73] He made the same argument in defending the settlement before the Senate Commerce Committee, when he declared, "I foresee in the near future the potential for substantial deregulation of the Long Lines function."[74] By 1991, however, Baxter acknowledged: "I absolutely did not foresee, and would have been horrified had I been able to

Baxter) [hereinafter *1982 Joint Hearings*].

67. *Justice Settles AT&T Case; Bell System Agrees to Divest Local Operating Companies*, 42 ANTITRUST & TRADE REG. REP. (BNA) (No. 1047) 82 (Jan. 14, 1982).

68. *Id.*

69. *Id.*

70. *Justice Department Publishes Competitive Impact Statement on Settlement with AT&T*, 42 ANTITRUST & TRADE REG. REP. (BNA) (No. 1052) 371 (Feb. 18, 1982).

71. *Justice Settles AT&T Case, supra* note 67, at 82.

72. United States v. American Tel. & Tel. Co., 552 F. Supp. at 172.

73. *1982 Joint Hearings, supra* note 66, at 81 (testimony of William F. Baxter).

74. *1982 Senate Commerce Hearings, supra* note 64, at 59 (testimony of William F. Baxter).

foresee, the extent to which regulation has continued."[75]

AT&T's Purpose for Making the Settlement

Why did AT&T agree to the draconian structural reorganization it had spent almost a decade and millions of dollars resisting?[76] Perhaps AT&T was discouraged by the prospect of further litigation and what was perceived as Judge Greene's hostility.[77] AT&T chairman Charles Brown thought that Judge Greene's ruling on AT&T's motion to dismiss signalled that he would ultimately decide against AT&T on the merits.[78] In 1991, however, Judge Greene repudiated the "general assumption I had decided to find against AT&T because of the denial of the company's motions to dismiss and the explanations I gave at the time."[79]

But the prospect of losing and having to appeal to the higher courts was daunting. Even with a strong case before the Supreme Court on the economics of regulation and predatory pricing, the company would be held in suspension for many years. Management perceived that it had to fall behind the new entrants in long-distance markets.

And there was another reason that AT&T was inclined to settle. AT&T's earnings from long-distance service, required by regulators for covering the common costs in both long-distance and local service, were being eroded by the price initiatives of the new independent long-distance carriers upon whom regulators had imposed lesser requirements for the use of their earnings. Consequently, AT&T let the Department of Justice do what the regulators would never have let the company do on its own: divest its low-profit local exchange operations so that it would be free to

---

75. William F. Baxter, Charles L. Brown, Stanley M. Besen & Henry Geller, *Questions and Answers with the Three Major Figures of Divestiture*, *in* AFTER THE BREAKUP: ASSESSING THE NEW POST-AT&T DIVESTITURE ERA 21, 23 (Barry G. Cole ed., Columbia University Press 1991) (statement of William F. Baxter) [hereinafter AFTER THE BREAKUP].

76. AFTER THE BREAKUP, *supra* note 75, at 40 (statement of Barry G. Cole).

77. *See* David Pauly, *Ma Bell's Big Breakup*, NEWSWEEK, Jan. 18, 1982, at 58.

78. AFTER THE BREAKUP, *supra* note 75, at 38 (statement of Charles L. Brown).

79. *Id.* at 41 (statement of Judge Harold Greene).

focus on profit-enhancing strategies in the long-distance and equipment markets. AT&T, by capitulating to the Justice Department (and thus "losing" the antitrust suit), won a reprieve from obligations to subsidize local service that it could not otherwise have avoided. Charles Brown explained in 1984:

> It had become clear that to gain access to new markets—and, in fact, to retain access to our existing markets—the Bell System would have to agree to some form of structural change . . . . [W]e concluded that getting rid of the terrible uncertainty and capitalizing on future market opportunities were more important than vindicating our past behavior in a marketplace that no longer existed.[80]

An AT&T focused on long-distance transport and switching could expand with high prospective returns while the operating companies languished as wire and cable connection providers with average public utility returns.[81] But such results were, as always, contingent on basic changes in regulation—for one, that earnings transfers from long-distance to local service would be eliminated, a development regulators were unwilling to permit before AT&T's divestiture.

At divestiture, AT&T shared the Justice Department's expectations that settlement would result in opening up long-distance markets. AT&T even appeared to welcome competition in those markets. In commenting on the appropriate size of the "local access and transport areas" (LATAs) that the decree would create, beyond the boundaries of which the operating companies would not be permitted to carry telephone calls, AT&T argued that LATAs should be big enough to "present an attractive market for potential new entrants" and to "assure that there [would] be multiple

---

80. Charles L. Brown, *A Personal Introduction*, in Disconnecting Bell, *supra* note 7, at 4.

81. *See* MacAvoy & Robinson, *Winning by Losing, supra* note 1, at 31–39; *see also* Louis B. Schwartz, *Stacked Competition and Phony Deregulation for AT&T: The Proposed Telecommunications Competition and Deregulation Act of 1981*, 3 Comm./Ent. 411 (1983).

interexchange carriers actually or potentially able to serve all telephone subscribers in the area."[82] Shortly after divestiture, Brown contended, "[I]t's obvious to the most zealous of competitors that we don't have market power in long-distance business."[83] He also asserted that AT&T's loss of market power was likely to be permanent, that AT&T would like to cut rates 30 to 40 percent, but that even reductions of those magnitudes would not restore its predivestiture market share.[84]

The promise of Justice Department support for future deregulation must have played a role as well.[85] For several years before divestiture, AT&T had sought legislation that would sanction deregulation of the firm's "effectively competitive" enterprises.[86] In fact, such legislation, supported by the Reagan administration, passed the Senate in the fall of 1981, months before the announcement of the AT&T settlement.[87] At that point in time, AT&T underestimated the strength of political opposition to deregulation; ultimately, the legislation failed in the House of Representatives. The road to deregulation through federal antitrust litigation and the Federal Communications Commission administrative rulings must have looked more promising. And subsequently, AT&T was freed from important aspects of commission and state "cost-of-service" rate regulation.

Yet deregulation did not materialize in the first decade after divestiture. Brown subsequently explained in 1991, "I did think more deregulation would take place, that regulatory bodies would back off a lot faster than has actually occurred."[88] Those unmet

82. AT&T Response to Comments and Objections Relating to the Proposed LATA Boundaries at 7, United States *v.* Western Elec. Co., No. 82–0192 (D.D.C. Nov. 23, 1982).

83. *AT&T "More Vulnerable" Than BOCs; AT&T Chairman Brown Charges Bias by FCC, Congress & Courts*, COMM. DAILY, Sept. 11, 1984, at 3.

84. *Id.*

85. AMERICAN TEL. & TEL. CO., 1983 ANNUAL REP. 12–13 (1984); *1982 Joint Hearings, supra* note 66, at 13 (testimony of Charles L. Brown); *1982 Senate Commerce Hearings, supra* note 64, at 7 (testimony of Charles L. Brown).

86. *See, e.g.*, Schwartz, *supra* note 81, at 411.

87. Howard J. Trienens, *Deregulation in the Telecommunications Industry: A Status Report*, 50 ANTITRUST L.J. 409, 423 (1982).

88. AFTER THE BREAKUP, *supra* note 75, at 26 (statement of Charles L. Brown).

expectations in turn spoke to the inefficacy of the divestiture. "As far as my expectations being realized," Brown observed, "I think the relatively slow pace at which federal and state regulation is decreasing is a disappointment and a major factor in why the divestiture setup has not worked as well as it might."[89]

Wishful Assessments since the Decree

For more than a decade after divestiture, long-distance markets have offered customers a choice of patronage with any one of three large nationwide long-distance service providers and a plethora of resellers or other smaller, facilities-based providers. Those conditions have allowed the authors of the decree, whose reputations for wisdom and expertise have been at stake, to conclude that long-distance markets are now competitive. Given that they expected the divestiture decree to produce competitive long-distance markets, their observation that competition is now prevalent is not surprising.

In 1982 Judge Greene found long-distance markets "quite competitive."[90] He affirmed that conclusion in 1987 by explaining that "competition now exists in the interexchange market, and that the entry of the Regional Companies into that market is not necessary to give it vitality."[91] In 1989 he again found that interexchange competition since the divestiture had, in fact, disipated the monopoly power that AT&T had at the time of the divestiture:

> The basic fact of life . . . is that . . . several large and effective interexchange carriers other than AT&T exist in all areas of the country, and the monopoly or quasi-monopoly situation that gave life and reason to the electronic publishing prohibition

89. *Id.* at 21.

90. United States *v.* American Tel. & Tel. Co., 552 F. Supp. 131, 189 n.234. At that time, Judge Greene briefly contemplated Bell operating company entry into interexchange but concluded that "the resulting increase in competition would not be substantial." *Id.* at 189.

91. United States *v.* Western Elec. Co., 673 F. Supp. 525, 550 (D.D.C. 1987).

on AT&T no longer exists.[92]

Further, in 1991, Judge Greene numbered among the greatest successes of the decree "the emergence of real competition in long-distance and the resulting substantial reductions in rates."[93]

The Justice Department saw competition in long-distance markets through a lens that expanded the coverage of Adam Smith's supply and demand very broadly indeed. In 1995 Assistant Attorney General Anne Bingaman said:

> The MFJ [Modification of Final Judgment] has benefitted the country spectacularly. Separating the long-distance market from the local monopoly has increased competition dramatically, as MCI, Sprint and hundreds of smaller carriers have vied with AT&T to provide long-distance service to businesses and residences. The *New York Times* recently reported that in 1994 more than 25 million residential customers changed long-distance carriers—spotlighting the MFJ's incredible success in bringing real choice to consumers. Residential long-distance rates have fallen some 50 percent since the break-up. Because of these lower prices, Americans are communicating with each other, by phone, fax and computer, more than ever before. We are closer to each other and in better touch with each other, for business and pleasure, because of the MFJ and its benefits. The impact of this change cannot be measured, but it unquestionably is profound and has changed the nation for the better.[94]

---

92. *See* United States *v.* Western Elec. Co., Civil Action No. 82-0192 (D.D.C. July 28, 1989).

93. AFTER THE BREAKUP, *supra* note 75, at 49 (statement of Judge Harold Greene).

94. Promoting Competition in Telecommunications (speech by Assistant Attorney General Anne K. Bingaman before the National Press Club, Washington, D.C. (Feb. 28, 1995) (available in 68 ANTITRUST AND TRADE REG. REP. (No. 1702) 312 (Mar. 2, 1995).

William Baxter has held to that enlarged view. He testified to Congress in 1994:

> [A]s soon as the long-distance and the local service monopoly were separated by divestiture, competition in long-distance became more vigorous. Every consumer in America has a choice of long-distance carriers—a choice that tens of thousands exercise daily. Business and consumers have benefitted from this competition. There are now four nationwide fiber optic networks for handling long-distance calls. Over the last 10 years, long-distance rates have been reduced by more than 60% in real dollar terms. And new services have expanded dramatically as long-distance competitors vie with each other to provide the newest technology.[95]

The FCC has generally subscribed to the Justice Department's position that divestiture should and therefore did lead to more competitive long-distance markets.[96] The Justice Department has stated that the decree would make regulation easier for the commission because it would reduce AT&T to more manageable dimensions.[97] Divestiture would facilitate regulatory changes

---

95. *1994 Senate Telecomm. Hearings, supra* note 59 (testimony of William F. Baxter).

96. *See* Response to Public Comments on Proposed Modification of Final Judgment, 47 FED. REG. 23,320 (May 27, 1982) (statement of Department of Justice).

97. In the words of one of the attorneys who filed the government case, "U.S. *v.* AT&T is as much about political control as economic power." BRITISH TELECOMMUNICATIONS UNION COMMITTEE, THE AMERICAN EXPERIENCE: A REPORT ON THE DILEMMA OF TELECOMMUNICATIONS IN THE U.S.A. 32 (1983). Those sentiments are echoed in Judge Greene's opinion approving the settlement:

> The legislators who enacted the [antitrust laws] voiced concerns beyond the effects of anticompetitive activity on the economy: they also greatly feared the impact of the large trusts on the nation's political system, and they regarded the power of these trusts as an evil to be eradicated . . . . The telecommunications industry plays a key role in modern economic, social, and political life . . . . [I]t is antithetical to our political and economic system for this key industry to be within the control of one com-

that the commission thought were necessary to advance further the scale of competitors while keeping a "level playing field."[98] And as the commission embraced that rhetoric, it stated that it found that long-distance markets had become competitive in reality. In 1986 the commission found that AT&T's ability to shift costs from unregulated to regulated activities was then limited by the competition that had developed in long-distance markets.[99] In 1990 the commission found that long-distance markets generally enjoyed "vigorous" competition,[100] and so the agency proposed to streamline regulation of AT&T's business services.[101] "Since the MFJ," the commission confidently asserted, "the long-distance industry has changed dramatically, becoming much more competitive."[102]

In an assessment of markets for business services, the FCC found in 1991 that "while AT&T may have certain first-in advantages, no one has shown that those advantages preclude the effective functioning of the business services market. On the contrary, we believe   .   .   .   that competition in business services is thriving, that AT&T's competitors are growing, and that consumers are benefitting from these occurrences."[103] The passage of time did not dampen that enthusiasm for the FCC's finding on competition in commercial services. In 1993 the commission concluded "that with the implementation of 800 number portability, AT&T's 800 services are now subject to substantial competition."[104] In 1994 the commission found that "[a]t this point in time

---

pany.
United States *v.* AT&T Co., 552 F. Supp. at 164–65.

98. *See* Dennis Patrick, *On the Road to Telephone Deregulation*, PUB. UTIL. FORT., Dec. 6, 1984, at 19.

99. Amendment of § 64.702 of the Commission's Rules and Regulations (Third Computer Inquiry), 104 F.C.C.2d 958 ¶¶ 84–85 (1986).

100. *Competition in Interstate, supra* note 62, at 2638 ¶ 94.

101. *Id.* at 2640 ¶ 95.

102. *Id.* at 2632 ¶ 46.

103. Competition in the Interstate Interexchange Marketplace, Report and Order, CC Dkt. No. 90-132, 6 F.C.C. Rcd. 5880, 5892 ¶ 61 (1991).

104. Competition in the Interstate Interexchange Marketplace, Second Report and Order, CC Dkt. No. 90-132, 8 F.C.C. Rcd. 3668, 3669 ¶ 10 (1993).

. . . interexchange competition is increasingly robust."[105] In 1995 the commission again found "that AT&T lacks the ability to exercise unilateral market power in the provision of [commercial] services and that there is sufficient competition among providers to justify moving AT&T's commercial services from price caps to streamlined regulation."[106]

CONCLUSION

Maintaining the illusion of competition serves the interests of all those still taking part in the largest divestiture in history. Competition was better for AT&T because divestiture would free it from the shackles of earnings diversion to subsidize the local exchange and, eventually, from long-distance regulation. It has not been freed, but chances are greater that it will still gain from further deregulation if there is agreement that the long-distance markets are competitive. At the same time, the current regulatory system works to the advantage of MCI and Sprint. Holding to the position that they are competitive helps them to preserve a status quo in which they set their prices outside the regulatory process. Thus, it is easy to see that the large three players in long-distance markets would find that describing the current markets as "competitive" is to their advantage.

But what about the regulators? The FCC, the Justice Department, and Judge Greene have had some stake in finding competition where there was none. Of course, it was possible that the commission, Justice, and Judge Greene viewed the extent of competition in long-distance markets in a way that was simply mistaken. Yet a simpler explanation is that expecting to find competition, given their premise that there should be competition, those parties

105. Amendment of Part 36 of the Commission's Rules and Establishment of a Joint Board, Notice of Inquiry, CC Dkt. No. 80-286, 9 F.C.C. Rcd. 7404, 7408 ¶ 5 (1994).

106. Revisions to Price Cap Rules for AT&T Corp., Report and Order, CC Dkt. No. 93-197, 10 F.C.C. Rcd. 3009, 3014 ¶ 16 (1995) [hereinafter *Price Cap Revisions*].

assumed that the pattern of behavior that they observed in long-distance markets was indeed competitive. In assessing the state of competition in long-distance markets, the Justice Department, the FCC, and Judge Greene did not make expert, objective observations about the competitiveness of the important markets. Instead, they made assertions that supported positive findings as to the wisdom of their own policies, past and present. That theme resonated in the self-congratulatory remarks of one commissioner in 1995:

> Our commitment to competition is pervasive and enduring. We have worked for more than 20 years to develop competition in the provision of long-distance services and customer-premises equipment . . . . The implementation of equal access has been expensive, but it has opened up competition in the long-distance market. [One result] has been that long-distance rates have declined dramatically over the same period.[107]

So long as they all believed that long-distance markets were becoming competitive, they did not need to admit that divestiture might have been, in some respects, a mistake. The commission did not need to admit that its efforts to introduce competition to long-distance markets came late to the complicated regulated pricing process of the three large service providers.[108] The commission

---

107. Fundamental Regulatory Principles for the Information Infrastructure, Remarks of Susan Ness, Commissioner, Federal Communications Commission, OECD Special Session, Paris (Apr. 3–4, 1995) (available in FCC LEXIS 2597 (Apr. 19, 1995)).

108. *See* Remarks by Richard M. Firestone, Chief, Common Carrier Bureau, Federal Communications Commission, 1992 World Communications Seminar (available in 1992 FCC LEXIS 811 (Feb. 11, 1992)):

> Telecommunications regulatory policy in the United States has undergone a fundamental change in course over the last decade, and I am pleased that the U.S. agency charged with the responsibility of regulating communications between our fifty states and internationally—the Federal Communications Commission—has

might also have sought to find conclusions that allowed it to postpone the day when it had to accept the fact that policies to develop competition (the goal of the antitrust decree) and policies to attain subsidies directed to "universal service" (the goal of public utility regulation) were incompatible. And, staying on the path toward more competition, without quite getting there, the FCC did not need to accept any diminution in its powers that might have come with deregulation.[109] If such a depiction of regulators marshaling their arguments to protect their authority is troublesome, consider the position of the commissioner wanting both success and the regulatory responsibility for continued success:

> One of this agency's proudest achievements is that it has fostered the development of a vibrant, diverse interexchange marketplace. That achievement did not happen without a good deal of work by the Commission to make the experiment in long-distance competition a success. We cannot take for granted that the long-distance competition we are so proud of will survive—or that local competition will grow and prosper—without continued effort on our part.[110]

been in the forefront of much that has been accomplished . . . .
[Since divestiture and equal access] the interstate long-distance industry is both more competitive—approximately 500 carrier entrants at last count—and more robust.

109. Statement of Reed E. Hundt, Chairman, Federal Communications Commission, Before the Comm. on Commerce, Science, and Transportation, U.S. Senate on S. 1822, the "Communications Act of 1994," and "Telecommunications Equipment Research and Manufacturing Competition Act of 1994," Public Notice, 1994 FCC LEXIS 835 (Feb. 23, 1994):

[C]ompetition must be managed and supervised by the FCC and state regulators who are charged with ensuring that the rates that consumers pay for service remain just and reasonable . . . . The divestiture of AT&T was the seminal event in the development of a truly competitive long-distance business.

110. Transport Rate Structure and Pricing Petition for Waiver of the Transport Rules filed by GTE Service Corporation, Report and Order and Further Notice of

The conclusion is that everyone in the policy formation process was better off espousing and then finding that competition was forthcoming from the application of antitrust and regulatory policies in long-distance markets. Except, of course, those who would still benefit from taking other approaches to actually establishing more competition in those markets. For them, the home and business subscribers to the services of the long-distance carriers, the question of current regulatory effectiveness remains open.

Proposed Rulemaking, CC Dkt. No. 91-213, 7 F.C.C. Rcd. 7006, 7117 (1992) (separate statement of Ervin S. Duggan).

3

Implementing Regulatory and Antitrust Policies on Developing Competition after 1984

REGULATION OF LONG-DISTANCE RATES and services in postdivestiture markets was necessarily going to affect the competitiveness of markets. The question was the nature and extent of that effect. The Department of Justice expected that divestiture would enable the Federal Communications Commission to deregulate interstate long-distance telecommunications. Assistant Attorney General William Baxter seemed to assume that the decree left the commission with relatively little role to play in long-distance markets and indeed had given it "no opportunity whatsoever" even to comment on the proposed settlement.[1] Baxter did expect that "long lines . . . at present and in the immediate future will continue to be regulated by the Federal Communications Commission," but projected that "AT&T, after the decree is approved and the reorganization occurs, will be, for the most part, an unregulated . . . and, I believe, a very vigorous competitor. . . . There is nothing about the long lines business in most markets in the United States which makes continued regulation inevitable."[2]

1. Hearing Before the Sen. Comm. on Commerce, Science, and Transportation, 97th Cong. 77–83 (1982). *See* GERALD W. BROCK, TELECOMMUNICATION POLICY FOR THE INFORMATION AGE: FROM MONOPOLY TO COMPETITION 164 (Harvard University Press 1994) [hereinafter TELECOMMUNICATION POLICY].

2. Hearing Before the Sen. Comm. on Commerce, Science, and Transportation, 97th Cong. 43 (1982) (testimony of William F. Baxter).

After divestiture the Federal Communications Commission undertook certain initiatives that proved those expectations to be incorrect. The commission's regulation of access charges on long-distance calls determined the relative size of the three large interexchange carriers. That is, by requiring AT&T to continue to pay access premiums and by setting ceilings and floors on AT&T's prices, its regulation promoted the relative growth of the second and third largest carriers. But rate setting in AT&T tariff submissions allowed the commission to retain its role as the central arbiter of the competitiveness of interfirm pricing behavior in long-distance markets.

Despite the expectations of the Department of Justice, what the commission has done cannot be characterized as "deregulation." The major suppliers in long-distance markets have not submitted tariff prices to the commission at levels that would be consistent with the actions of the invisible hand of competition. Rather, the commission has kept a visible thumb under price levels that has reduced price differences. Oddly, despite repeated insistence that divestiture has produced robust competition in long-distance markets, the commission continued to keep its thumb there over the ten years after divestiture.

ANTITRUST DIVESTITURE AND RESTRICTIONS ON ENTRY INTO LONG-DISTANCE MARKETS

There is a new "virtual" public agency that has played a key role in determining the competitiveness of long-distance markets. Judge Greene's court has set out a regulatory rule that prevented the Bell operating companies from entering interstate long-distance markets. Operating company long-distance service offerings had to remain within local access and transport areas (LATAs); in effect, they were limited to long-distance services in local (intraLATA) toll markets.

The Bell operating companies, however, did apply persistently to the judgment court for waivers of those limits. Their first substantial initiative was for the purpose of entering cellular phone service markets throughout the country. Under the decree, they were required to hand off cellular calls to long-distance companies just as they did landline calls in regular long-distance service. Judge

Greene granted integrated service waiver requests for nine metro-politan complexes of local exchange providers in 1983 that extended beyond LATA boundaries, and in 1987 granted NYNEX a waiver request to provide interLATA cellular services in the Mid-Atlantic region. By 1992, the court had granted over sixty requests, in the name of "competitive parity" or "community of interest," that for the most part made alignments between cellular service areas and LATA territories of local exchange providers.[3]

But those initiatives did not go to testing limits on entry of the Bell operating companies into long-distance wireline service markets beyond local calling region boundaries. The applicable section of the court's Modification of Final Judgment, section VIII, item C, states that the ban on long-distance services "shall be removed upon a showing by the petitioning Bell operating company that there is no substantial possibility that it could use its power to impede competition in the market it seeks to enter." Twice since the judgment a Bell operating company has petitioned the Department of Justice (in 1987 and in 1994) to remove that restriction; neither petition succeeded in convincing Judge Greene to relax the interexchange restriction. In 1986 the Bell operating companies petitioned Judge Greene directly for a general "clarification" of long-distance market entry restrictions, the effort was rebuffed as an attempt to achieve interexchange entry authorization through an underhanded process.

The first petition to enter a specific set of interLATA service markets was initiated in 1986 when certain Bell operating companies requested authority to provide interLATA services outside their own service territories. Judge Greene rejected that petition in the same year.[4] U S West, Bell Atlantic, and Pacific Telesis appealed to obtain a reversal of the court's decision on grounds that it barred the Bell operating companies from providing extraregional exchange services without prior court approval. In August 1986 the D.C. Circuit Court determined that the companies could offer exchange services outside their respective regions not connected to

---

3. *See* PETER HUBER, MICHAEL KELLOGG & JOHN THORNE, THE GEODESIC NETWORK II: REPORT ON COMPETITION IN THE TELEPHONE INDUSTRY (Geodesic Co. 1992) [hereinafter GEODESIC NETWORK II].

4. United States *v.* Western Elec. Co., 627 F. Supp. 1090 (D.D.C. 1986).

their in-region local exchange services. The court held that the Modification of Final Judgment did not impose restraints on the areas in which the Bell operating companies could provide service, nor did the circumstances of divestiture support territorial restrictions imposed on exchange services.[5]

The first test of the ban on interLATA entry within region was undertaken in 1987 as part of Judge Greene's triennial review of the performance of affected companies required under the decree. The Department of Justice petitioned the court to eliminate interexchange restrictions, although it later partially reversed itself by declaring that interexchange services should be approved on a "case-by-case" basis. It was joined by all the operating companies seeking to enter long-distance interexchange markets pursuant to section VIII(C).[6] AT&T objected to the removal of the interexchange services restrictions, Judge Greene denied the petition, and the Bell operating companies appealed. The appellate court's opinion affirmed Judge Greene's opinion; the court found that the long-distance restriction had been properly determined under section VIII(C).[7] The appellate panel (Abner J. Mikva, Harry T. Edwards, and Lawrence H. Silberman) also said that Judge Greene had to defer to the Justice Department's expert "economic analysis and predictions of market behavior."[8] The court also found that only the Bell operating companies, not the Department of Justice, could seek revisions, and that the Bell operating companies "did not satisfy their burden in this Triennial Review of showing that there was no substantial possibility that they could use their monopoly power to impede competition."[9]

In April 1994, Ameritech submitted a separate petition seeking the relaxation of limits on its entry into long-distance markets across LATAs in its upper midwest service region. That mid-

---

5. United States *v.* Western Elec. Co., 797 F.2d 1082 (D.C. Cir. 1986); *DC Appeals Court Says Regional Phone Firms May Expand Service,* 166 DAILY REP. FOR EXEC., Aug. 27, 1986, at A9.

6. United States *v.* Western Elec. Co., 673 F. Supp. 525 (D.D.C. 1987).

7. United States *v.* Western Elec. Co., 900 F.2d 283 (D.C. Cir.), *cert. denied,* 498 U.S. 911 (1990).

8. *Id.* at 294.

9. *Id.* at 300.

western operating company petitioned the Department of Justice, along with the Federal Communications Commission and the Illinois Commerce Commission, to be allowed to enter interLATA long-distance markets, given that it would "unbundle" its local network to all entrants into its local exchange markets including the long-distance carriers. The response of incumbent long-distance carriers was that even with unbundled services Ameritech would still have an advantage because, according to AT&T, it would still have the only local loop to 99 percent of the customers and thus would maintain the local monopoly.[10]

The Department of Justice solicited responses from interested parties in December 1994 and approved a plan for Ameritech entry into long-distance service that was filed with Judge Greene in April 1995. Ameritech and the department proposed that Judge Greene waive the interexchange restriction as local entry became "competitive" in two local markets—Chicago, Illinois, and Grand Rapids, Michigan—which together had four million customers and $3 billion in long-distance revenues.[11] Under the proposal, the department would monitor the development of competition and ultimately determine its sufficiency. Even with agreement at that stage, the within-state operating companies of Ameritech still needed a waiver from the Federal Communications Commission to attain the flexibility in rate tariffs they needed to meet entrants' prices. Other required preconditions included dialing parity, number portability, and state regulatory approval for prices for Ameritech to charge entrants seeking to resell its local exchange offerings. In general, as years passed, the proposal was greatly reduced in scope to selling less than facilities-based service in Ameritech's relevant interLATA markets to increase chances for approval.[12]

Ameritech's petition was still under review when Congress passed the Telecommunications Act of 1996. In the space of those three years, other operating companies sought removal of all of the

10. *Id.* at 297; David Rubenstein, *Ameritech Seeks Entry into Long Distance,* ILLINOIS LEGAL TIMES, Apr. 1994, at 1.

11. Karen Donovan, *Move over, Ms. Bingaman, New Trustbuster Is in DC,* NAT'L LAW J., Apr. 24, 1995, at B1.

12. *Justice Approves Plan to Allow Bell Company into Long-Distance,* DAILY REP. FOR EXEC., Apr. 4, 1995, at A64.

Modification of Final Judgment's restrictions. Four of the seven Bell operating companies (NYNEX, Southwestern Bell, BellSouth, and Bell Atlantic) requested in July 1994 that Judge Greene vacate the agreement's restrictions since its goals had been "fully accomplished."[13] The companies cited new forms of price controls and new regulations ensuring equal access as fundamental changes fostering competition in the interexchange marketplace. That petition, too, was still under consideration when the 1996 legislation passed.

In addition, Pacific Telesis (initially a party to the July 1994 motion to vacate) chose instead to initiate actions to open entry into long-distance service by proposing new state and federal legislation. Its California initiative is of particular interest; the resulting legislation "commands" the California Public Utilities Commission to grant Pacific Telesis entry into intrastate long-distance markets between LATAs. That legislation was in response to a California Public Utilities Commission announcement that it intended to open local toll service to competition. But the California Public Utilities Commission could not so proceed to open up interLATA markets under the Modification of Final Judgment, so that Pacific Telesis simultaneously had to pursue federal legislation to open entry across LATAs so as to meet the new state statute requirements. To some extent the federal Telecommunications Act of 1996 met those requirements. But if Congress failed to open entry for Pacific Telesis to interLATA markets by January 1995 (which indeed it did), the California Public Utilities Commission was required to order PacTel to seek a waiver from Judge Greene.[14] In February 1995 Pacific Telesis asked the Justice Department for support in seeking a waiver that would allow it to offer long-distance telephone service within California's eleven LATAs.[15] By the time the federal legislation was enacted a year later, such a waiver had not been issued.

Those initiatives have involved not only local carriers but also the incumbent long-distance carriers and the Justice Department. Their actions have sought to forestall the emergence of new sources of supply of the scale of Ameritech and NYNEX into re-

---

13. *Bell Companies Ask Court to Vacate Decree in AT&T Case,"* 67 ANTITRUST TRADE REP. (BNA) (No. 1672) 62 (July 14, 1994).

14. Jennifer Thelen, *Dialing Direct*, RECORDER, July 22, 1994, at 1.

15. *Baby Bell Seeks Help on Waiver*, N.Y. TIMES, Feb. 1, 1995, at D4.

gional long-distance service markets. The incumbent long-distance carriers have been more than wary of attempts of the Bell operating companies to enter the interexchange marketplace. In March 1995 Judge Greene issued an opinion on an MCI motion for an order directing BellSouth and other operating companies to cease development and deployment of a nationwide, linked database network capable of performing interexchange service functions as part of the operating companies' 800 services. In that case, Judge Greene cited an FCC report and order of April 21, 1989, that specifically permitted the Bell operating companies to provide the functions alleged to be violations of the Modification of Final Judgment. Accordingly, he denied MCI's motion.[16]

Meanwhile, the Department of Justice became more partisan on the side of preventing interexchange entry. While it finally supported a narrow version of the Ameritech petition, in March 1995 the department announced new guidelines that the operating companies should use when seeking a waiver from the Modification of Final Judgment. They included requirements that the petitioner provide findings that state regulators had removed local barriers to competition, that there was mutual compensation and interconnection arrangements between local and interexchange carriers, that local toll dialing parity, number portability, and access to poles and conduits all existed, and that local exchange carriers had set up separate subsidiaries for long-distance services. Such findings were all subject to controversy; that they would have been required at all was indicative of the department's position that entry should be made difficult.

Last of all was the effort of potential entrants to seek permission by other routings, principally off the face of the planet. In October 1995 a group of Bell operating companies including Ameritech, Bell Atlantic, NYNEX, and Southwestern Bell submitted a waiver request to offer direct broadcast satellite transmission of video service to customers. Such transmission would use new technology and provide new services outside the realm of the divestiture proceeding. That service offering was considered an "interLATA"

16. United States *v.* Western Elec. Co., CI No. 82-0192, filed March 5, 1992, 767 F. Supp. 308 (D.D.C. 1991).

service, which the Bell operating companies could not provide without a waiver from the judgment court.[17] As of the enactment of the Telecommunications Act of 1996, Judge Greene had not ruled on that waiver request.

REGULATORY POLICY ON ACCESS
CHARGES AND SETTLEMENTS

Divestiture required the federal and state regulatory commissions to develop new policy on long-distance contributions to cover local exchange costs. Before divestiture, the Ozark Plan of the agencies diverted a substantial part of AT&T's long-distance earnings to cover the joint and common costs attributed to local exchange service. In fact, the price-cost margins on AT&T long-distance calls had increased to more than 70 percent in the ten years before divestiture,[18] and AT&T's share of "contributions" to cover systemwide costs had increased steadily from 6 percent in 1955 to 32 percent in 1978.[19] After divestiture, given the revenue diversions from gains in market shares of other long-distance carriers, the Federal Communications Commission had to develop new transfer payment schemes that extended beyond the AT&T and Bell operating company settle-

17. *Five Bell Companies Seeking Permission to Offer DBS Service*, DAILY REP. FOR EXEC., Mar. 1, 1995, at A40.

18. *Cf.* The Historical Cost Study, Defendants' Ex. D-T-427, United States *v.* American Tel. & Tel. Co., 552 F. Supp. 131 (D.D.C. 1982). The price-cost margin for long-distance service is based on the average price and the incremental direct cost of a long-distance call; the price-cost margin for local service is based on the average price of the major local services and the incremental direct costs of those local services.

19. Paul W. MacAvoy & Kenneth Robinson, *Winning by Losing: The AT&T Settlement and Its Impact on Telecommunications,* 1 YALE J. ON REG. 1, 7 (1983). Roger Noll and Susan Smart also make that point: "Between the late 1960s and 1984, the fraction of non-traffic-sensitive local exchange costs paid from long-distance revenues increased from 10 to 26 percent, at which time the Federal Communications Commission froze the federal share at 25 percent. Had [the Ozark Plan] not been in place, by the early 1980s nearly another dollar per month of local exchange costs would have been collected somewhere else in the price structure, and most probably in large measure from the basic monthly rate." Roger Noll & Susan Smart, *Pricing of Telephone Services, in* AFTER THE BREAK-UP: ASSESSING THE NEW POST-AT&T DIVESTITURE ERA 88 (Barry Cole ed., Columbia University Press 1991).

ment process and that would allow AT&T to respond to entry by reducing its high price-cost margins on long-distance services. The commission replaced the separations process internal to the Bell System with access charges that all interexchange carriers paid to the local exchange companies and line charges that customers paid to the local exchange companies.

Access Charges

The Modification of Final Judgment directly specified that access charges paid by interexchange carriers to local exchange carriers would replace the separations and settlements system.[20] Ultimately, however, the FCC's rulings provided the steps to be taken in setting new rates for access services that the operating companies provided to the long-distance carriers. In anticipation of entry into long-distance service markets, in 1980 the commission tried to develop an access charge plan for the new carriers that would preserve the AT&T subsidy from its long-distance services to local exchange.[21] The announcement of pending divestiture in 1982 caused the commission to reconsider that plan. Staff economists at the FCC's Office of Plans and Policy urged the commission to develop a new approach that would "rationalize the industry's pricing practices, improve efficiency, and create opportunities for full utilization of market forces."[22] In short, the commission should shift contributions to access charges that all long-distance carriers would pay equally for locally originating calls at the long-distance point of presence.

But the logic for what to charge whom had to go further. Access is (1) a service of the local exchange provider to interexchange carriers, but ultimately (2) a service to the end user enabling her to reach the interexchange provider. The FCC proposed to impose not only an access charge on the interexchange providers but also flat-rate fees on end users as a subscriber line charge (SLC). The 1983 plan would recover non-traffic-sensitive costs such as the cost of lines through per-line charges and traffic-

---

20. TELECOMMUNICATION POLICY, *supra* note 1, at 174.
21. *Id.*
22. *Id.* at 185.

sensitive costs such as switching costs by a charge that varied with usage.[23] The commission explained:

> Provision of telephone services involves two marginal costs. One varies with the traffic level. The other varies with the number of access lines demanded. For this reason, efficient pricing requires both usage sensitive and non-usage sensitive charges for recovery of access costs. . . . Prices based upon the true cost characteristics of telephone company plant are necessary both to make a decision on whether use of the alternative technologies is appropriate and to make a decision on whether to substitute telecommunications for other activities.[24]

Even so, all those in the policy formation process clearly perceived the per-line charge to be an increase in local rates, for "[e]ach dollar of SLC removed a little over $1 billion of revenue requirement from the usage-based carrier access charges and required individual customers to pay an additional $1.00 per month to the local telephone company independent of the customer's volume of usage."[25] The commission's first proposal was to have the Bell operating companies collect line charges on residential subscribers that started at $2.00 per month and increased rapidly; similarly, they were to collect line charges on business subscribers that started at $4.00 per month and also increased at a rapid rate over the next few years.[26] That plan, in theory, raised monthly bills for home consumers and reduced costs of long-distance carriers by billions of dollars per year.

Those charges met with strong opposition from Congress and Judge Greene's divestiture court. The latter "noted with consid-

---

23. MICHAEL K. KELLOGG, JOHN THORNE & PETER W. HUBER, FEDERAL TELE-COMMUNICATIONS LAW §9.6.3 (Little, Brown & Co. 1992) [hereinafter FEDERAL TELECOMMUNICATIONS LAW].

24. MTS and WATS Market-Structure, Third Report and Order, CC Dkt. No. 78-72, 93 F.C.C.2d 241, 251, 252 ¶¶ 27–28 (1983) [hereinafter *Access Order*].

25. TELECOMMUNICATION POLICY, *supra* note 1, at 189.

26. *Access Order, supra* note 24, at 353.

erable surprise and some dismay that the Federal Communications Commission, far from using the access charge tool as a means for easing the burdens on the users of local telephone service, has opted instead . . . to saddle the local subscribers with the access costs of interexchange carriers . . . . [T]he agency's action runs directly counter to one of the decree's principal assumptions and purposes—that the fostering of competition in the telecommunication field need not and should not be the cause of increases in local telephone rates."[27] Judge Greene, of course, had no authority to prevent the commission's action. Further, the D.C. Circuit rejected a related state regulators' challenge to the commission's authority to set subscriber line charges.[28]

Pressure from Congress and the Senate forced the commission to partly yield. In further proceedings, the FCC set an initial level of $4.00 per month, later lowered to $3.50 per month, on the subscriber line charge on the premise that the charge would not be increased. The House and the Senate, responding to the complaint of the other long-distance carriers that the access charge plan would drastically increase their costs, had urged the commission to give them a large discount.[29] Indeed, a discount was justified as long as their customers had to dial more digits to connect at their point of presence. But the FCC decided on a discount of 55 percent to be phased out as equal quality access became available.[30] The AT&T access charge premium should have just compensated for the company's ability to provide better quality access; but the extra charge for that better access was in fact enough to induce substantial numbers of consumers to shift to MCI and Sprint's inferior access services.[31]

27. United States *v.* Western Elec. Co., 569 F. Supp. 990, at 997–99.

28. National Ass'n of Regulatory Util. Comm'rs *v.* F.C.C., 737 F.2d 1095 (D.C. Cir. 1984), *cert. denied*, 469 U.S. 1227 (1985).

29. TELECOMMUNICATION POLICY, *supra* note 1, at 198–203.

30. MTS and WATS Market Structure, Memorandum Opinion and Order, CC Dkt. No. 78-72, 97 F.C.C.2d 834, 861 ¶¶ 81–85 (1984).

31. *See* Paul W. MacAvoy & Kenneth Robinson, *Losing by Judicial Policymaking: The First Year of the AT&T Divestiture,* 2 YALE J. ON REG. 163, 251 (1985). The extent of the shift is assessed in share of revenues in the next chapter.

Separations and Settlements

Access charges did not eliminate AT&T's payments of separations and settlements to local exchange companies. The FCC began soon after divestiture to reconsider the process by which earnings attributed to the recovery of joint and common costs were assigned to interstate or intrastate jurisdictions. The commission knew that the interstate share of costs had been inflated under the Ozark Plan.[32] Pending reforms, the FCC froze the share of each company's costs that would be attributed to the interstate jurisdiction at 1981 levels; those shares varied across companies from 85 to 25 percent.[33] To reduce the size of the fund requirement to cover common costs, the FCC also required all carriers to contribute to a pool called the "Universal Service Fund" that would be paid out to high-cost companies providing service at averaged rates in low-density locations.[34] That pool was to be funded by various flat-rate and usage-based charges imposed on the interexchange carriers, but particularly by the carrier common line charge.[35]

Separations adjustments along those lines were a limited compromise. They moved interexchange prices toward costs but maintained price averaging that led to earnings transfers from low to high-cost services. FCC Commissioner Anne Jones dissented:

> The days are numbered for regulators who believe they can mandate economically irrational behavior in the telephone industry. It is unrealistic to persist in the belief that dynamic telecommunications markets will adjust to a regulator's transition timetable to preserve "equities" among affected market participants. "Equity"-driven policies may be sustainable in a slow-growth, static-technology industry. They are simply not viable in a dynamic growth industry

32. Amendment of Part 67 of the Commission's Rules and Establishment of a Joint Board, Decision and Order, CC Dkt. No. 80-286, 89 F.C.C.2d 1, 4–5 ¶ 7 (1982).

33. *Id.* at 4–5 ¶¶ 7–9.

34. *Access Order, supra* note 24, at 278–79, 281–82 ¶¶ 123, 134–37.

35. *Id.* at 283–91 ¶¶ 138–75; NARUC *v.* FCC, 737 F.2d at 1130.

such as telecommunications.[36]

Ultimately, the FCC, supported by state commissioners in low-cost states, sought to end the pooling program but not the subsidies.[37] In early 1987 the joint board of commissions working on postdivestiture policies announced a depooling plan.[38] That body of regulators proposed that line charges increase and that the mandatory pooling requirement be abolished over time.[39] The major carriers were to withdraw from the pool but continue long-term payments to subsidize the carriers remaining in the pool.[40] The commission agreed not to increase subscriber line charges for residential customers above $3.50 per month. As a result, depooling occurred in 1989.[41]

Under rules in force since 1989, the fund is supported by charges paid by interexchange carriers that use local exchange switches, if the interexchange carriers have 5 percent or more of presubscribed subscriber lines.[42] The charge is a monthly per-line charge and is treated as a specific rate element in access charge tariffs.[43] The local carriers that still participate in the pool all charge the same rates, even though their costs to provide services vary from company to company. Each company receives part of the pooled revenues to cover costs. And the FCC has initiated apparently endless proceedings on pool allocations.[44] In 1993 the commis-

36. *Joint Board, supra* note 32, 89 F.C.C.2d 2 (dissenting statement of Commissioner Anne P. Jones).

37. MTS and WATS Market Structure and Amendment of Part 67 of the Commission's Rules and Establishment of a Joint Board, 50 FED. REG. 939 (Jan. 8, 1985), adopted, 49 FED. REG. 48,325, 48,335–36 (Dec. 12, 1984).

38. MTS and WATS Market Structure and Amendment of Part 67 of the Commission's Rules and Establishment of a Joint Board, Report and Order, CC Dkt. No. 78-72, 80-286, 2 F.C.C. Rcd. 2953 (1987).

39. *Id.* at 2957 ¶ 30.

40. *Id.* at 2957–58 ¶¶ 32–36.

41. TELECOMMUNICATION POLICY, *supra* note 1, at 212.

42. Amendment of Part 69 of the Commission's Rules Relating to the Assessment of Charges for the Universal Service Fund and Lifeline Assistance, Notice of Proposed Rulemaking, CC Dkt. No. 78-72, 80-286, 4 F.C.C. Rcd. 2041, 2042 ¶ 15. (1988).

43. 47 C.F.R. §§ 69.116, 69.117.

44. *See* Amendment of Part 36 of the Commission's Rules and Establishment of a Joint Board, Notice of Inquiry, CC Dkt. No. 80-286, 9 F.C.C. Rcd. 7404 (1994);

sion noted that the fund had grown from $445 million in 1986 to over $700 million and imposed a cap on future growth.[45] AT&T complained that it was still paying a disproportionate share; and both the Commerce Department and Congress considered changes to funding universal service.[46]

State Regulators and Intrastate Toll Rates

Pending court approval of divestiture, the Bell operating companies filed an unprecedented $10.8 billion in local rate increase requests with state public utility commissions nationwide. The companies rationalized those requests as necessary to recover revenue shortfalls that would be caused by changes in payments following divestiture.[47] But the companies had other reasons for the requests, such as the adoption of accelerated depreciation practices authorized earlier by the FCC.[48] Further, however, the restructuring of the industry itself provided a schedule for phasing in changes in cost recovery practices that increased prices but were still acceptable to the regulators and the public.

Divestiture had to have an impact on local rates. The question was, however, the extent of that effect. Assistant Attorney General Baxter took the position that divestiture need not increase

Amendment of Part 36 of the Commission's Rule and Establishment of a Joint Board, Notice of Proposed Rulemaking and Notice of Inquiry, CC Dkt. No. 80-286, 1995 F.C.C. LEXIS 4697 (July 13, 1994).

45. Amendment of Part 36 of the Commission's Rules and Establishment of a Joint Board, Report and Order, CC Dkt. No. 80-286, 9 F.C.C. Rcd. 303 ¶ 3 (1993).

46. *Commerce Department Considers Universal Service Proposals*, 2 WASH. TELECOMM. NEWS, Dec. 26, 1994.

47. *See* K. GORDON & JOHN R. HARING, THE EFFECTS OF HIGHER TELEPHONE PRICES ON UNIVERSAL SERVICE 61 (FCC Office of Plans and Policy Working Paper, 1984).

48. *See* Amendment of Part 31, Uniform System of Accounts for Class A and Class B Telephone Companies, Memorandum Opinion and Order, CC Dkt. No. 79-105, 89 F.C.C.2d 1094 (1982), *reconsid.*, 92 F.C.C.2d 864 (1983), *aff'd sub nom.* Virginia State Corp. Comm'n v. FCC, 737 F.2d 388 (4th Cir. 1984); Petition of the State of Michigan Concerning the Effects of Certain Federal Decisions on Local Telephone Service, Order, CC Dkt. No. 83-788, 96 F.C.C.2d 491 (1983); GORDON & HARING, *supra* note 47, at 22–23.

local rates.[49] His theory was that there were no earnings transfers from long-distance to local exchange service in the separations process—and that even if there were, the commission could continue to generate the required amount in higher access charges:

> It is not at all clear to me that the fund flow in the direction of the local operating company that results from [the] cost allocation process is substantially more than or perhaps more at all than the funds that flow in the other direction through the license fee contract the [local operating companies] purchase of equipment [from Western Electric] . . . . [R]egulators have the authority to set . . . access charges wherever they choose to set them, and there is not the slightest doubt in the world that if they wish to do so, they can set them high enough to recapture for the local companies precisely those revenues that would have been received through the separations process under the old way of doing things.[50]

Those presumptions have been difficult to establish. Earnings paid over from long-distance to local exchange operations came to several billion dollars per year.[51] At the time of divestiture, each minute of long-distance service generated about fourteen cents of subsidy to local service rates.[52] AT&T's tariffs for twenty years prior had been set to generate high toll price-cost margins, so that net earnings from those services would provide contributions to cover systemwide joint costs and thereby keep down rates on local exchange services. But there have been no findings that showed, in

---

49. TELECOMMUNICATION POLICY, *supra* note 1, at 180.

50. Hearing Before the Sen. Comm. on Commerce, Science, and Transportation, 97th Cong. 61–62 (1982) (testimony of William F. Baxter), *in* TELECOMMUNICATION POLICY, *supra* note 1, at 182.

51. TELECOMMUNICATION POLICY, *supra* note 1, at 182.

52. DAVID M. SAPPINGTON & DENNIS L. WEISMAN, DESIGNING INCENTIVE REGULATION FOR THE TELECOMMUNICATIONS INDUSTRY 48 (MIT Press & AEI Press 1996) [hereinafter DESIGNING INCENTIVE REGULATION].

the opposite direction, excessive payments of the operating companies for AT&T equipment.

Moreover, the FCC recognized, should regulators choose to set access charges high enough to continue that transfer of cash flow to local exchange providers, they faced a significant probability of bypass by large subscribers that built their own long-distance to home office networks. Additionally, one of the anticipated benefits of competition in long-distance markets, that prices would be more in line with direct costs, would not be realized if the pass-through of access charges inflated initial prices. If local basic residential rates were to continue to be kept down, then contributions would have to come from other market sources. Political pressure was minimized by the adoption of federal and state "lifeline" programs and the Universal Service Fund to limit the impact of local rate increases on low-income subscribers.[53] But state regulators still had the onerous responsibility for funding local residential service, given that they set prices in the local exchange and toll service markets.

For the most part, state regulators controlled pricing of intraLATA telephone services.[54] Under the divestiture decree, the country had been divided into 161 LATAs large enough to include both local exchange and long-distance (toll) traffic. State regulators allowed intraLATA toll prices to achieve levels significantly above direct incremental costs while designating the resident Bell operating company the only carrier of intraLATA long-distance traffic.[55] That is, any customer dialing a 1 + long-distance call within a LATA for completion in that LATA selected the Bell operating company as the carrier of choice. But, as pressures for entry increased over time, the commissions one by one allowed the long-distance carriers to provide alternative service on intraLATA calls, albeit only after

---

53. INGO VOGELSANG & BRIDGER M. MITCHELL, TELECOMMUNICATIONS COMPETITION: THE LAST TEN MILES 77 (MIT Press & AEI Press 1996) [hereinafter TELECOMMUNICATIONS COMPETITION].

54. *Id.* at 74.

55. Ever since the costs of the local network began to increase markedly relative to the costs of providing long-distance service, "[s]tate regulations have generally chosen to increase rates for special business services, intrastate toll and enhanced services before increasing rates for basic residential local exchange services." *Id.* at 76. *See* National Ass'n of Regulatory Util. Comm'rs, Bulletin 15 (1986).

the subscriber first dialed an extra access code.

Further, state regulators held up the prices charged for intraLATA access.[56] Median intrastate carrier common line charges were about 10 percent lower than interstate charges in 1985, but by 1990 they were twice the interstate charges. Twenty states, mainly those with high rural populations, had charges more than double the interstate average access charge.[57]

Access for AT&T versus the Other Common Carriers

Before divestiture, the other carriers had paid AT&T for access in originating or terminating calls pursuant to negotiated agreements; on average, they paid substantially less for access than AT&T's Long Lines settlements. The larger carriers such as MCI increased in size relative to AT&T, but their success came from access costs enough lower than AT&T's to compensate for AT&T's advantages from scale and extensive integration. At least one analyst's position was that "MCI's pre-divestiture high profits were mainly the result of its advantageous rates for local access."[58] The proof of that emerged in the year of divestiture, when MCI's profits disappeared with rising access costs and AT&T's new lower price level that resulted from the shift from the settlements to the access charge system:

> During 1984 MCI's gross revenue increased by 30 percent to almost $2 billion, but access costs increased from 17.2 percent of gross revenue in 1983 to 24.5 percent of revenue in 1984. While MCI's access cost was increasing, AT&T's prices were forced down to show consumer benefit from the access charge plan, and therefore MCI was required to reduce its prices to remain competitive. MCI's pretax profit rate dropped from 18.5 percent of revenue in 1983 to 2.6 percent of revenue in 1984.

56. *Id.*
57. TELECOMMUNICATIONS COMPETITION, *supra* note 53, at 112.
58. TELECOMMUNICATION POLICY, *supra* note 1, at 208.

. . . By late 1984 MCI stock had plunged to one-quarter of its 1983 high.[59]

MCI was the largest and strongest of the non-AT&T long-distance carriers. Smaller interexchange companies were worse off. It began to appear that not many of those carriers were going to be able to operate in postdivestiture long-distance markets. But then, in the late 1980s, the commission intervened to ensure that the smaller carriers would not pay so much for access, even for equal access, as did AT&T.

The logic of the FCC's position was based on a new concept of equal access. The obligation of a common carrier to offer other carriers the right to interconnect with its network can be said to follow from common carrier law generally: what it came to was that alternative carriers could be "customers," and when buying carriage, they were entitled to service on nondiscriminatory terms with respect to other customers.[60] In 1971 the FCC had introduced the concept of "equal access" by declaring that monopoly carriers must interconnect with entrants:

> [W]here a carrier has monopoly control over essential facilities we will not condone any policy or practice whereby such carrier would discriminate in favor of an affiliated carrier or show favoritism among competitors.[61]

The consent decree imposed a consistent "equal-access" obligation on the divested Bell operating companies by requiring them to provide access "equal in type, quality and price to that provided to

---

59. *Id.* at 209.

60. FEDERAL TELECOMMUNICATIONS LAW, *supra* note 23, at §12.7.

61. Establishment of Policies and Procedures for Consideration of Application to Provide Specialized Common Carrier Services in the Domestic Public Point-to-Point Microwave Radio Service, First Report and Order, Dkt. No. 18920, 29 F.C.C.2d 870, 940 ¶ 157 (1971); Establishment of Policies and Procedures for Consideration of Application to Provide Specialized Common Carrier Services in the Domestic Public Point-to-Point Microwave Radio Service, Notice of Inquiry, Dkt. No. 18920, 24 F.C.C.2d 318, 347 ¶ 67 (1970).

AT&T and its affiliates."[62] They were directed to update their networks to provide equal access in virtually all central switching offices by September 1986.[63] Inspired by that commandment, shortly after divestiture, the FCC directed all local exchange carriers to begin the changes necessary.[64] At the time of divestiture, there were no equal access lines. By 1985, 43 percent of lines had been converted. By 1990, 93 percent of lines were converted, including 95 percent of Bell operating company lines.[65] And in 1995 the commission found that 97 percent of lines had been converted.

The FCC also took steps to ensure equal access to companies that offered "800" and "900" billing services. At one time, any company that wanted to change long-distance companies also had to change its 800 number because routing information was encoded in the number itself; numbers were not "portable" from one carrier to another.[66] In 1991 the commission concluded that full competition in the 800 market would not develop until numbers were portable.[67] In 1993 the FCC asserted that "with the implementation of 800 number portability, AT&T's 800 services are now subject to substantial competition."[68] The FCC also took steps to establish equal access for providers of calling cards.[69]

But beyond the open network, the critical step was to invoke the equal-charge requirement. The FCC had determined that it would slowly move access charges toward costs. The divestiture decree required:

62. Modification of Final Judgment §II(A), *cited in* United States *v.* AT&T, 552 F. Supp. 225, 227.

63. *See* United States *v.* AT&T, 552 F. Supp. 233.

64. MTS and WATS Market Structure Phase III, Report and Order, CC Dkt. No. 78-72, 100 F.C.C.2d 860, 861 ¶ 3 (1985).

65. Competition in the Interstate Interexchange Marketplace, Notice of Proposed Rulemaking, CC Dkt. No. 90-132, 5 F.C.C. Rcd. 2627, 2632 ¶ 45 (1990).

66. *See* Provision of Access for 800 Service, Memorandum Opinion and Order, CC Dkt. No. 86-10, 6 F.C.C. Rcd. 5421-22 ¶ 3 (1991).

67. Competition in the Interstate Interexchange Marketplace, Report and Order, CC Dkt. No. 90-132, 6 F.C.C. Rcd. 5880, 5904 ¶ 145 (1991) [hereinafter *Interexchange Competition*].

68. Competition in the Interstate Interexchange Marketplace, Second Report and Order, CC Dkt. No. 90-132, 8 F.C.C. Rcd. 3668, 3669 ¶ 10 (1993).

69. *Interexchange Competition, supra* note 67, at 2632 ¶¶ 77–81.

Each tariff for exchange access shall be filed on an unbundled basis specifying each type of service, element by element, and no tariff shall require an interexchange carrier to pay for types of exchange access that it does not utilize. The charges for each type of exchange access shall be cost justified and any differences in charges to carriers shall be cost justified on the basis of differences in services provided.[70]

But the other carriers believed that they would be disadvantaged if they were to pay equal access charges. They would be paying more than they had paid under the exchange agreements. But the local Bell operating companies could provide access to AT&T at lower costs than to the other carriers, because AT&T's lines merged with the Bell operating companies' switching facilities, so that AT&T was entitled on cost savings grounds to volume discounts. Even so, the decree required the other carriers to pay the same rates for access as AT&T:

Notwithstanding the requirements of paragraph (2), from the date of reorganization specified in section I until September 1, 1991, the charges for delivery or receipt of traffic of the same type between end offices and facilities of interexchange carriers within an exchange area, or within reasonable subzones of an exchange area, shall be equal, per unit of traffic delivered or received, for all interexchange carriers; provided, that the facilities of any interexchange carrier within five miles of an AT&T class 4 switch shall, with respect to end offices served by such class 4 switch, be considered to be in the same subzone as such class 4 switch.[71]

70. Modification of Final Judgment, App. B ¶ B(2), *cited in* United States *v.* AT&T, 552 F. Supp. 131.
71. Decree App. B ¶ B(3).

That "equal-charge rule" was set to expire in September 1991,[72] and it conflicted with the FCC's *Access Order*, which proscribed a rate structure for transport charges that reflected the commission's finding that transport costs were sensitive to both usage and distance.[73] Nevertheless, the FCC agreed to waive its rules to permit AT&T and the Bell operating companies to comply with the Modification of Final Judgment.[74]

As the expiration of the equal-charge rule loomed, the other facilities-based common carriers demanded relief from the FCC.[75] Sprint claimed that bringing access charges into line with access costs would raise its charges by 10 percent, while AT&T's would fall by 6 percent. Sprint emphasized the advantages that volume discounts would give AT&T, simply because "its enormous size over other carriers makes it most likely to have the volumes necessary in any given location to take full advantage of these discounts."[76] AT&T projected that abandoning the equal-charge rule would give it switched access costs 15 percent lower than midsized carriers' access costs and 26 percent lower than smaller carriers' access costs.[77] CompTel complained that AT&T's cost advantages would generate incremental operating earnings that would come to $698 million annually, "twice the combined 1988 net income of those AT&T rivals that were profitable that year. That amount is eight times the combined 1988 net income of third tier carriers with revenues in excess of $10 million."[78] CompTel concluded that,

72. Decree App. B ¶ B(3).

73. *Access Order, supra* note 24, at 309, 313 ¶¶ 230, 241.

74. *See* American Tel. and Tel. Co., Petition for Waiver of Sections 69.1(b), 69.3(e), 69.4(b)(7) and (8), 69.101, 69.111 and 69.112 of the Commission's Rules and Regulations, 94 F.C.C.2d 545, 547 ¶ 4 (1983); *Reconsideration Order*, 97 F.C.C.2d at 862 ¶ 88 (waiver extended through May 31, 1985); MTS and WATS Market Structure, Mem. Op. and Order, CC Dkt. No. 78-72, Phase I, 50 FED. REG. 9633 ¶ 7 (1985) (waiver extended until further notice).

75. GEODESIC NETWORK II, *supra* note 3, at 3.24–3.26.

76. Reply Comments of Sprint at 6, Expanded Interconnection with Local Telephone Companies, No. 91-141 (FCC Sept. 20, 1991).

77. *See* MTS and WATS Market Structure, Phase I, Order and Further Notice of Proposed Rulemaking, CC Dkt. No. 78-72, 6 F.C.C. Rcd. 5341, 5342 n.15 (1991) [hereinafter *Phase I Order*].

78. Comments and Request for Further Proceedings of CompTel, MTS and WATS Market Structure, No. 78-72, at 33 (FCC Feb. 22, 1991).

without the equal-charge rule, "there is absolutely no possibility of long-run competition."[79] Abolition of the equal-charge rule "would wipe out the razor thin margins under which the smaller [long-distance] carriers are doing business these days."[80] CompTel argued that the equal-charge rule could not ever be abolished if AT&T's smaller competitors were to survive—trying to phase out the rule "would result in a slow death rather than a quick death."[81] The FCC in response extended the equal-charge rule temporarily[82] but ultimately concluded that "the equal charge rate structure cannot remain in place if customers are to receive the benefits of switched transport competition."[83]

Yet in late 1992 the commission went further in the same direction by requiring access rates that promoted "full and fair interexchange competition."[84] The FCC refused to take any action that could "endanger the availability of pluralistic supply in the interexchange market"[85] and kept the equal-charge system in place from November 1993 to October 1995.

In the end the FCC failed to come up with permanent rules to replace the interim rules and extended the October 1995 deadline. The commission cited Bell operating company estimates that the new rates would lower AT&T's switched access costs by 0.6 percent, would raise midsized carriers' costs 0.9 percent, and would raise smaller carriers' costs 1.8 percent.[86] The FCC also found that "[b]ecause total switched access costs account on average for only approximately 40 percent of an interexchange carrier's total costs, assuming the carrier is facilities-based, the impact would be slightly

---

79. *On Regulatory Front, Smaller Carriers See Major Battles in 1992*, LONG DISTANCE OUTLOOK, Mar. 1992, at 3 (quoting CompTel president James Smith).

80. *Id.*

81. *Id.*

82. *Phase I Order, supra* note 77, at 5344; *see also The Little Guys of Long-Distance Are Mighty Nervous*, BUS. WK., June 3, 1991, at 29.

83. Transport Rate Structure and Pricing Petition for Waiver of the Transport Rules filed by GTE Service Corporation, Report and Order and Further Notice of Proposed Rulemaking, CC Dkt. No. 91-213, 7 F.C.C. Rcd. 7006, 7008 ¶ 2 (1992).

84. *Id.* at 7009 ¶ 5.

85. *Id.* at 7008 ¶ 5.

86. *Id.* at 7041 ¶ 67.

less than half those percentages.[87] The extension de facto has established interstate access charges that result in all carriers' having the same access charges and thus virtually the same operating costs.

Price Caps on Access Charges

On January 1, 1991, the FCC moved the local carriers' access charges from rate-of-return regulation to the new price cap regulatory process.[88] Price caps were made mandatory for the Bell operating companies and for GTE Corporation. Smaller carriers could choose whether or not to be regulated under a price cap system, but all price cap carriers, voluntary or mandatory, were required to participate on an "all-or-nothing" basis—all affiliates had to enter one or the other system.[89]

Under price caps, the FCC divided the different elements of access into four "baskets," for common-line, traffic-sensitive, special-access, and interexchange access.[90] The commission capped average price increases in each basket at a maximum equal to the economywide inflation rate minus an "X-factor" that measured relative industry change in productivity.[91] The FCC's estimates of productivity for the industry in excess of that for the economy were from –2.6 percent to +6.6 percent per year, but company-to-company productivity varied. The FCC's 1991 price cap plan permitted local carriers to select from a 4.3 percent to a 3.3 percent offset; if the local carrier selected the more challenging 4.3 percent, it could retain more of its profits under a less onerous requirement to share excess net returns with customers.[92]

87. *Id.* at 7042 ¶ 68.

88. Policy and Rules Concerning Rates for Dominant Carriers, Second Report and Order, CC Dkt. No. 87-313, 5 F.C.C. Rcd. 6786 [hereinafter *LEC Price Cap Order*], and Erratum, 5 F.C.C. Rcd. 7664 (1990), *mod'd on recons.*, 6 F.C.C. Rcd. 2637 (1991) [hereinafter *LEC Price Cap Reconsideration Order*].

89. *LEC Price Cap Order, supra* note 88, at 6789 ¶ 18.

90. *Id.* at 6788 ¶ 14. Service categories are used in the traffic-sensitive basket—(1) local switching, (2) local transport, and (3) information—and in the special-access basket—(1) voice grade/WATS/metallic/telegraph, (2) audio/video, (3) high capacity/Digital Data Service, and (4) wideband data/wideband analog.

91. *Id.* at 6796–99 ¶¶ 75–101.

92. *LEC Price Cap Order, supra* note 88, at 6799 ¶¶ 100–02; *LEC Price Cap*

Within each of the baskets, the commission further categorized services, and each category had its own pricing constraints ("bands"). Those constraints, which set a ceiling and a floor on specific prices (for most services, the bands were set at plus or minus 5 percent), were designed to prevent the local exchange carriers from compensating for a decrease in one set of prices within a basket by increasing prices on another set.[93] Further, it placed a cap on carrier common line charges that depended not on dollar revenues and costs, but on minutes per line and annual growth of minutes per line.

There were streamlined procedures for approving tariffs in which prices did not exceed the cap and that fell within the bands; such tariffs could take effect without a review proceeding on fourteen days' notice. But local carriers were required to continue to file cost-support data for tariffs outside those constraints.[94]

In 1994 the FCC modified its rules to move transport services[95] from the basket for traffic-sensitive charges to a new "trunking" basket for transport and special-access services.[96] The avowed purpose of that change was to limit any local carrier's ability to offset lower rates for more competitive services with higher rates for less competitive services. Then, in 1995, the commission announced that the local carriers would have a choice of offset productivity factors of 4.0, 4.7, and 5.3 percent.[97] The local exchange carriers that elected the 5.3 percent factor would not be subject to the sharing requirement. The FCC also announced that it would lower band floors for some service categories.

Reconsideration Order, supra note 88, at 2641–42 ¶¶ 6–8.

93. *See* 47 C.F.R. §§ 61.41–61.43, 61.45–61.47.

94. *LEC Price Cap Order, supra* note 88, at 6811 ¶ 198.

95. Transport, a component of interstate switched access, consists of local transmission between customer points of presence and local exchange carrier end offices, where local switching occurs.

96. Transport Rate Structure and Pricing, Second Report and Order, CC Dkt. No. 91-213, 9 F.C.C. Rcd. 615, 622 ¶ 12 (1994).

97. Price Cap Performance Review for Local Exchange Carriers, Notice of Proposed Rulemaking, CC Dkt. No. 94-1, 9 F.C.C. Rcd. 1687 (1994) [hereinafter *1994 Performance Review*]; Price Cap Performance Review for Local Exchange Carriers, First Report and Order, CC Dkt. No. 94-1, 77 Rad. Reg. 2d (P & F) 783, 819 ¶¶ 198–200 (1995).

What are the competitive implications of those changes? During the first three years of price caps, the local carriers kept their access charges at or below the applicable ceilings, which implied decreases of $1.5 billion in total charges to the long-distance carriers. Of that total, $373 million were the result of pricing below caps on various exchange service offerings.[98] With productivity advances, access providers' profits increased under price cap regulation. Initial price cap rates were targeted at an 11.25 percent return, and by 1992, the most recent year for which there are estimates, the overall rate of return for price cap local carriers had risen to 12.25 percent, and all price cap carriers earned above 11.25 percent. The most recent access charge filings propose $1.2 billion in further reductions.[99] End-user charges would increase by $13.8 million; carrier common line charges would decrease by $550.8 million; traffic-sensitive charges would decrease by $283.1 million; and rates in the trunking basket would decrease by $388.0 million.

TARIFF SETTING AND ENTRY CONTROL

Before divestiture, statutory powers to license service providers and to require the filing of tariffs had given the FCC the power to determine the number and relative size of carriers in long-distance telephone service markets. First, the commission could determine who would and would not enter those markets.[100] All common carriers, wire-line or radio-based, fell within Title II of the Communications Act.[101] Title II includes section 214, the commission's basic licensing power over common carriers, which barred construction of new lines unless the FCC finds that the additions would serve the public's "convenience and necessity."[102] But there were limits on

98. *1994 Performance Review, supra* note 97, at 1691 ¶ 25.

99. 1995 Annual Access Tariff Filings of Price Cap Carriers, Memorandum Opinion and Order Suspending Rates, 1995 F.C.C. LEXIS 4976 ¶ 2 (July 21, 1995).

100. *See generally* Richard E. Wiley, *The End of Monopoly: Regulatory Change and the Promotion of Competition, in* DISCONNECTING BELL: THE IMPACT OF THE AT&T DIVESTITURE 23, 24 (H. Shooshan ed., Pergamon 1984).

101. *See, e.g.,* National Ass'n of Regulatory Util. Comm'rs v. FCC, 525 F.2d 630 (D.C. Cir. 1975) (discussing regulatory scheme adopted for private and common-carriage cellular services). *See generally* FEDERAL TELECOMMUNICATIONS LAW, *supra* note 23, at §12.3.

102. 47 U.S.C. §214(a). Private radio-based carriers must also be licensed,

using that authority to determine what carriers could offer. In 1977 the D.C. Circuit Court review of the MCI application to provide Execunet service (*Execunet I*) specified that the commission could not retroactively apply conditions on section 214 authorizations to restrict competition.[103] The upshot was that any carrier holding section 214 authorization could offer switched long-distance services in interstate markets.[104]

Even so, the FCC could still determine on what price and service terms common carriers offered their services. Section 203 of the Communications Act required all carriers to file tariffs, or "schedules showing all charges for itself and its connecting carriers."[105] As a general rule, such regulatory oversight as to the prices charged by all providers of long-distance services proved to be cumbersome. The FCC was not able to deal with large numbers of tariff filings; after *Execunet I*, the commission's response to filings became prolonged and prompted the D.C. Circuit Court to hold that the Communications Act required that "rates . . . be finally decided

under Title III. 47 U.S.C. §301. *See, e.g.,* Allocation of Frequencies to the Various Classes of Non-Government Services in the Radio Spectrum from 10 Kilocycles to 30,000,000 Kilocycles, 39 F.C.C. 298 (1948); National Rural Telecommunications Cooperative *v.* Southern Satellite Systems, Inc., 7 F.C.C. Rcd. 3213 (1992). Private wire-line networks could perhaps also be licensed by the commission under its "ancillary jurisdiction," although the Communications Act does not expressly contemplate such networks and the current judiciary may be more hostile to an expansive view of the commission's ancillary jurisdiction than in the past. "Undoubtedly, private interstate communications services rendered by a common carrier remain within the purview of the commission, if only pursuant to the commission's general title I jurisdiction which authorizes commission regulation that is 'reasonably ancillary' to the exercise of specifically delegated powers under the Act." Southwestern Bell Telephone Co. *v.* FCC, 19 F.3d 1475, 1481 (D.C. Cir. 1994).

103. MCI Telecom. Corp. *v.* FCC (*Execunet I*), 561 F.2d 365, 374 (D.C. Cir. 1977), *cert. denied*, 434 U.S. 1040 (1978).

104. *Cf.* MTS and WATS Market Structure, Report and Third Supplemental Notice of Inquiry and Proposed Rulemaking, CC Dkt. No. 78-72, 81 F.C.C.2d 177 (1980), 93 F.C.C.2d 241, *modified on recons.* 97 F.C.C.2d 682 (1983), *modified on further recons.* 97 F.C.C.2d 834, *aff'd in principal part and remanded in part*, National Ass'n of Regulatory Util. Comm'rs *v.* F.C.C., 737 F.2d 1095 (D.C. Cir. 1984), *cert. denied*, 469 U.S. 1227 (1985).

105. 47 U.S.C. §203(a); see also *id.* at § 204 (giving the commission the power to suspend tariffs); *id.* at §205 (giving the commission the power to prescribe "just and reasonable" charges and practices if it finds a tariff in violation of Title II).

within a reasonable time encompassing months, occasionally a year or two, but not several years or a decade."[106] Consistent with those developments, in 1980 the commission ruled that all carriers would henceforth be classified as "nondominant" or "dominant."[107]

Nondominant and Dominant Carriers

In 1980 the FCC ruled that nondominant carriers were those that lacked market power to raise prices, restrict output, or impose unreasonable or discriminatory charges.[108] The commission streamlined regulation of nondominant carriers by reducing the ninety-day notice of a tariff filing to fourteen days. The presumption was that the commission would not investigate or suspend the tariffs.[109]

In 1982 the FCC adopted a policy of "forbearance" for some nondominant carriers, by which it declined to require them to file tariffs under section 203 or to comply with section 214.[110] After divestiture in 1984, the commission extended that policy to all domestic nondominant carriers[111] and by 1985 decided that they should not be required to file any tariffs.[112] The grounds for that new poli-

106. *See* MCI *v.* FCC, 627 F.2d 322, 340 (D.C. Cir. 1980).

107. Policy and Rules Concerning Rates for Competitive Common Carrier Services and Facilities Authorizations, Notice of Inquiry and Proposed Rulemaking, CC Dkt. No. 79-252, 77 F.C.C.2d 308 (1979); First Report and Order, 85 F.C.C.2d 1 (1980) [hereinafter *First Report and Order*]; Further Notice of Proposed Rulemaking, 84 F.C.C.2d 445 (1981) [hereinafter *Rates for Competitive Further Notice*]; Second Report, 91 F.C.C.2d 59 (1982) [hereinafter *Second Report*], *recons.* 93 F.C.C.2d 54 (1983); Second Further Notice of Proposed Rulemaking, 47 FED. REG. 17,308 (1982); Third Further Notice of Proposed Rulemaking, 48 FED. REG. 28,292 (1983); Third Report and Order, 48 FED. REG. 46,791 (1983); Fourth Report and Order, 95 F.C.C.2d 554 (1983) [hereinafter *Fourth Report*]; Fourth Further Notice of Proposed Rulemaking, 96 F.C.C.2d 922 (1984) [hereinafter *Fourth Further Notice*]; Fifth Report and Order, 98 F.C.C.2d 1191 (1984) [hereinafter *Fifth Report*]; Sixth Report and Order, 99 F.C.C.2d 1020 (1985) [hereinafter *Sixth Report*], *reversed and remanded sub nom.* MCI Telecommunications Corp. *v.* FCC, 765 F.2d 1186 (D.C. Cir. 1985).

108. *First Report and Order, supra* note 107, at 20–21 ¶¶ 15–16.

109. *Id.* at 35–38 ¶¶ 102–11.

110. *Second Report, supra* note 107, at 73 ¶ 5.

111. *Fifth Report, supra* note 107, at 557 ¶ 10.

112. *Fourth Further Notice, supra* note 107, at 923–24 ¶ 1; *Sixth Report, supra* note 107, at 1034 ¶ 11.

cy were that the FCC was concerned that its tariff-filing requirements could facilitate collusive pricing,[113] a prospect reduced by
allowing nondominant carriers to keep their prices confidential.[114]
MCI, a nondominant carrier, objected to not submitting tariffs,[115]
and the D.C. Circuit Court overruled the commission in a decision
that found that the Communications Act left the FCC with no dis-
cretion to "prohibit the filing of tariffs that, by statute, every common carrier shall file."[116] But a second D.C. Circuit Court opinion
in 1992 overruled the commission's decision to exempt
nondominant carriers from tariffing requirements.[117] The commission then made it clear that it intended to streamline tariffing for
nondominant carriers as much as possible, so that, since 1993,
whenever a nondominant carrier filed a tariff, it became effective in
one day.[118]

   Those decisions left AT&T in a class of tariff regulation by
itself. In 1979 the Commission ruled that AT&T would be treated
as a "dominant" carrier and so would not enjoy the streamlined
regulation subsequently applied to MCI and Sprint.[119] The Department of Justice may have assumed that divestiture would change
how the commission regulated AT&T. The FCC, however, refused
to adopt a policy of streamlined regulation for AT&T after divestiture.[120] In 1989 when the commission replaced rate-of-return regu-

113. *Sixth Report, supra* note 107, at 1030–32 ¶ 18.

114. *Id.* at 1034 ¶ 23.

115. *Id.* at 1020 n.9.

116. MCI *v.* FCC, 765 F.2d at 1186 (1985).

117. AT&T *v.* FCC, 978 F.2d 727 (D.C. Cir. 1992).

118. Tariff Filing Requirements for Nondominant Common Carriers, Notice of
Proposed Rulemaking, CC Dkt. No. 93-36, 8 F.C.C. Rcd. 1395 ¶ 13 (1993). In
addition, later *see* 47 C.F.R. §61.23(c); Tariff Filing Requirements for Nondominant
Common Carriers, Mem. Op. and Order, CC Dkt. 93-36, 8 F.C.C. Rcd. 6752 ¶ 3
(1993) [hereinafter *Tariff Filing Requirements for Nondominant Carriers*].

119. *See, e.g.*, Policy and Rules Concerning Rates for Dominant Carriers, Report and Order and Second Further Notice of Proposed Rulemaking, CC Dkt. No.
87-313, 4 F.C.C. Rcd. 2873, 2887–88 n. 197 (1989) [hereinafter *Rates for Dominant
Carriers*]; *Interexchange Competition, supra* note 67, at 5903 ¶ 30; Remarks of
Alfred C. Sikes, Commission Chairman, Feb. 15, 1990 (1990 F.C.C. LEXIS 862)
("Today, AT&T . . . [is] still required to file voluminous data, to get permission
before it offers many price discounts, and, among the interstate carriers, its regulatory treatment remains unique.").

120. *Interexchange Competition, supra* note 67, at 5903 ¶ 30; Policy and Rules

lation for AT&T with price caps, AT&T was still the "dominant" interexchange carrier.[121] In 1993 AT&T petitioned the commission to be reclassified as a nondominant carrier; the company asserted that it lacked the market power that would still justify restraint under existing regulation.[122]

AT&T's unique position was eliminated when the FCC unanimously granted that petition on October 12, 1995.[123] AT&T was freed from most price cap regulation, was allowed to file tariffs on one-day's notice, no longer was required to report carrier-to-carrier contracts, was authorized to extend service to any domestic point, and did not have to meet the requirement to submit cost support data for proposed rate changes. The commission found that AT&T lacked "market power in the interstate, domestic, interexchange market."[124] Two arguments marked that finding. The first was the broad definition of AT&T's market; the second was the rejection of price leadership as a pattern of behavior to be associated with dominance. In the nondominance order, the commission found that all interstate, domestic, interexchange telecommunications services comprised a single product market relevant for determining whether a carrier had "(sufficient) market power . . . to control prices."[125] The commission did not explain but "agreed with AT&T that in this case we should use the all interstate domestic interexchange services market definition" previously adopted.[126]

Concerning Rates for Dominant Carriers, Memorandum Opinion and Order, CC Dkt. No. 87-313, 6 F.C.C. Rcd. 4819 (1991).

121. *See, e.g., Interexchange Competition, supra* note 67, at 5903 ¶ 30; *Rates for Dominant Carriers, supra* note 119, at 2943, 2996; Policy and Rules Concerning Rates for Dominant Carriers, Further Notice of Proposed Rulemaking, CC Dkt. No. 87-313, 3 F.C.C. Rcd. 3195, 3235–36 (1988) [hereinafter *Rates for Dominant Further Notice*].

122. Motion for Reclassification of American Telephone and Telegraph Company as a Non-Dominant Carrier, CC Dkt. No. 79-252 (Sept. 22, 1993). See also AT&T April 24, 1995, *Ex Parte* Filing.

123. Motion of AT&T Corp. to Be Reclassified as a Non-Dominant Carrier, CC Dkt. No. 95-427 (Oct. 13, 1995). AT&T's request to be reclassified as a nondominant in regard to the provision of international services was deferred to another proceeding.

124. *Id*. at ¶ 74.

125. *Id*.

126. *Id*. at ¶ 21.

That definition allowed the FCC to conflate revenue share across different home and business service markets to arrive at a judgment of AT&T's lower market share. The commission also noted that AT&T's residential rates fell between 15 percent and 28 percent in nominal terms and took that, and the availability of numerous discount plans, as evidence of pricing competition. Even more striking, the commission used a definition of market dominance that recognized dominance only when there was a monopoly. The Bell operating companies submitted evidence that cooperative pricing had rendered the industry a three-firm, noncompetitive oligopoly, in which AT&T, MCI, and Sprint coordinated price changes.[127] Although the FCC recognized that characterization, the commission found that the evidence was "conflicting and inconclusive as to the issue of tacit price coordination."[128] To the extent the condition did exist, however, it would be "a problem generic to the interexchange industry and not specific to AT&T."[129] The commission asserted that "because they relate to the industry as a whole, these issues do not preclude our concluding that AT&T lacks the power to raise residential prices unilaterally above competitive levels."[130] No carrier now has dominant status.

The Shift to Price Cap Regulation

At the time of divestiture, AT&T was subject to public utility regulatory practices and procedures of both state and federal agencies. The company submitted cost studies to support requests for tariff rate changes. It was allowed to charge consumers enough to recover operating and capital costs, plus a reasonable return on its investments.[131] After a half century of rate cases, the problems with rate-of-return regulation were well known; limiting revenues to "costs of service" generated inefficient investments so as to increase total earnings and reduce incentives to hold down staff and line employment.[132] Even more basic, the system proved to be a force for ex-

---

127. *Id.* at ¶ 81.
128. *Id.* at ¶ 83.
129. *Id.*
130. *Id.*
131. FEDERAL TELECOMMUNICATIONS LAW, *supra* note 23, at § 9.2.
132. The theory of excess capitalization was developed in Harvey Averch and

panding capital-intensive local services and subsidizing those services with earnings on long-distance services.

Price cap regulation developed as the alternative to rate-of-return regulation in the postdivestiture decade in all regulated industries. Under the new system, regulators chose a price level (essentially the current level) and then in succeeding years applied a percentage change determined by an inflation index net of an index of relative productivity growth. The telephone company under those rules could increase its earnings by controlling costs and increasing productivity at a rate higher than the index rate.[133]

In May 1989 the FCC adopted a system of price caps for AT&T,[134] the "dominant" interexchange carrier,[135] that would take effect in July 1989.[136] The commission had determined that AT&T should have more pricing flexibility to respond to the pricing initiatives for share gain by the entrant carriers.[137] New price cap tariffs would take effect on July 1 of each year, after a forty-five-day notice period (later reduced to fourteen days for in-band rates). The commission was actually rather slow in adopting the new procedure. State commissions had already provided full pricing flexibility for AT&T for interLATA services in thirteen states, while commissions in sixteen more states had begun to allow prices to move within specified ranges without cost-based rate proceedings. Commissions in six more states allowed partial pricing flexibility for AT&T's MTS or WATS services.[138] Most states had reduced notice periods for rate changes from ten to thirty days, with some differing by the direction of the change (for example, thirty days for increases, one day for decreases).

The FCC not only lagged behind the states but also did not adopt a pure price cap plan. Instead, it separated AT&T's services

Leland L. Johnson, *Behavior of the Firm Under Regulatory Constraint*, 52 AM. ECON. REV. 1053 (1962).

133. DESIGNING INCENTIVE REGULATION, *supra* note 52, at 312–16.

134. *Rates for Dominant Carriers*, *supra* note 119, at 2877 ¶ 3.

135. *See, e.g., Interexchange Competition*, *supra* note 67, at 5903 ¶ 30; *Rates for Dominant Carriers*, *supra* note 119, at 2943 ¶ 133, 2996 ¶ 238; *Rates for Dominant Further Notice*, *supra* note 121, at 3235–36 ¶ 69.

136. *Rates for Dominant Carriers*, *supra* note 119, at 2876 ¶ 3.

137. *See, e.g., id.* at 2893 ¶ 37, 2922–24 ¶¶ 100–05, 2939–43 ¶¶ 125–33.

138. *Id.* at 2927 n. 183, 2930 ¶¶ 109–10.

into "baskets." At first, the commission suggested a single basket,[139] then two baskets—one for public switched services and one for private-line services.[140] Ultimately, however, responding to competitor's fears, the FCC established three baskets.[141] Basket one was to apply full caps to services for small business and residential subscribers ("the grandma basket"). Basket two was for 800 services (inbound WATS). Basket three was for AT&T's other business services, such as outbound WATS and virtual network services, used mainly by large business customers and thus most often targeted by competitors.[142] For each basket, the FCC established a price cap index representing a weighted average of the actual prices to be charged for services. The company could change rates for services within each basket if the weighted average of all prices remained below the index.

The FCC further subdivided the baskets into service categories and set a ceiling and a floor index price for those service categories that established the acceptable price "band"[143] limiting the range within which AT&T could raise or lower prices for individual service elements in each category. For instance, the residential service average rate could not increase by more than 1 percent per year relative to the change in the index,[144] although the commission had recently authorized an exception to that limit.[145] The upper and lower bands allowed movement of around 5 percent for most service categories.

The purpose of the separate baskets and bands was to "isolat[e] less competitive services" to "prevent their use as a

---

139. Policy and Rules Concerning Rates for Dominant Carriers, Notice of Proposed Rulemaking, CC Dkt. No. 87-313, 2 F.C.C. Rcd. 5208 (1987).

140. *Rates for Dominant Further Notice, supra* note 121, at 3352–53 ¶ 280.

141. *Rates for Dominant Carriers, supra* note 119, at 2897 ¶¶ 48–51.

142. *Id.* at 2897 ¶¶ 48-51. *See* TELECOMMUNICATION POLICY, *supra* note 1, at 272.

143. Policy and Rules Concerning Rates for Dominant Carriers, Mem. Op. and Order on Recons., CC Dkt. No. 87-313, 6 F.C.C. Rec. 665, 666 ¶ 8 (1991) [hereinafter *Rates Reconsideration*]; *Rates for Dominant Carriers, supra* note 119, at 2898 ¶ 52.

144. *Rates for Dominant Carriers, supra* note 119, at 3054 ¶ 364.

145. AT&T Corporation's Petition for Waiver of Section 61.47(f)(2) of the Commission's Rules, Order, 1995 F.C.C. LEXIS 4262 (June 29, 1995).

source of cross-subsidies," and to "discourage predation."[146] The commission seemed particularly concerned that AT&T would drop its prices below the floors specified in the bands and warned that it would guard against "precipitous price decreases" that might have an "anticompetitive effect."[147] The FCC also took the position that it would disallow price decreases within the bands if they were anticompetitive under "relevant antitrust analysis."[148]

The FCC emphasized that the move to price caps still constrained AT&T's ability to engage in "anticompetitive pricing actions"[149] such as predatory pricing.[150] It explained that the service bands would "address any residual concerns about price manipulation by AT&T detrimental to its competitors"[151] and would "provide protection to [AT&T's] competitors from injurious pricing actions."[152] Protecting competition meant protecting competitors.[153]

Ceiling prices under the plan took AT&T's existing rates as a starting point.[154] AT&T was permitted to raise prices by the gross domestic product inflation rate,[155] but only after that rate was reduced by a "productivity offset" factor of 2.5 percent.[156] The FCC also required the rate to be decreased by an additional 0.5 percent "consumer productivity dividend," intended to cause AT&T to pass along cost savings from some part of its own higher level of increased efficiency.[157] To monitor AT&T's compliance with that plan, the commission required AT&T to file annual price cap tariffs.[158] The commission did not prohibit tariffs that deviated from

146. *Rates for Dominant Carriers, supra* note 119, at 3065, 3056 ¶ 368, ¶ 387.
147. *Rates Reconsideration, supra* note 143, at 666 ¶ 8; *Rates for Dominant Carriers, supra* note 119, at 3111–12, 3114 ¶ 390.
148. *Rates for Dominant Carriers, supra* note 119, at 3115 ¶ 389.
149. *Id.* at 2941 n.238; *Rates Reconsideration, supra* note 143, at 669 ¶ 32.
150. *Rates Reconsideration, supra* note 143, at 667; *Rates for Dominant Carriers, supra* note 119, at 3066 ¶ 389.
151. *Rates for Dominant Carriers, supra* note 119, at 3059 ¶ 374.
152. *Rates for Dominant Further Notice, supra* note 121, at 3355 ¶ 285.
153. *See, e.g., id.* at 3200–01 ¶ 6; *Rates for Dominant Carriers, supra* note 119, at 2886 ¶ 25, 3065–66 ¶¶ 387–91.
154. *Rates for Dominant Carriers, supra* note 119, at 3084–89 ¶¶ 424–30.
155. *Id.* at 2969–74 ¶¶ 186–97.
156. *Id.* at 1989–97 ¶¶ 221–39.
157. *Id.* at 2894, 3001 ¶ 249.
158. *Id.* at 3093 ¶ 440.

price bands but did subject them to regulatory scrutiny for potentially adverse effects on competitors.[159]

That procedure established that AT&T set "posted" prices for all classes of service that could be used as the benchmark for *pro forma* tariffs subsequently submitted by the other carriers. Then other carriers could not chisel that price schedule with discounts to gain share. The benchmark allowed responses by AT&T that could make chiseling unprofitable; AT&T could legally react to other suppliers' lower rates by putting through responsive cuts if they were within a specified range of the average rate for that basket of services. The range for AT&T was broad; for example, basket one had six categories consisting of domestic day, domestic evening, domestic night/weekend, international MTS, operator and credit card, and the "discount" Reach Out America services. AT&T could decrease rates for those categories by 5 percent per year, after adjusting for the percentage change in the price cap index, which could further reduce price by 5 percent or more.[160] Thus, AT&T could put in place a substantial rate response—a cut of 10 percent or more—without having to provide notice, at least in selected categories, where shares were prominently spread among the three largest carriers. While tariffs prevented "predation," they had in place the flexibility to warn the smaller carriers against strategic discounting to shift market share.

At the same time—as part and parcel of those complicated trigger mechanisms—when AT&T submitted tariffs, other carriers could respond before the tariffs took effect. That process precluded any competitive gain for AT&T from an own-price-reduction initiative. The what and when in the tariffs of the largest carrier established discipline in the price-change practices of all three large carriers.

The FCC decided that it could provide even more flexibility in tariff setting for business service offerings. In 1990 the commission announced that because services "at the high end of the market . . . [are] the most vigorously competitive," it would limit the

159. *See, e.g., Rates for Dominant Further Notice, supra* note 121, at 667 ¶ 15; *Rates for Dominant Carriers, supra* note 119, at 3065–66 ¶¶ 387–89.

160. A 4 percent rate of change in the cap applied to domestic evening and domestic night/weekend. *Rates for Dominant Carriers, supra* note 119, at 3054 ¶364.

control process over prices for those services.[161] In 1991 the FCC found that "the public interest would best be served by more limited advance review of AT&T's business service filings, including the complaint process and our authority to initiate investigations and find tariffs unlawful after they take effect."[162] In November of that year the commission eliminated basket-three caps and replaced them by rates with automatic fourteen-day approval (except for those involving service on analog private lines).[163] The commission allowed AT&T to offer those business services by private contract rather than by tariff, although the company still had to file the contract terms fourteen days in advance.[164] The contracts had to comply with Communications Act requirements, such as the "reasonable rates" requirement and the prohibition on discrimination.[165] In May 1993 the FCC eliminated price caps on basket-two services, except for 800 directory service. Citing "substantial" competition, the agency moved commercial long-distance services remaining in basket one from price cap regulation in January 1995.[166]

Even so, the commission held the position for ten years that AT&T was still a dominant carrier. Unlike Sprint, MCI, and other smaller carriers, whose tariffs could become effective on one day's notice, AT&T had to subject its tariffs to the FCC's "advance review."[167] The commission reserved the right to "suspend and/or reject tariffs where necessary," even after those tariffs had taken effect.[168]

FACILITATING COLLUSION

In markets with two or three large-sized suppliers, the sales and

161. *Interexchange Competition, supra* note 67, at 2628 ¶ 2.

162. *Id.* at 5882 ¶ 9.

163. *Id.* at 5894 ¶ 73. Basket three holds ProAmerica, WATS, Megacom, SDN, other switched services, voice grade and below private line service, and other private line service. *Id.* at 5881 & n.4.

164. *Id.* at 5897 ¶ 72.

165. *Id.* at 5897 ¶ 91, 5902–03 ¶¶ 126–28.

166. Revisions to Price Cap Rules for AT&T Corp., Rep. and Order, CC Dkt. No. 93-197, 10 F.C.C. Rcd. 3009–11, ¶ 5 (1995).

167. *Interexchange Competition, supra* note 67, at 5882 ¶ 9, 5893–94 ¶ 72.

168. *Id.* at 5894 ¶ 74.

revenue levels of any one depend on the actions of the others as to pricing of services. One such carrier would have to be aware of others' prices and anticipate others' reactions to its price offerings in the tariffs. There are quite different ways, however, in which those providers could interact.

The threshold assumption is that they act collectively to set rate levels that increase market revenues. They would cooperate, or make adjustments to each other's presence short of cooperation, to set a commonly advantageous price level. But that holds only if each is assured that none of the others adopts price cutting as an initiative to gain market share.

Regulatory procedures in place after 1984 in long-distance markets have been of the type that assist in the (informal) adoption of such an approach. Tariff submission processes favored acceptance of AT&T's tariffs as the benchmark. Over time, the three large facilities-based carriers, AT&T, MCI, and Sprint, issued tariffs with pricing terms that became more publicly identical.

Signaling

The FCC was well aware that its tariffing process had the potential to be used by one carrier to signal others what its prices would be before actually charging those prices. Since the early 1980s, the commission had repeatedly expressed concern that tariffing under section 203 of the Communications Act suppressed price initiatives of any one of the carriers. The reasons were straightforward: the tariff required that terms and conditions of a carrier's service offerings be published before they were to go into effect; and the carrier could not deviate from tariffed prices when they were in effect. In 1983, when the commission embarked on its "forbearance" policy,[169] it explained that it sought to eliminate all tariff filings by MCI and Sprint[170] because that would provide "an excellent mechanism for inducing competitive pricing."[171] The FCC found that "traditional tariff regulation of nondominant carriers is at odds with the

---

169. *Fourth Report, supra* note 107, at 554.

170. *Rates for Competitive Further Notice, supra* note 107, at 445, 478–79 ¶ 87 (1981).

171. *Id.* at 454 ¶ 26.

purposes of the [Communications] Act because it inhibits price competition, service innovation, and the ability of firms to respond quickly to market trends."[172] Indeed, the commission later concluded that the tariff process encouraged nondominant carriers to follow AT&T's lead in setting their rates.[173] The Department of Justice expressed a similar concern in 1990 that the tariffing process promoted tacit collusion among AT&T, MCI, and Sprint.[174]

Permissive detariffing would have made it possible for MCI and Sprint to offer their services with price discounts that challenged AT&T's prices. But those two other carriers declined permissiveness and instead continued to offer their services only under tariff. MCI's challenge to the FCC's prohibition is particularly telling in that context; in a competitive market, one would think that MCI would seek to be relieved of the burden of filing tariffs.[175] That the industry was engaged in "umbrella pricing," as described by the commission itself, was evident:

> [O]ne firm behaves as a price-searcher and the others as price-takers. The price-searcher finds a price he likes; the others take that price as a given in deciding how much to supply, expanding their supply the higher the given price. The price-searcher takes these supply decisions into account (*i.e.,* he anticipates the reactions of the fringe to the price he chooses) in deciding what price he likes. He, of course, prefers a high price, but the higher the price, the less he sells as consumers substitute other goods and the competing products of fringe suppliers. So he must balance the gains and losses of a

172. *Second Report, supra* note 107, at 59, 65 ¶ 12 (1982).

173. By late 1993, in its attempt to reestablish detariffing after remand from D.C. Circuit, the FCC repeated its warning, but with a distinct variation in wording: "traditional tariff regulation of nondominant carriers . . . is *actually counterproductive* since it can inhibit price competition, service innovation, entry into the market, and the ability of carriers to respond quickly to market trends." *Tariff Filing Requirements for Nondominant Carriers, supra* note 118, at 6752 ¶ 2 (emphasis added).

174. Reply Comments of the U.S. Department of Justice, CC Dkt. No. 90-132, at 41, 44–46 (filed Sept. 28, 1990).

175. MCI *v.* FCC, 765 F.2d 1186 (D.C. Cir. 1985).

higher price in deciding what price maximizes his profit.[176]

The carriers' tariff submission practices themselves contributed further to cooperative pricing patterns. After 1990, AT&T submitted tariffs once or twice per year on repeated dates, to be followed by quite similar submissions from MCI and Sprint. For example, AT&T submitted its standard tariff for message toll service with an index price of 23.3 cents per minute at the end of 1990 for customers making calls to points from 400 to 2,000 miles distant, during the daytime working week (those specifications for "representative" subscriber usage are described, as are the tariffs, in chapter 6). MCI submitted its revised tariff with an index priced at 22.2 cents, and Sprint submitted a revised tariff priced at 22.4 cents per minute, for the same representative service package. Between 1991 and 1993, AT&T, in each new tariff, initiated a change in that index price that MCI and Sprint followed with changes that became more and more similar. By December 1993, AT&T was charging 23.5 cents, MCI was charging 23.4 cents, and Sprint was charging 23.5 cents per minute for that service. The narrowing of the difference between AT&T's prices and those of the other two large carriers further indicated how price caps in those markets actually have worked. In mid-1984 AT&T's prices were 10 to 20 percent higher than its competitors'. By 1987, the gap was only about 5 percent; by the end of 1995 the gap was close to zero for MTS standard services (as shown in chapter 6).

That sequence of submissions with price convergence was not just in tariffs for basket-one services. It was present in outbound WATS and after 1991 in Inbound WATS as well. Remarkably, even in virtual network services, for which subscriber self-provision of service afforded a significant competitive alternative, AT&T submitted tariffs that generated price changes from 1990 to 1993 that MCI followed with its own changes different by only 0.6 to 0.8 cents per minute.

176. FCC, WHAT MAKES THE DOMINANT FIRM DOMINANT? 3–4 (OPP Working Paper No. 25) (Apr. 1989).

Delays and Other Nonsense

The tariffing process provided competitors with the mechanism for imposing delays and litigation costs on a carrier making a deviant submission. The carriers have employed a procedure by which to file an objection to another's tariff to ensure that another carrier did not move out from under the pricing umbrella. In 1987 AT&T filed Tariff 12, a one-customer contract, showing a single set of prices for services integrated into a private network designed for General Electric Telecommunications Network (GETN).[177] MCI and Sprint objected on grounds that AT&T had offered an index price for that bundle of services less than the sum of the prices to customers buying parts of the bundle so that the tariff was discriminatory. The companies' concern, however, was more likely that AT&T was pricing service to GETN at a low level.[178] AT&T revised the tariff by taking out the express reference to GETN[179] and making the offering available to "similarly situated" customers.[180] MCI challenged the commission's ruling approving that tariff, and the D.C. Circuit Court remanded the proceeding to the FCC,[181] which again approved the tariff by ruling that the offering was not per se discriminatory.[182]

AT&T's Tariff 15, designed to allow AT&T to tailor servic-

177. AT&T Request for Waiver of Rules Regarding Proposed Custom Designed Integrated Service, 2 F.C.C. Rcd. 3915 (1987).

178. AT&T Response to Tariff F.C.C. No. 12, 4 F.C.C. Rcd. 5430, 5431 ¶ 10 (1988); MCI Petition to Reject, AT&T Communications, Revisions to Tariff F.C.C. No. 12, Transmittal No. 1592, at 10–11 (FCC May 19, 1989) (complaining that AT&T's offerings propose significant price reductions); Sprint Petition to Reject or Alternatively Suspend and Investigate, AT&T Communications, Revisions to Tariff F.C.C. No. 12, Transmittal No. 1592, at 16–17 (FCC May 19, 1989) (complaining that under the offerings AT&T's expenses have been reduced without justification).

179. AT&T Communications Tariff F.C.C. Nos. 10 and 12, 2 F.C.C. Rcd. 5493, 5493 n.6. (1983).

180. AT&T, Revisions to Tariff F.C.C. No. 12, 4 F.C.C. Rcd. 4932, 4938 ¶ 60, *recons. denied*, 4 F.C.C. Rcd. 7928 (1989), *rev'd and remanded*, MCI v. FCC, 917 F.2d 30, 37 (D.C. Cir. 1990); AT&T Communications, Revisions to Tariff F.C.C. No. 12, 4 F.C.C. Rcd. 5430 ¶ 2.

181. MCI v. FCC, 917 F.2d at 30.

182. AT&T Communications, Revisions to Tariff F.C.C. No. 12, 6 F.C.C. Rcd. 7039, 7055 ¶ 87 (1991).

es further to large customers able to self-supply at least parts of the network, faced the same objections from other carriers.[183] Sprint complained that AT&T was "effectively underpricing" Sprint's comparable services.[184] MCI objected that the offering threatened "an effectively competitive interexchange market."[185] The FCC found the tariff not unlawful but suspended it following an order from the D.C. Circuit.[186] Similarly, responses to AT&T's Tariff 16 for large volume services to be provided to the Defense Department faced an MCI challenge[187] in which the company complained that "AT&T [was] shielding rates that are unreasonably discriminatory" and that Tariff 16 constituted "predatory pricing."[188] Martin Marietta and MCI complained that AT&T's proposal to provide Federal Telecommunications Service 2000 offered an illegal rebate[189] and that AT&T was pricing below costs.[190]

183. AT&T Communications, Tariff F.C.C. No. 15, Competitive Pricing Plans—Holiday Rate Plan, 4 F.C.C. Rcd. 7933 (1989), *recons. denied,* 5 F.C.C. Rcd. 1821 (1990); *see also* AT&T Communications, Revisions to Tariff F.C.C. No. 15, Competitive Pricing Plan No. 17, 6 F.C.C. Rcd. 5353 (1991); AT&T Communications, Revisions to Tariff F.C.C. No. 15, Competitive Pricing Plan 5—La Quinta Motor Inns, Inc., 5 F.C.C. Rcd. 4581, 4582 ¶¶ 7-10 (1990); AT&T Communications, Tariff F.C.C. No. 15, Competitive Pricing Plan No. 2—Resort Condominiums Int'l, 6 F.C.C. Rcd. 5648, 5649-50 ¶¶ 9-11 (1991), *remanded,* AT&T v. FCC, No. 91-1504 (D.C. Cir. Jan. 21, 1992); AT&T Communications, Tariff F.C.C. No. 15, Competitive Pricing Plan No. 2—Resort Condominiums Int'l, 7 F.C.C. Rcd. 3036 (1992).

184. AT&T Communications, Revisions to Tariff F.C.C. No. 15, Competitive Pricing Plan No. 17, 6 F.C.C. Rcd. 5353 ¶ 8 (1991); Opposition of Sprint, AT&T Communications, Tariff F.C.C. No. 15, No. 90-327 (FCC Nov. 21, 1991).

185. MCI Opposition to Direct Case, AT&T Communications, Tariff F.C.C. No. 15, No. 90-27, at 1 (FCC Nov. 21, 1991).

186. AT&T Communications, Tariff F.C.C. No. 15, 7 F.C.C. Rcd. 818, 819 ¶8 (1992).

187. AT&T Communications, Tariff F.C.C. No. 16, 4 F.C.C. Rcd. 2231 (1989); *see also* AT&T Communications, Revisions to Tariff F.C.C. No. 16, 5 F.C.C. Rcd. 468 (1990).

188. 4 F.C.C. Rcd. at 2231 ¶ 4; *see also* 5 F.C.C. Rcd. at 468 ¶ 3-4; MCI Telecommunications Corp., Comments in Opposition, AT&T Application for "Special Permission" No. 511 to Waive Requirement That Proposed AT&T Tariff F.C.C. No. 16 Federal Telecommunications Service 2000 (FTS 2000) Rates Be Published, at 2 (FCC Feb. 10, 1989); WilTel, Petition to Reject or Suspend and Investigate, AT&T Communications Tariff F.C.C. No. 16, Transmittal No. 1555, at 3 (FCC Apr. 14, 1989).

189. AT&T Communications, Revisions to Tariff F.C.C. No. 16, 4 F.C.C. Rcd.

The FCC's procedures related to price setting were complemented by other, less notorious case practices. From 1987 to 1994, AT&T made transmittals to revise tariffs that changed service offerings to large users. Those had the potential of destabilizing tariffs across carriers, and in all the major transmittals the response of MCI, Sprint, or both was to object to the tariffs. In 1986 in transmittals 434 and 435, AT&T proposed to revise its Tariffs 2, 9, and 10 to allow customers to access its class-four switch at discount rates; MCI and Sprint in response took the position that doing so gave AT&T an unfair competitive advantage in its WATS offerings. In 1987 in response to Transmittals 1063 and 1064—to reduce tariff rates on both MTS and WATS—Sprint stated that the reductions were merely to shift cost recovery from more- to less-competitive service categories. In 1988 in special rate offerings for services to hotel chains (the "Hospitality Network Services"), respondents to transmittal 7386 called for "competitive necessity" tests. Further tests were to determine whether proposed prices were unduly discriminatory in Transmittal 1445 in 1988, based on flawed projections in Transmittal 1552 in 1988 and targeted to favor specific customers in Transmittal 2032 in 1989.

Over the eight years, AT&T filed thirty-six major transmittals for revised service offerings that elicited similar responses from the other major carriers. The FCC held hearings and in most cases rejected the responses of the other carriers objecting to the offering. In a number of specific cases, involving the allegation that AT&T was bundling services to offer with its 800 services for which it had a dominant position, the commission rejected or required revisions in the submittal, as in Transmittals 3525 and 3571 in 1992. The general thrust of the results of those practices was that AT&T, by

5043, 5044 n.4 (1989). *See* Petition of Martin Marietta to Reject or Suspend, AT&T Communications, Tariff No. 16, Transmittal No. 1555, at 18 n.26 (FCC Apr. 14, 1989).

190. "AT&T's FTS 2000 rates are not compensatory, the carrier's other rate payers will be unreasonably burdened, and competition was unfairly restrained." Petition to Reject of Martin Marietta Corp., AT&T Communications, Tariff F.C.C. No. 16 FTS 2000, Transmittal 1555, at 12 (FCC Apr. 14, 1989). Marietta Corp. added, "[U]nder any reasonable standard, AT&T intends to provide FTS 2000 services at a loss." *Id.* at 2.

delay or rejection, was required to hold to its main tariffs, for any variations on well-established services, until the other large carriers could bring similar services in line.

Those cases added up. In 1989 the FCC's Office of Plans and Policy found that its regulatory apparatus provided carriers with a forum for "self-serving attempts to sustain an outmoded regime of regulation that supplies protection from competition."[191] Alfred Sikes, then the chairman, complained that tariff procedures "limit the ability of a major competitor—AT&T—to compete. Current procedures afford many ways to energize the regulatory process to block price reductions potentially offered by AT&T. Most importantly, that holds prices artificially higher, and reduces customer choice."[192] "It is a reasonable supposition," Alfred Kahn concluded, "that the apparent failure of competition itself to produce substantial price reductions in long-distance telephony has been attributable in important measure to continued regulatory handicapping of AT&T and sheltering of its competitors."[193]

Then how do those procedures involving caps and tariffs fit together to affect competition? In theory, price caps as imposed on an existing three-firm market would prevent monopoly price levels from being set collectively and would provide incentives to operate efficiently.[194] That is the theory, but in fact there are three major aspects of regulation to the contrary. First, caps on access charges make all carriers' costs the same. In markets with three carriers providing homogeneous services under conditions of uniform operating costs, the incentive for each is to have price ceilings become cemented in place from below. It is in the collective interest of those carriers and the regulator that ceilings also become floors. Second, that is especially the case for new service offerings where

191. FCC, WHAT MAKES THE DOMINANT FIRM DOMINANT? 11–12 (OPP Working Paper No. 25) (Apr. 1989).

192. Hearing Before the House Subcomm. on Telecommunications and Finance, Comm. on Energy and Commerce, 102d Cong., 1st Sess. (June 19, 1991) (statement of Alfred C. Sikes, FCC Chairman), 1991 F.C.C. LEXIS 4212.

193. Alfred Kahn, The Necessary Conditions of Effective Competition for Local Transport, Comment of Bell Atlantic, Expanded Interconnection with Local Telephone Company Facilities, No. 91-141, at 12 (FCC Aug. 6, 1991).

194. WILLIAM J. BAUMOL & J. GREGORY SIDAK, TOWARD COMPETITION IN LOCAL TELEPHONY 51 (MIT Press & AEI Press 1994).

regulatory constraints in the tariff submission process prevent the largest firm from growing relative to the rest of the market. Third, each carrier's filing of tariffs stabilizes intercarrier informational exchange across long-distance markets. The commission, by certifying price floors and ceilings at levels for any one carrier that are preemptively reviewed by all carriers, generates not a price umbrella but a shared price level for all carriers.

Tracing Regulation's Role in Price Level Changes since Divestiture

Indexes of average prices for long-distance services have decreased 50 percent since divestiture. That decline is often cited as proof that regulation by divesting AT&T of its operating companies and by fostering entry has caused competitive pricing to break out in those markets.[195] But industry analysts, even including the commission, have linked the decline in price levels to reductions in access charges.[196] Moreover, long-distance carriers did not pass along all such reductions in lower prices, as they would have if there were competitive pricing.

Changes in access charges have followed FCC mandates. Since divestiture, the commission partly replaced access charges by flat-rate line charges like the subscriber line charge. As a result, the access charges paid by AT&T and the other carriers were mandated to decrease.[197] Access charges indeed fell as a percentage of local carrier revenues. In 1984 the long-distance carriers paid out 24 percent of revenues to local exchange carriers in access charges (see table 1-1). The same was true in 1987.[198] But by 1991, long-dis-

195. Hearing Before the House Subcomm. on Telecommunications & Finance, Comm. on Energy and Commerce, 102d Cong., 1st Sess. (May 10, 1995) (Statement of Robert E. Allen, Chairman and Chief Executive Officer of AT&T Corp.).

196. In the AT&T Price Cap Order, the FCC observed, "The single force most responsible for driving down long-distance rates over the last several years has been the reduction of access charges." *Rates for Dominant Carriers, supra* note 119, at 3054 ¶ 365.

197. *Id.* at 3132–33 ¶¶ 532–39.

198. AT&T Communications, CC Dkt. No. 87-611, Direct Case of AT&T, Attachment 3 (filed January 28, 1988). Approximately 84.6 percent of AT&T's total nonaccess costs were interstate costs. Attachment 3, *Rates for Dominant Carriers,*

tance companies paid only about 22 percent of their revenues to local exchange companies.[199] If rates were reduced by the same amount as access charges, then the percentage would remain the same over those same periods. That the percentage fell can only be explained by the fact that those carriers did not pass on all of the access cost reductions to consumers.

Alternative analyses agree with that judgment. A 1992 study found that between 1984 and 1992, access charges fell by $10.13 billion, but only $8.22 billion of that was passed on in rate reductions.[200] That study concluded that "reductions in carrier access charges more than accounted for reductions in AT&T's toll prices."[201] In Alfred Kahn's words, "[the mandated access charge reductions] produced enormous net economic benefits, but it was they, and not competition itself, that caused prices to decline and demand to grow more rapidly than it would otherwise have done."[202] The 1992 study also found that between 1972 and 1984, inflation-adjusted interstate toll rates, net of changes in access charges, fell by 6.2 percent per year, twice as fast than in the seven years after divestiture.[203]

The FCC assumed that the price cap adjustments mechanism would prevent AT&T from withholding cost savings. Under price cap regulation, access charge reductions are treated as exogenous events. Lower access charges would automatically reduce AT&T's price cap and force the firm to reduce prices. But the price cap is not reduced by AT&T's cost savings when they exceed that associated with the productivity adjustment factor, or when the service is in a basket without caps. Also prices are not reduced by the regulatory process when AT&T substitutes competitive access service providers for local carrier access services. Such alternatives provided a growing segment of local access service, as their route miles

supra note 119, at 2961 ¶ 168.

    199. GEODESIC NETWORK II, *supra* note 3, at 3.22–3.23; but *see* table 1–1.

    200. WILLIAM TAYLOR, EFFECTS OF COMPETITIVE ENTRY IN THE U.S. INTERSTATE TOLL MARKETS: AN UPDATE 1 (National Economic Research Associates, May 28, 1992).

    201. *Id.*

    202. Kahn, *supra* note 193, at 12.

    203. TAYLOR, *supra* note 200.

increased from 133 in 1987 to 2,071 in 1991, and fiber miles from 7,770 to 105,148 over the same period.[204]

The final reason why regulated rate reductions did not achieve the pass-through of cost reductions is that the FCC refused to recognize that its policies did not achieve that result. In assessing compliance with the price cap process in 1995, the commission found that the regulated local carriers' interstate access charges were $1.5 billion lower than at the time price caps were instituted.[205] In 1995 the FCC rejected the argument that interexchange carriers had not passed on those savings to consumers:

> We also conclude that the interexchange carriers have passed on the savings they have received from lower interstate exchange access charges to end-users. The AT&T price cap plan requires AT&T to treat changes in the access charge rates it pays to LECs as exogenous and pass through any savings from reductions in those charges to residential service basket customers. This may be accomplished through the use of optional calling plans, promotions and discounts from the basic rates. Our recent performance review of the AT&T price cap plan indicated that AT&T has passed on these cost reductions to its customers. Although basic rates have remained relatively high, AT&T has passed on its savings from lower access charges in the form of optional calling plans and other discounts and promotions. We also have no reason to believe that AT&T's long distance competitors have not been forced by competition to follow suit. Thus, although the data BellSouth offered to show that basic long distance rates have not decreased may be correct, that data fails to capture the effect of optional call-

---

204. J. KRAUSHAAR, FEDERAL COMMUNICATIONS COMMISSION, FIBER DEPLOY-MENT UPDATE, 1991 (March 1992); J. GROSS, DONALDSON LUFKIN & JENRETTE, REPORT NO. 1226863, LOCAL TELEPHONE COMPETITION (May 18, 1992).

205. Notice, 9 F.C.C. Rcd. 1691 ¶ 25 (1995).

ing plans and other discounts.[206]

But optional calling plans did not offer the subscriber a lower price on the same service; rather, they reduced price on inferior offpeak service. Prices on those plans did fit into the index, and they did offer lower charges for an inferior service. The commission played with the index and made changes in the index fit its explanation.

CONCLUSION

Long-distance telephone regulation since divestiture has kept the price structure for that service in place but has not made it competitive. The FCC has not expressly admitted that its actions, particularly its reluctance to abandon the equal-charge rule and to deregulate AT&T's residential services, have fostered market sharing. As Huber said, "[T]hat [other carriers] seem to thrive under Commission regulation probably proves much more about regulation than about competition."[207]

Of course, it is possible that the FCC is merely overcautious or reluctant to abandon its earlier commitments to foster the development of MCI and Sprint. It is possible that those carriers' insistence that deregulation would be a disaster for them is correct. But the long-distance companies have been pushed and pulled to employ the tariffing process to interact with one another in their markets in ways that foster the collective development of noncompetitive price levels. As Sappington and Weisman have pointed out, the commission's regulatory policies have practically required collusion: "If AT&T competes too aggressively and thereby manages to gain a larger share of long-distance markets, it faces the prospect of asymmetric regulatory constraints."[208] And they note that "competitors may refrain from aggressive battle in the marketplace if the reward for winning the battle is the privilege of facing AT&T on equal terms."[209] The system of Federal Communications Commission regulation in the first decade after divestiture was not designed to

---

206. 77 Rad. Reg. 2d (P&F) 783, 795 ¶ 61 (1995).
207. GEODESIC NETWORK II, *supra* note 3, at 3.19.
208. DESIGNING INCENTIVE REGULATION, *supra* note 52, at 220.
209. *Id.*

complete an evolution to competitive markets. It was, perhaps, under the circumstances the best possible system to preserve and develop entrant carriers after decades of AT&T dominance. But the question still to be raised at this point is the extent to which regulation and antitrust "worked" to make prices at least partially competitive.

4

Concentration Levels and Service Provider Conduct in Long-Distance Markets after 1984

THE RELATIVE SIZES OF THE THREE LARGEST service providers, based on their shares of long-distance revenues, changed substantially in the first five years after the divestiture decree. Initially, AT&T dominated provision of service, with almost all of those revenues. AT&T still had more than 90 percent of interLATA toll revenues, while MCI and Sprint had 5 and 3 percent, respectively. But from 1984 to 1989, while AT&T's ranking stayed the same, its share decreased by 20 percent, and MCI and Sprint's shares increased by eight and six percentage points, respectively.

Subsequently, from 1990 to 1993, the shares of the three large providers stabilized. AT&T did lose three percentage points to MCI, but none to Sprint. Even so, the share reallocation process that had substantially increased the relative size of the second and third firms in the 1980s ceased. By the end of 1993 AT&T had 65 percent, while MCI and Sprint together had 29 percent of interLATA service revenues.[1] That pattern of concentration[2] did not

---

1. FCC, LONG-DISTANCE MARKET SHARES, FOURTH QUARTER (1993), tables 5 and 6.

2. The measure of "concentration" in this chapter is the Herfindahl-Hirschman index (HHI), equal to the sum of the squared shares of firm sales, with shares in decimal terms. That index enables one to make comparisons of concentration between that for an "equivalent" number of equal-sized firms and that observed in a market when shares are not in fact equal. The HHI ranges from one to zero, with one

vary across the four largest service markets; the initial loss of market share for AT&T in message toll services (MTS), outbound wide-area telecommunications services (WATS), inbound WATS (800 number services), and virtual network services (VNS) in the late 1980s was much the same and was followed by stability in share in the early 1990s.

Although the antitrust decree itself did not mandate reductions in AT&T's market shares, the application of the decree and the regulatory practices and procedures then in place provided exceptional opportunity for other carriers to take additional shares. AT&T's tariffs were subject to regulatory processes that did not apply to other carriers; those processes made AT&T's prices relatively inflexible. Access charges paid by all three toll service providers to local exchange carriers were set to favor the non-AT&T carriers. That AT&T was required to pay more for access than MCI and Sprint[3] was intended to compensate subscribers for MCI and Sprint's lower-quality access. But AT&T's higher access costs induced customers to shift to MCI and Sprint's services.[4] Only when the FCC equalized access charges at the end of the 1980s was that incentive for customers to shift eliminated.

The stability in revenue shares after 1989 was consistent with an important change in the FCC's regulatory procedures. The

---

indicating that a single firm makes all the sales and zero indicating that an infinite number of firms is present. The reciprocal of HHI is the number of equivalent, equal-sized firms; if

$$HHI = \sum_{i=1}^{n} S_i^2$$

for share S_i of firm i and each of n firms is of equal size, so that $S_i = 1/n$, then *HHI* $= \Sigma \, (1/n)^2 = 1/n$.

3. For example, in 1983 specialized common carriers paid an access charge only 45 percent that of AT&T's charge. Paul W. MacAvoy & Kenneth Robinson, *Winning by Losing: The AT&T Settlement and Its Impact on Telecommunications*, 1 YALE J. ON REG. 1, 34 (1983) [hereinafter *Winning by Losing*]. That same percentage discount held through 1987 for less-than-equal access connections.

4. *See* Paul W. MacAvoy & Kenneth Robinson, *Losing by Judicial Policymaking: The First Year of the AT&T Divestiture*, 2 YALE J. ON REG. 251 (1985).

commission at that point in time had imposed price-cap controls on AT&T tariffs.[5] Henceforth, AT&T could initiate price increases or decreases in reaction to changes in other suppliers' prices on short notice. The cap on the percent rate of change in the index price greatly enhanced the range of AT&T's price flexibility. AT&T could decrease rates in markets by up to 5 percent, not including the change in the price cap, which could add 5 percent of further reduction.[6] Those conditions changed the relationship among the three large carriers so as to allow an effective AT&T response to strategic discounting of rates that would prevent gains from shifting market share. AT&T could respond to tariffs MCI or Sprint submitted to the commission before the rates took effect and thus could preclude those companies from gaining share as a result of their pricing initiatives. In effect, the new procedures for tariff regulation established the basis for realizing stability in shares. Price caps facilitated a new collective discipline among the three large carriers.[7]

CONCENTRATION IN KEY NATIONAL INTERLATA MARKETS

The services provided by the three major carriers in the four most important markets are described as follows:

- *Message Toll Service*: calls from local exchange networks by residential and small business consumers.
- *Outbound WATS*: voice or data business calls using either switched or dedicated access based on numerous rather than individual calls from that source.
- *Inbound WATS (800 Service)*: the receipt of long-distance voice or data business calls using either switched or

---

5. Policy and Rules Concerning Rates for Dominant Carriers, Report and Order and Second Further Notice of Proposed Rulemaking, CC Dkt. No. 87-313, 4 F.C.C. Rcd. 2873 (1989).

6. *Id*. at 3054.

7. That discipline was earlier anticipated theoretically. *Cf*. DAVID S. SIBLEY & SIMON J. WILKIE, A REPEATED GAME OF PRICE CAP REGULATION (University of Texas Working Paper, revised January 1996).

dedicated access.

- *Virtual Network Services*: services provided in bulk to business customers using common carrier switching facilities as a user network indistinguishable from a facilities-based private network.

Revenue shares for the three largest carriers for those four classifications of service markets became more equal in the 1980s and either stabilized, or equalized at a much reduced rate, in the first half of the 1990s.[8] The Herfindahl-Hirschman index, or HHI, for nationwide MTS service was 0.76 in 1985 (the equivalent of that for 1.3 equal-sized firms), declined to 0.54 in 1990 (the equivalent of 1.9 equal-sized firms), and then declined further but very gradually to 0.50 (two equal-sized firms) over the first four years of the 1990s.

Business services break down into three key sets of markets: inbound (800 number service) WATS, outbound WATS, and virtual network services. The HHI for inbound WATS was initially 1.0 in 1985, given that AT&T was the only carrier to offer interLATA 800 services, but fell rapidly upon the entry of the other two carriers to 0.53 (1.9 equal-sized firms) by 1990 and stabilized at that level from 1990 to 1993. Concentration in outbound WATS services nationwide was below that in inbound WATS at the end of the nine-year period. The HHI for outbound WATS equaled 0.75 (1.3 equal-sized firms) in 1986, declined until 1991, and then stabilized at the relatively low level of 0.3 (3.3 equal-sized firms).[9] Concentration in markets for virtual network services was similar to

8. The data in this analysis were obtained from Multinational Business Services, Inc., based on historical series on revenues by company and class of service. Those were compiled from filings made with the FCC and state public utilities commissions, corporate reports, Wall Street analysts' reports, academic publications, interviews with corporate officials, and information obtained from federal and state regulatory agencies through Freedom of Information Act requests.

9. The HHI for each market from 1991 to 1993 has been estimated based on the assumption that the trend behavior for the total toll services applies on specific services. That is, a specific toll has been regressed on total toll shares and extrapolated for the later period from the regression coefficient for total toll and from later-period total toll assimilations. Such a procedure is used because data on specific service shares are not available after 1990.

that in inbound WATS but not outbound WATS services; the HHI declined from 0.65 in 1986 to 0.47 in 1989 (the equivalent of 2.1 equal-sized firms), where it remained throughout the early 1990s.

Figure 4–1 shows index levels in those four markets from 1985 to 1993. They reveal systematic reductions in concentration in all markets that converge to an HHI of 0.5 (except for outbound WATS, where the level was close to 0.3). For message toll service, the reduction in the HHI was equivalent to the addition of one-half an identical-sized firm, so that by 1993 there were two equal-sized sources of supply. For virtual network services, the index change was equivalent to the addition of three-quarters of a firm, which left the market with slightly more than two equal-sized firms. For inbound WATS, the declines in the HHI characterize the market structure as that associated with a transition from one to two same-sized firms. But for outbound WATS, the changes took the HHI from one-and-one-third equal-sized firms to the equivalent of three equal-sized firms. Those changes in shares in each of the sets of

FIGURE 4–1

HERFINDAHL INDEXES IN FOUR SETS
OF LONG-DISTANCE MARKETS

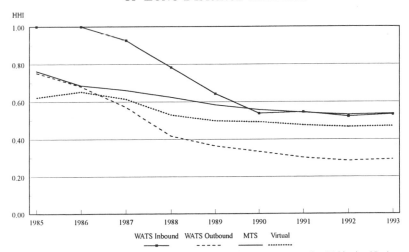

Source: The HHIs for the 1985 to 1990 period are based on company by company revenues from Multinational Business Services, Inc., *Interexchange Competition in the Price Cap Era: A Quantitative Analysis by Major Carrier, Service and Market Basket* (Washington, D.C.: 1990) at B-1 to B-8. The HHIs for the 1991 to 1993 period are estimated from a regression model in which HHI values in specific classes of service have been regressed for long-distance market shares. This is necessary because company-specific data by class of service are available only for 1985 to 1990.

markets mostly took place before 1990. Henceforth, those markets operated as if there were a static structure in service supply, or as if there were two equal-sized firms in message toll and in inbound and network WATS business services, but three equal-sized firms in outbound WATS business services.

CONCENTRATION IN INTERLATA
MARKETS IN CALIFORNIA

Since 1984, InterLATA market shares in California have been determined by the same market and regulatory conditions as in the rest of the country. The shares of the major facilities-based carriers of interLATA toll service revenues in California from 1984 to 1991 (in table 4–1) indicate a six percentage point annual decline for AT&T from 1984 to 1989 and a two-and-one-half percentage point annual decline from 1990 to 1991. MCI's share increased rapidly from 1984 to 1990, while Sprint's share increased from 1984 to 1986 and then stabilized. The HHI shows a similar pattern, that is,

TABLE 4–1 SHARES (%) OF TOTAL MINUTES-OF-USE OF INTERLATA SERVICE IN CALIFORNIA			
Year	AT&T	MCI	Sprint	HHI
1984	100	0	0	1.00
1985	88	5	6	0.78
1986	80	8	10	0.66
1987	77	9	11	0.61
1988	75	11	11	0.59
1989	70	14	12	0.52
1990	67	17	12	0.49
1991	65	18	13	0.47

Source: California Public Utilities Commission, Commission Advisory and Compliance Division, REPORT ON 1991 CALIFORNIA INTEREXCHANGE MARKET MONITORING PLAN (December 1993), exhibit 5.

a rapid decline from 1984 to 1989, followed by a leveling off in 1990 and 1991, at least in relative terms.

Even so, shares of revenues in specific markets were not the same in California as across the country. The HHI for interstate outbound WATS in 1985 was at the level of .75 (1.3 equal-sized firms), fell relatively rapidly, and then stabilized at .30 (3.3 equal-sized firms) by 1993.[10] The HHI for intrastate outbound WATS shows a different pattern; it fell from 0.98 in 1986 to 0.19 in 1989 and then rose to 0.33 by 1992.[11] The HHI for intrastate inbound WATS, initially at 0.99 in 1986, fell to 0.36 by 1992, and then reached the low value of 0.34 by 1993. Comparison of that with interstate inbound WATS shows that share concentration of interstate exceeded that of intrastate in most years, but the differences were not large or as consistent as those for MTS and outbound WATS.

CONCENTRATION IN INTERNATIONAL LONG-DISTANCE MARKETS

A description of the structure of international markets has to begin with defining the product and geographic dimensions of those markets. The two primary products considered here are international message toll services (IMTS) and international wide-area toll services (IWATS). The first are for residential and small business

10. The HHI for outbound WATS from 1991 to 1994 is calculated by assuming the same trend behavior as for total toll services. That assumption causes the HHI for outbound WATS to decline from 0.33 in 1990 to 0.27 in 1994. That would imply that AT&T's market share declined by as much as one-fourth in that period. Such a decline, in my view, is extremely unlikely. It is more likely that the HHI for outbound WATS is currently in the range of 0.3 to 0.4, given the known value of 0.37 for intrastate outbound WATS in 1992, but specific data to indicate that are not available for the interstate market after 1990.

11. One reason for the different pattern is that the interstate HHI series does not account for shares of resellers, while the intrastate HHI series compiled by the California PUC does include resellers. The California PUC was able to remove resellers for one year, 1992, and the facilities-based intrastate HHI for that year equaled 0.37, approximately the same as the interstate HHI. The decline in the HHI to 0.19 in 1989 may be due to the presence of resellers, whose relative importance in the market diminished after 1990.

customers; the second are services for high-volume business customers. International message toll is not a good substitute for IWATS for high-volume business customers, nor is IWATS a substitute for IMTS for residential customers, given that each requires inconvenient usage levels to achieve price parity. An additional important international service is discount IMTS service, for which carriers charge a fixed monthly fee and then offer lower rates per minute for use in offpeak periods. Discount IMTS plans offer lower rates than standard IMTS to customers making a sufficiently large number of calls to the extent that the larger call volume spreads the customer's cost of the monthly charge, and to the extent that those calls originate in offpeak periods.

The geographic dimensions of those markets can be specified by example. Consider a customer desiring to place a call from the United States to Canada. For that customer, the option to call a number in Germany is not a substitute, nor would a triangular call from the United States to Germany to Canada be a cost-effective alternative. Therefore, specific country pairs form relevant markets for international outbound calls from the United States. Given such a condition, the important markets are focused on national capitals or population centers of foreign destination countries to which U.S. customers place large volumes of calls. The pairs of the United States with eight foreign countries account for approximately 55 percent of the total outbound U.S. international calls.[12] Table 4–2 shows those country pairs and the 1993 volume of minutes billed in the United States in descending order.

The toll volume shares in the mid-1980s for AT&T, MCI, and Sprint together mostly exceeded 90 percent.[13] Table 4–3 shows that concentration in supply, as measured by the HHI, was higher than in domestic service markets. The HHI levels were at or near one in 1985, given AT&T's monopoly position,[14] but then fell

12. The only country of the top ten in revenue with the United States that was excluded was South Korea, which ranked eighth in 1993. *See* STATISTICS OF COMMUNICATIONS COMMON CARRIERS, 1993/1994 edition.

13. The commission does not publish data on carriers' revenues by type of service, for example, IMTS or IWATS. The shares estimated here are carriers' percentages of total international toll service revenues for outbound calls from the United Sates to a specific foreign country.

14. Market share data were obtained from the FCC's INTERNATIONAL TELECOM-

TABLE 4–2 SELECTED COUNTRY PAIRS AND VOLUME OF MINUTES BILLED IN THE UNITED STATES	
United States to:	Millions of Minutes Billed
Canada	2,493
Mexico	1,398
United Kingdom	799
Germany	572
Japan	397
France	263
Dominican Republic	253
Italy	229

Source: STATISTICS OF COMMUNICATIONS COMMON CARRIERS, 1993/1994 edition.

rapidly in those eight country pairs from 1988 to 1993. In fact, the HHI series in the six country pairs for which complete data are available indicate three quite different patterns of decline. In services to the United Kingdom, Italy, and Japan, the HHI declined at a steady rate over the period, while in Germany and the Dominican Republic it remained at or near one for several years before declining sharply. Finally, the HHI for France fell rapidly from 1985 to 1987 and then declined at a more gradual rate. The resulting levels of the HHI differed across countries within a fairly

MUNICATIONS DATA REPORT § 43.61 (various years). The commission did not collect data for Canada and Mexico before 1991.

Table 4-3
The Herfindahl-Hirschman Index for Outbound
U.S. Service to Selected Countries

U.S. to:	1985	1986	1987	1988	1989	1990	1991	1992	1993
Canada	n/a	n/a	n/a	n/a	n/a	n/a	0.51	0.44	0.42
Mexico	n/a	n/a	n/a	n/a	n/a	n/a	0.64	0.59	0.55
U.K.	0.91	0.78	0.73	0.68	0.61	0.57	0.54	0.52	0.50
Germany	1.00	1.00	1.00	0.86	0.73	0.68	0.67	0.62	0.56
Japan	1.00	0.96	0.80	0.71	0.64	0.57	0.56	0.52	0.43
France	1.00	0.89	0.69	0.66	0.61	0.56	0.54	0.52	0.49
Dominican Republic	1.00	0.95	0.93	0.97	0.82	0.73	0.70	0.67	0.52
Italy	1.00	0.97	0.83	0.76	0.71	0.65	0.64	0.60	0.56

Source: Market share data were obtained from the FCC's International Telecommunications Data Report, § 43.61 (various years).

narrow range. By 1993, the HHIs were as low as 0.42 for Canada (the equivalent of 2.4 equal-sized firms) to as high as 0.56 for Germany and Italy (the equivalent of 1.8 equal-sized firms). But in each country pair market, MCI and Sprint shares increased during the 1990s at the expense of AT&T, so that shares of the three firms converged.[15]

EXPLANATIONS FOR CHANGES
IN CONCENTRATION

At the time the consent decree was drafted, there was controversy as to how long it would take for long-distance markets to experience significant declines in carrier concentration. But in 1983 MacAvoy and Robinson predicted that the consent decree would confer share gain advantages on AT&T.[16] While it has turned out that long-distance markets remained highly concentrated, from all appearances they were in the process of becoming less concentrated in the late 1980s. MCI and, perhaps, Sprint, were trying then to take market share from AT&T. That ceased to be the case in the 1990s as shares became much more stable.

There were good market-based reasons for that pattern of share behavior. Technology of telecommunications switching and transmission was advancing at a rapid and unpredictable pace. Microwave supplanted much of coaxial cable transport; its cost characteristics differed from those of the wireline technology that preceded it. Microwave was less capital-intensive and made entry of smaller carriers in long-distance transport economically feasible. Huber noted, "The basic building block in microwave transmission is a radio capable of handling 12 voice calls; [since] long-distance networks typically carry a lot more traffic than that, ... transmission costs rise as traffic volumes increase—which in economic terms means that radio-based services are not 'natural monopolies'."[17] Those new systems should have led to relative

15. Canada, Japan, and Italy are the only countries where facilities-based carriers other than MCI and Sprint gained market share from AT&T. In those countries, facilities-based carriers other than AT&T, MCI, and Sprint accounted for 3.1 to 5.6 percent of the market by 1993.

16. MacAvoy & Robinson, *Winning by Losing, supra* note 3, at 31.

17. PETER W. HUBER, MICHAEL K. KELLOGG & JOHN THORNE, THE GEODESIC

growth of smaller carriers.

But even in the early years after divestiture, carriers were replacing microwave transmission with fiber-optic networks. Fiber-optic technology lowered the cost per message minute mile, but such savings were derived from expansion of throughput per unit of capital. Thus, Huber argued, long-distance transmission by fiber-optic cable developed significant new natural monopoly characteristics to provision of service:

> Lightwave transmission . . . requires . . . investment up front, with tiny marginal costs thereafter. The carrier spends billions before the network generates a penny of revenue; but once in operation, the network can carry billions of minutes of traffic at pennies or less per minute. The marginal cost of carrying an extra minute of traffic is very close to zero.[18]

Each of the nationwide facilities-based carriers—AT&T, MCI, and Sprint—currently has enough fiber capacity to carry all of the nation's long-distance traffic. By the late 1980s, Sprint alone had "far more capacity than it could possibly hope to utilize in the near-term," and "full provisioning of Sprint's fiber network would equip Sprint to handle . . . traffic . . . well in excess of AT&T's total switched traffic volume for the year."[19] In 1995 the FCC reported:

> [M]uch of the network capacity owned by the long-distance carriers is fiber optic technology, which is capable of expansion to serve increasingly larger amounts of traffic at relatively low cost. In 1993, AT&T owned 47 percent of the total fiber miles while serving 60 percent of the minutes of use of the interexchange market. In contrast, all other

NETWORK II: REPORT ON COMPETITION IN THE TELEPHONE INDUSTRY 3.3 (The Geodesic Co., 1992) [hereinafter GEODESIC NETWORK II].

18. *Id.* at 3.4.

19. Competition in the Interstate Interexchange Marketplace, Report and Order, CC Dkt. No. 90-132, 6 F.C.C. Rcd. 5880, 5888 ¶ 44 (1991).

interexchange carriers owned 53 percent of the total-fiber miles while serving 40 percent of the interexchange market. It therefore appears that AT&T's competitors have a greater supply of unused fiber capacity than AT&T.[20]

New generations of fiber-optic technology further increased the existing network's capacity.[21] Since the introduction of fiber, technological advances have increased installed capacity from 45 megabits per second to 90 megabits per second, to 540 megabits per second, then to 1.2 gigabits per second and now to 2.4 gigabits per second.[22] In 1994 Sprint announced deployment of synchronous optical network (SONET) rings, which would carry information at 2.4 gigabits per second and expected to complete deployment of rings throughout its national network by the end of 1996.[23] Sprint has since deployed about 23,000 miles of SONET fiber.[24] MCI announced deployment of SONET the same year[25] and now has also deployed 23,000 miles of SONET fiber.[26] AT&T's announcement followed in 1995.[27] Along with its use of SONET, AT&T will employ wave division multiplexing—a means of assigning multiple signals on the same fiber path to different wavelengths—that will increase the capacity in parts of its network to about 20 gigabits per second.[28] MCI has already begun to deploy wave division

20. Revisions to Price Cap Rules for AT&T Corp., Report and Order, CC Dkt. No. 93-197, 10 F.C.C. Rcd. 3009, 3017 ¶ 23 (1995) [hereinafter *Price Cap Revisions*].

21. Emmanuel DeSurvire, *Lightwave Communications: The Fifth Generation,* SCI. AM., Jan. 1992, at 114.

22. John T. Mulqueen, *Ten Years of Change,* COMM. WK., Jan. 3, 1994, at 8.

23. Christine Heckart, *SONET Strategies: Sprint Has Ring Fling,* NETWORK WORLD, May 16, 1994, at 45.

24. Tom Williams, *Carriers Pick up Speed on SONET Deployment; Synchronous Optical Network Transport Architecture,* TELEPHONY, May 15, 1995, at 32.

25. Paul Weichselbaum, *MCI's Broadband Telecommunications Solutions for Demanding Imaging Apps; MCI Communications Corp.,* ADVANCED IMAGING, June 1994, at 42.

26. Williams, *supra* note 24, at 32.

27. Dan O'Shea, *AT&T Forges Ahead with Network Upgrades,* TELEPHONY, June 12, 1995, at 12.

28. *Id.*

multiplexing and expects to increase network capacity to 7.5 gigabits per second.[29] Each gigabit per second increase in capacity lowers the costs of carrying additional bits on established networks by an order of magnitude.

The technological conditions for long-distance services are now such that the three large carriers have significant cost advantages over any entirely new entrants and also over current small carriers. The fixed costs of rights of way and installation of fiber-optic cable stand as a barrier to other potential carriers. Any one of the existing networks could carry all of the nation's long-distance traffic at lower cost than any new entrant, so that incumbents could repel that entrant from the long-distance market business by signaling decreases in prices.

Further, AT&T probably is the carrier with the greatest cost advantages, stemming from the size of its network: With its fiber system costs spread over larger message volumes, its unit operating costs converge to a level only slightly in excess of its access charges per call. Between 1990 and 1993, AT&T's fiber miles grew from 0.9 to 1.2 million miles; over the same period, MCI's grew from 0.4 to 0.6 and Sprint's grew from 0.45 to 0.47 million miles.[30] AT&T realizes further cost advantages in switching and access, again because of its volume of calls. In 1991 CompTel, the trade association of smaller interexchange carriers, insisted that if the FCC allowed access charges to be based on cost, AT&T would enjoy advantages amounting to $698 million per year, "twice the combined 1988 net income of those AT&T rivals that were profitable that year. That amount is eight times the combined 1988 net income of third tier carriers with revenues in excess of $10 million."[31]

---

29. MCI COMMUNICATIONS CORP., MCI PRESS RELEASE: MCI DEPLOYS TECHNOLOGY CAPABLE OF INCREASING CAPACITY BY FIFTY PERCENT WITHOUT NEW FIBER, Aug. 30, 1995; *MCI Hopes to Boost Network Capacity 50% Through New Method,* WALL ST. J., Aug. 31, 1995, at B5.

30. FCC FIBER DEPLOYMENT UPDATE—END OF YEAR 1994, table 2 (July 1995); *see also Price Cap Revisions, supra* note 20, at 3017–18 ¶¶ 24–25.

31. Comments and Request for Further Proceedings of CompTel, MTS and WATS Market Structure, No. 78-72, at 33 (FCC Feb. 22, 1991).

CompTel added that AT&T's advantages "[prevent] carriers from using available interexchange transmission capacity to discipline AT&T in any way."[32] Sprint agreed; it found that volume discounts "favor AT&T in practice simply because its enormous size advantage over other carriers makes it most likely to have the volumes necessary in any given location to take full advantage of these discounts."[33] CompTel found that access charges were 1.04 cents per minute lower for any carrier with a 65 percent market share over any carrier with a 10 percent share and that a carrier must control at least 25 percent of the market to compete with AT&T.[34] Otherwise the carrier could not "approach the switched transport cost of AT&T."[35] Investment analysts familiar with the revenues and costs of the interexchange carriers have reached similar conclusions.[36]

Market shares stabilized after 1990 as the fiber networks were completed. AT&T had 63 percent, and MCI *plus* Sprint had 30 percent, of all long-distance revenues by the end of 1993.[37] AT&T had 47 percent of the total fiber miles, compared with all other long-

32. *Id.* at 4. CompTel adds that "[i]f AT&T takes all the monopoly profits made possible by current access imbalances, the appearance of 'competition' might survive because some firms would still have room to offer service despite their cost disadvantages. But AT&T would control that competition, not the Commission." *Id.* at 23.

33. Reply Comments of Sprint, Expanded Interconnection with Local Telephone Companies, No. 91-141, at 6 (FCC Sept. 20, 1991); *see also* Comments of WilTel, MTS and WATS Market Structure, Transport Rate Structure and Pricing, No. 91-213, at 34–35 (FCC Nov. 22, 1991).

34. *See* Comments and Request for Further Proceedings of CompTel, MTS and WATS Market Structure, No. 78-72, at 22 (FCC Feb. 22, 1991).

35. *Id.*

36. *See, e.g.,* MERRILL LYNCH, UNITED STATES TELECOM SERVICES: LONG DISTANCE SECOND-TIER: PUMP UP THE VOLUME 9 (Oct. 13, 1993) (three major long-distance providers exhibit oligopolistic behavior and stable pricing); BROWN BROTHERS HARRIMAN & CO., AT&T BASIC REPORT 7 (Mar. 31, 1992) (should FCC establish cost-based access charges, it "would benefit AT&T more than its competitors"); RAYMOND JAMES & ASSOCS., INC., TELECOMMUNICATIONS INDUSTRY REPORT: OUTLOOK FOR THE INTERSTATE ACCESS CHARGE 3 (Feb. 10, 1992) (bringing access charges to costs would be "a positive for AT&T, and a negative for AT&T's interexchange competitors").

37. FCC LONG-DISTANCE MARKET SHARES, FOURTH QUARTER (1993), tables 5, 6.

distance carriers, which had 53 percent of the fiber miles.[38] The disparity between revenue and capacity shares has lead to the speculation that shares stabilized because "[i]n 1990, AT&T openly declared its intention to stabilize its share position. By 1992, the company had resolved to 'grow share' and 'at the same time . . . retain the margins in our business.' . . . However unwelcome the fact may be to policy makers of various shades, AT&T can, and does, unilaterally decide what share it will hold or cede in the long-distance market."[39]

An industry analyst wrote in 1991 that "it is difficult to imagine how MCI and Sprint will take meaningful share from AT&T now that AT&T has demonstrated it doesn't want to lose any more share."[40] Other carriers held similar views: Sprint in 1990 described the FCC's belief that AT&T's market share would erode further as "unfounded."[41] AT&T, said Sprint in 1991, had shown that it could "flex its economic muscle to halt erosion of its market share."[42]

The reality of today's long-distance markets is that the gains from scale in new technologies have turned out to be significant. Now that each of the three large interexchange carriers has the capacity to serve as a monopoly, mutual destruction would follow from each individual firm's taking price to levels where the firm would gain market share. Since AT&T probably has the lowest cost, it would hardly be profitable for MCI and Sprint to contest AT&T's shares in any of the key message toll or business service markets.

38. *Price Cap Revisions, supra* note 20, at 3017 ¶ 23.

39. GEODESIC NETWORK II, *supra* note 17, at 3.10 (quoting *AT&T MTS Volume, Revenues up in First Quarter, Pelson Says, in* THE REPORT ON AT&T, May 4, 1992, at 11).

40. PAINE WEBBER INC., INDUSTRY REPORT NO. 1105870, LONG-DISTANCE INDUSTRY 2, 4 (Feb. 25, 1991).

41. Reply Comments of Sprint, Competition in the Interstate Interexchange Marketplace, No. 90-132, at 47 (FCC Sept. 18, 1990).

42. Comments of Sprint, MTS and WATS Market Structure, No. 78-72, at ii (FCC Feb. 22, 1991).

Changes in Concentration and
Conduct of the Major Carriers

In markets with from two to three large carriers, the level of service activity of any one firm depends on the conduct or strategies of the others as to their pricing and service offerings. Any one carrier has to anticipate the actions of the others with respect to price structures inherent in their tariffs and the effects of those actions on its own prices and service levels. Together, the three large carriers had the capacity to determine the nature and extent of offerings through the four large markets both domestically and on outbound traffic from the United States. But the extent to which they determined price levels as a result depended on the nature of their interactions on their separate and collective conduct.

There are quite different ways in which the three large providers could interact. In a dynamic setting, in very general terms, they could set out strategies implying that they would cooperate in their separate tariff submissions, or make adjustments to each other's presence short of cooperation, or compete by setting out independent tariffs designed to take away market share. The implications for the competitiveness of prices would be quite different across those general strategies.

With cooperation, service providers' tariffs would be close to identical on the critical dimensions of price schedules and service offerings. Any one tariff would be established to set out that carrier's price schedule so that its price-cost margins would result in no changes in revenue shares of the individual firms. But when they do not cooperate to that extent, price-cost margins would decline as carriers take market share away from each other. That is, changes in concentration determine noncooperative price-cost margins (or $(p - mc)/p = f(HHI)$). That relationship of price level to the number of equal-sized firms is not yet specified, however. It still depends on the type of noncooperative interfirm behavior. When each provider takes current levels of others' shares as given and reduces its index price-cost margin to increase its share, company-to-company margins converge; they decline from the monopoly level to lower levels proportional to the HHI. That is, each carrier sets prices so that price-cost margins are equal to the HHI divided by the elasticity of market demand $[(p - mc)/p = HHI/e]$. But with service providers' seeking actively to reduce others' shares of service, price-cost margins would be driven to zero ($(p - mc)/p = 0$ for a price index designated as p and incremental costs including access charges as mc). In other words, the dynamics of price competitiveness depend on the specific company strategy as to share taking from others in various markets.[43]

But there are market conditions that favor the assumption that one strategy is being utilized over another. The historical changes that have taken place in market shares, and in regulation, provide credence for certain hypotheses as to the more likely strategies. When one carrier is responsible for almost all of the sales volume, and regulatory conditions result in a floor under that carrier's prices, then the other two would most plausibly seek to increase their market shares. A successful strategy of that genre should lead to more equal shares but also to declines in price-cost margins. When shares of the second and third largest firms increase to levels more comparable to if not the same as that of the largest firm, and regulation eliminates price floors for the largest firm, the second and third firms would not clearly be advantaged from further individual initiatives to increase their shares. With two to three equal-sized firms, any one can credibly threaten its rivals with large price reductions if those rivals seek to have shares further redistributed. As shares equalize, the original carrier's threat to cut prices to halt its loss of share becomes much more credible (since its inframarginal losses are less from doing so). It is more credible to expect that each firm sets out its own tariff, with the preconception that all firms will do the same, to maintain previous

---

43. Bresnahan asserts, "[E]ven such simple theories as Cournot, Bertrand, and collusion lead to very different $h(n)$ in $[p - mc(q/n) = h(n)]$ for per-firm output q/n and equal-sized firms n, where the 'toughness of price competition' refers to 'the slope of $h(n)$ not its level.'" Timothy J. Bresnahan, *Sutton's Sunk Costs and Market Structure: Price Competition, Advertising, and the Evolution of Concentration*, 23 RAND J. ECON. 137 (1992). Since the cooperative strategy is more profitable than the competitive one, other things being equal, cooperative-type results may be the goal for individual firms, even if a noncooperative framework is in place to avoid accusations of collusion in violation of antitrust laws. *Id.* But full competitive "toughness," as the second and third providers increased share, would imply falling price-cost margins, and no competitive "toughness" with inbound share stability would imply no reduction in higher than competitive margins.

shares.[44]

The alternative hypothesis is that competitive pricing takes hold as further equalization of shares leads to more intense rivalry to gain additional share. That set of strategies to shift percentage points of share would lead to deep discount tariffs to supplant prices in standard tariffs. As shares destabilize, margins decline sharply.

Model constructs support the development of the first hypothesis. Sibley and Wilkie analyze the behavior of duopolists in repeated games, one of which is under regulation in a case where the regulatory regime changes at a known time to a price cap control process.[45] That switch stabilizes shares and price-cost margins. According to the authors, the FCC's switch in July 1989 from a rate-of-return to price cap regime should have been the cause for price increases. At that point, AT&T's prices were in effect "grandfathered" into the price cap system. Those prices were set before the change in regime, under asymmetrically applied rate-of-return regulation, at levels based on the condition that AT&T could not cut prices in response to competitive initiatives of other carriers. But the new price cap regime sustains cooperative outcomes by making the threat of responsive price cuts credible. Assuming that the regime is put in place at a known time, the lag between announcement and implementation allows any nondominant firm to signal its intentions for its behavior after the price cap regime begins. The nondominant firm finds it advantageous to announce a strategic price initiative designed to induce a higher joint-profit equilibrium. The leader or dominant firm should infer that the other firm will adopt only such strategies. Such a model demonstrates that, at the onset of price caps, the regulated firm will set out its price strategy so as to increase price levels, and the unregulated firm will set its price at that or a higher level.

In summary, it appears that technology and regulatory conditions in markets for long-distance telecommunications have changed in directions that favored adoption of the first set of

44. *Cf.* Daniel Orr & Paul MacAvoy, *Price Strategies to Promote Cartel Stability*, 32 ECONOMICA 186 (1965), where general conditions are given in table 2 for three equal-sized firms or their equivalent (that is, HHI = 0.33) to have stable tacit collusion.

45. SIBLEY & WILKIE, *supra* note 7.

strategies. The three large carriers' marginal costs of providing service have become virtually the same, given that access charges for local exchange were the same after 1990 and that other operating costs have been minimal. The growth of each carrier's capacity has been so extensive that each firm could have provided the entire interexchange volume of services, which makes credible the threat of any one of the three to take rates to marginal costs. Those emerging conditions provided each carrier with more incentive to choose price levels that limit incursions in the revenue shares of each of the carriers in each of the key markets.

The carriers' practices in submitting tariffs to the FCC contributed to developing such stability. Each of the large service providers has offered an array of calling plans under tariffs submitted periodically to the commission. The procedure has been that AT&T submits tariffs first and then has been followed by MCI and Sprint. From 1990 to 1993, AT&T in each new tariff initiated a change that MCI and Sprint followed; their changes increasingly converged. By December 1993, AT&T, MCI, and Sprint arrived at virtually the same index price level for message toll services across the country.

That sequence of submissions with price convergence was also present in outbound WATS and after 1991 in inbound WATS. Remarkably, even in virtual network services for which subscriber self-provision of service provides a competitive alternative, the AT&T tariffs generated price changes from 1990 to 1993 that MCI followed with only a single exception.

THE CONDUCT FRAMEWORK FOR
ANALYZING PRICING BEHAVIOR

Given those conditions, it is possible to posit certain hypothetical relationships between changes in concentration and in price-cost margins across markets for long-distance services. Depending on the extent of interactivity among individual price setters, margins should decline more or less rapidly than share concentration declines. The general framework for setting out such expectations on changes in margins based on declining concentration is $[(p - mc)/p = -ms\,(1+v)/e]$, where ms is firm market share, e is market elasticity of demand, and v is the conjectural variation among firms.[46] For identical price-cost margins across firms, that condition is $[(p - mc)/p = -HHI(1+v)/e]$, and the conjectural variation term ranges from $(1 - HHI)/HHI$ for perfect collective interaction among firms to -1 for the fully competitive interaction. As adjustments in price-cost margins are made as a result of declines in the HHI, a further hypothesis is that the conjectural variation would also decline. Whether price-cost margins fall to zero or only proportionally to the fall in the HHI ($v=0$), the conclusion would be that markets become more competitive. Postdivestiture market behavior characterized in that way would show that price-cost margins decline not only as concentration declines, but at a more rapid rate.[47]

46. For reference to the use of v as the conjectural variation term, see J. A. Brander & A. Zhang, *Market Conduct in the Airline Industry: An Empirical Investigation*, 21 RAND J. ECON. 569 (1990).

47. That is, $\partial[(p - mc)/p]/\partial HHI = -(1+v)/e - (HHI/e)\partial v/\partial HHI > 0$.

5

Testing for Competitiveness in Changes in Price-Cost Margins

THE "COMPETITIVENESS" of service providers in long-distance markets can be assessed in terms of changes in price-cost margins for the key services from 1984 to 1994. Their prices have been specified in standard tariffs submitted to the Federal Communications Commission or in various discount plan tariffs that quote percentage discounts in standard plans. In addition, prices for business services on dedicated facilities have been specified as percentage reductions of tariff prices for standard business services. Price indexes for representative calls for six classes of services offered by AT&T, MCI, and Sprint have been constructed from tariffs of each of those carriers. The direct measure of the price-cost margin, specified as $[(p - mc)/p]$ in the last chapter, requires estimates of marginal costs as well. Those costs have been estimated as the sum of access charges levied by the local carrier for passing on messages to the long-distance carrier and operating expenses incurred from use of a carrier network to switch and transport those messages. Approximations for the two parts of that cost element have been used to estimate price-cost margins first for standard services and then separately for discount plans, for services nationwide, for services in California, and finally for international services outbound from the United States.

Each of those estimations can be taken in turn. The first step in constructing price indexes is to specify calling patterns for a representative consumer and then price those patterns from the relevant tariffs. Representative calling patterns are shown in table 5-1. The prices for those calls on each of six classes of standard service have been estimated from tariffs as specified in that table.[1] The calling pattern assumptions fit customers located on the East Coast. For estimating prices in California, however, the assumed calling pattern has been adjusted. The important differences are: (1) the distance calls travel is greater for California-based than for East Coast customers and (2) the time-of-day distribution of calls is earlier in the day for customers located in California. It is also assumed that the customer is located in the 415 area code (San Francisco) and that he makes calls to each area code outside California with equal probability.

Estimated prices per minute for the representative call on various carriers and services appear in table 5-2. They show that there were index price reductions in the late 1980s and index price increases in the early 1990s. The increases in the 1990s took place, moreover, when costs at the margin were declining.

Marginal costs have been estimated as the change in total costs resulting from an incremental change in existing service levels. For all long-distance services, those costs comprise access charges for calls based on tariffed rates for access switched services per conversation minute as obtained from the FCC. Pacific Telesis provided the access charges for dedicated services that were used to calculate all classes of interstate dedicated access costs for outbound and inbound services that are not switched. Access charges for intrastate, interLATA calls' tariffed rates per minute were obtained from Pacific Telesis for both switched and dedicated (outbound and inbound) access.[2]

---

1. The price indexes were calculated based on data provided by HTL Telemanagement, Ltd., by taking the assumed calling patterns and applying them to tariffs that AT&T, MCI, and Sprint maintain on file at the Federal Communications Commission.

2. The sources of access charge estimates over time are listed below following the type of service. Interstate MTS: FCC, MONITORING REPORT, 1994, table 5.11. Intrastate MTS: Pacific Telesis tariffs. Interstate WATS outbound switched: FCC, MONITORING REPORT, 1994, table 5.11. Interstate WATS outbound dedicated, open end of call: FCC, MONITORING REPORT, 1994, table 5.11; closed end of call: Pacific Telesis tariffs. Intrastate WATS outbound switched: Pacific Telesis tariffs. Intrastate WATS outbound dedicated: Pacific Telesis tariffs. Interstate WATS inbound

TABLE 5–1			
USAGE ASSUMPTIONS IN CALCULATING AN INDEX PRICE			

Distribution of Calls by Mileage			
Miles	Distribution		
0–55	6%		
56–292	8%		
293–430	6%		
431–925	30%		
926–1,910	33%		
1,911–3,000	17%		

Time-of-Day Distribution			
Day	85%		
Evening	10%		
Night/Weekend	5%		

Virtual Networks			
	On-Net	Off-Net	
Originating	80%	20%	
Terminating	25%	75%	

Tariff Sources:		Provider:	
Service Type	AT&T	MCI	Sprint
MTS	MTS	Execunet	Dial "1"
WATS Outbound-Switched	PRO WATS	Prism Plus	Dial "1" WATS Advantage
WATS Outbound-Dedicated	MEGACOM	Prism I	Ultra WATS
WATS Inbound-Switched	800 Ready Line	Business Line	FONLINE
WATS Inbound-Dedicated	800 MEGA-COM	800 Direct	Ultra 800
Virtual Network	SDN	Vnet	VPN

switched: FCC, MONITORING REPORT, 1994, table 5.11. Interstate WATS inbound dedicated, open end of call: FCC, MONITORING REPORT, 1994, table 5.11; closed end of call: Pacific Telesis tariffs. Intrastate WATS inbound switched: Pacific Telesis tariffs. Intrastate WATS inbound dedicated: Pacific Telesis tariffs.

TABLE 5–2			
PRICE PER MINUTE BY CARRIER AND SERVICE			
A. MTS			
Date	AT&T	MCI	Sprint
1/1/87	0.298		
3/1/87		0.289	0.289
1/1/88	0.265		
3/1/88		0.256	0.259
1/1/89	0.254	0.244	0.250
5/1/89		0.227	0.234
8/1/89		0.228	0.229
12/1/89		0.228	
12/15/89			0.230
1/1/90	0.233		
2/1/90		0.223	0.228
8/1/90		0.222	0.224
1/1/91	0.228		
2/1/91		0.222	
3/1/91		0.222	
6/3/91			0.228
7/1/91	0.227		
8/1/91			0.227
12/1/91		0.223	

TABLE 5–2 (CTD.)			
PRICE PER MINUTE BY CARRIER AND SERVICE			
A. MTS			
Date	AT&T	MCI	Sprint
1/2/92	0.228		
1/16/92		0.224	
3/1/92			0.228
6/1/92	0.227		
6/18/92		0.225	
9/1/92		0.223	
11/1/92			0.227
2/19/93	0.228		
3/4/93		0.225	
4/1/93			0.228
6/26/93		0.227	
8/1/93	0.229		
9/29/93	0.235	0.234	
10/1/93			0.235
1/19/94		0.234	
1/14/94	0.256		
1/19/94		0.255	0.256

TABLE 5–2 (CTD.) PRICE PER MINUTE BY CARRIER AND SERVICE			
B. WATS SWITCHED INBOUND (200 HOURS PER MONTH)			
Date	AT&T	MCI	Sprint
7/1/87	0.252		
1/1/88	0.219	0.221	
3/1/88		0.221	
12/1/88	0.215		
2/1/89			0.189
4/5/89	0.214		
5/1/89		0.194	
6/1/89			0.187
7/1/89	0.210		
2/1/91	0.211	0.197	
3/1/91			0.193
9/5/91	0.213		
10/1/91		0.199	
11/1/91	0.217	0.202	
1/1/92			0.197
6/1/92	0.220		
6/4/92		0.206	
7/1/92			0.203
11/1/92	0.224	0.214	0.212
8/1/93	0.232		
8/6/93		0.221	0.221
12/1/93	0.230		
1/1/94		0.219	0.222
2/1/94	0.239	0.227	0.231

TABLE 5–2 (CTD.) PRICE PER MINUTE BY CARRIER AND SERVICE			
C. WATS SWITCHED OUTBOUND (200 HOURS PER MONTH)			
Date	AT&T	MCI	Sprint
1/1/87	0.258		
7/1/87	0.249		
11/1/87			0.211
1/1/88	0.237		
3/1/88			0.199
8/1/88			0.199
11/1/88		0.211	
12/1/88	0.228		
1/5/89			0.202
2/1/89		0.209	
3/1/89	0.230		
4/1/89	0.219		
5/1/89		0.204	
6/1/89			0.191
9/6/89	0.214		
10/1/89		0.199	
11/20/89	0.213		
1/5/90			0.197
2/1/90		0.198	
4/5/90			0.196
7/27/90	0.217		

TABLE 5–2 (CTD.) PRICE PER MINUTE BY CARRIER AND SERVICE			
C. WATS SWITCHED OUTBOUND (200 HOURS PER MONTH)			
Date	AT&T	MCI	Sprint
8/1/90		0.201	
8/5/90			0.199
1/3/91		0.204	
2/1/91	0.221	0.209	
5/3/91			0.200
6/30/91	0.223		
1/3/92	0.225		
2/1/92		0.211	
2/3/92			0.203
6/1/92	0.227		
6/3/92			0.217
6/4/92		0.216	
7/3/92			0.215
11/1/92		0.215	
5/1/93		0.226	
5/3/93			0.219
8/1/93	0.235	0.237	
8/6/93			0.232
1/4/94	0.236		
2/1/94	0.244	0.249	0.241

TABLE 5–2 (CTD.)			
PRICE PER MINUTE BY CARRIER AND SERVICE			
D. VIRTUAL NETWORK (10,000 HOURS PER MONTH)			
Date	AT&T	MCI	Sprint
1/1/87	0.167		
1/1/88	0.141		0.139
11/1/88		0.131	
12/1/88	0.132		
1/5/89			0.129
2/1/89		0.116	
4/1/89	0.127		
4/19/89		0.113	
6/1/89			0.121
6/29/89	0.123		
7/1/89		0.108	
8/1/89			0.113
11/3/89			0.113
12/1/89		0.116	
3/11/90	0.123		
6/1/90			0.121
7/27/90	0.125		
8/1/90		0.118	

TABLE 5–2 (CTD.) PRICE PER MINUTE BY CARRIER AND SERVICE			
D. VIRTUAL NETWORK (10,000 HOURS PER MONTH)			
Date	AT&T	MCI	Sprint
9/1/90	0.167		0.122
11/1/90			0.122
4/1/91		0.116	
4/22/91	0.124		
12/16/91	0.126		
1/1/92		0.118	0.125
4/1/92		0.118	
6/1/92	0.132		
6/4/92		0.124	
7/1/92			0.130
3/1/93		0.126	
4/1/93	0.134		0.134
6/1/93		0.128	
8/1/93	0.139		
8/3/93		0.128	
8/6/93			0.139
2/1/94	0.144	0.137	0.138
Source: As described in the text and *supra* note 1.			

Estimates of the network operating costs per minute for a long-distance call have been reported by AT&T for WATS outbound and WATS inbound (800) services as shown in table 5–3.[3]

---

3. *See* Direct Testimony of John Sumpter on Behalf of AT&T Communications of California, Inc., Application of AT&T Communications of California, Inc. (U 5002 C) for Authority to Provide Intrastate AT&T 800 READYLINE Service, June 18, 1990.

Wharton Econometric Forecasting Associates (WEFA) report that the network cost of service equals $0.01 per minute, which supports those AT&T cost estimates.[4] The marginal cost estimates here are based on AT&T's estimates of operating costs for switched and dedicated WATS outbound and inbound services and WEFA's estimate of operating costs for MTS standard and discount services.

TABLE 5–3
AT&T ESTIMATES OF LONG-RUN NETWORK COSTS
FOR LONG-DISTANCE CALLS (DOLLARS PER MINUTE)

WATS Outbound Switched	WATS Outbound Dedicated	WATS Inbound Switched	WATS Inbound Dedicated
Pro WATS	Megacom WATS	READYLINE 800	Megacom 800
$0.0101	$0.0130	$0.0108	$0.0129

Source: Testimony of John Sumpter on Behalf of AT&T Comm. of California, Inc., Application of AT&T Comm. of California, Inc. (U 5002 C) for Authority to Provide Intrastate AT&T 800 READYLINE Service, June 18, 1990.

Access charges and network operating costs together comprise marginal costs that vary according to the types of services provided. Table 5–4 indicates the extent of variation between switched and dedicated services. The costs of switched interstate calls are greater because operating expenditures and access charges are higher. That table also indicates the significant decline in marginal costs over the ten-year period—by more than 50 percent for each type of service. Marginal costs declined over that period because state and federal regulatory decisions reduced access charges by more than ten cents per minute for switched and five cents per minute for dedicated services.

4. WHARTON ECONOMETRIC FORECASTING ASSOCIATES, ECONOMIC IMPACT OF ELIMINATING THE LINE-OF-BUSINESS RESTRICTIONS ON THE BELL COMPANIES (July 1993) at 20–21 (citing Bellcore data).

TABLE 5–4
ESTIMATED MARGINAL COSTS OF A REPRESENTATIVE
INTERSTATE LONG-DISTANCE MESSAGE

	Switched Service	Dedicated Outbound Service	Dedicated Inbound Service
Date	($ per message minute)		
5/26/84	0.183	0.105	0.099
1/15/85	0.187	0.107	0.101
6/1/85	0.172	0.099	0.094
10/1/85	0.164	0.096	0.091
6/1/86	0.150	0.096	0.091
1/1/87	0.134	0.096	0.090
7/1/87	0.125	0.096	0.090
1/1/88	0.116	0.093	0.088
12/1/88	0.106	0.084	0.079
2/15/89	0.105	0.082	0.078
4/1/89	0.101	0.066	0.063
1/1/90	0.088	0.058	0.055
7/1/90	0.085	0.054	0.051
1/1/91	0.082	0.052	0.099
7/1/91	0.080	0.051	0.048
7/1/92	0.078	0.049	0.047
7/1/93	0.077	0.050	0.047
Source: *Supra* note 2.			

The estimated price and marginal cost indexes provide the data required to calculate price-cost margins for each service for each year. Price-cost margins are estimated here as the difference between the price and cost indexes as a percentage of the price index. Margins are analyzed first for standard services and then for discount plans. Next, margins are examined for long-distance services within California. Finally, margins are analyzed for a sample of important outbound U.S. international markets.

THE DYNAMICS OF PRICE-COST
MARGINS AND MARKET SHARES

The price-cost margins and HHI estimates for the four major classifications of service markets appear below.[5] For message toll service (in figure 5-1) price-cost margins were constant over time and slightly variant across the three firms in the 1980s. Margins both increased and converged for the three firms in the 1990s—a reflection of the underlying increased similarity not only in access charges but also in the firms' standard tariff prices. Market concentration, as measured by the HHI, decreased from a level of 0.76 in 1985 to 0.54 in 1993. Those changes over time produced an inverse relation between profit margins and the HHI. Price-cost margins increased as concentration declined.

For WATS switched inbound access, as in figure 5-2, margins differed among the three firms from 1982 to 1989. AT&T's price-cost margins were consistently higher than those of MCI and Sprint. But as the two smaller carriers established inbound service comparable to that of AT&T, and as they began to pay the same access charges, their margin levels became more similar until in 1993 they had become virtually identical. As margins converged, they increased to 70 percent of prices. Because of AT&T's monopoly in that service at the time of divestiture, the HHI for inbound WATS was 1.0 in 1986 but decreased rapidly to 0.55 in 1990, after which it stabilized at 0.53 by 1993. Thus, inbound WATS pricing margins increased to high levels as concentration declined significantly.

5. While it is customary to measure the HHI in units (thousands), based on shares in whole numbers, it is assumed here that shares are percentages (thousandths) for convenience in placing the HHI and margins on the same diagram.

FIGURE 5-1
PRICE-COST MARGINS AND MARKET CONCENTRATION—MTS

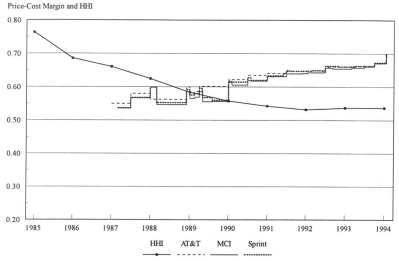

Sources: Marginal costs from FCC and WEFA, rates from HTL Telemanagement, Ltd., and market concentration from Multinational Business Services, Inc.

FIGURE 5-2
PRICE-COST MARGINS AND MARKET CONCENTRATION—
WATS SWITCHED INBOUND

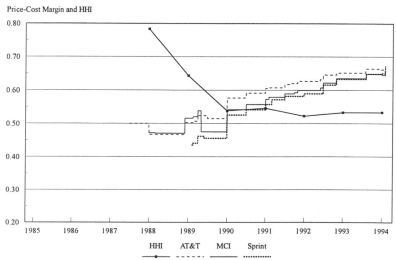

Note: Service for 200 hours per month.
Sources: Marginal costs from FCC and AT&T, rates from HTL Telemanagement, Ltd., and market concentration from Multinational Business Services, Inc.

For outbound WATS with switched access, as illustrated in figure 5-3, the price-cost margins of AT&T, MCI, and Sprint followed a path of steady increases during the late 1980s and early 1990s—from 55 percent to 60 percent initially and to 75 percent in 1994. Margins of the three suppliers converged following the establishment of uniformity in prices. Concentration in shares as indicated by the HHI declined rapidly from 1985 to 1988 from a level of 0.75 to 0.42 and thereafter stabilized at 0.30, the equivalent of three-and-one-third equal-sized firms. Again, as for inbound WATS, margins rose to high levels as the three large service providers moved toward much more equal shares of revenues.

FIGURE 5–3
PRICE-COST MARGINS AND MARKET CONCENTRATION—
WATS SWITCHED OUTBOUND

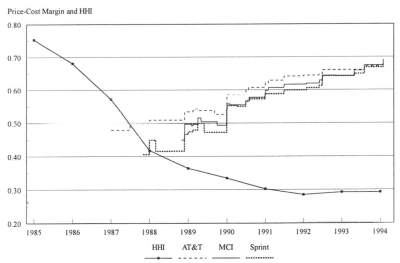

Note: Service for 200 hours per month.
Sources: Marginal costs from FCC and AT&T, rates from HTL Telemanagement, Ltd., and market concentration from Multinational Business Services, Inc.

Virtual network services offered to large-volume business users were available at prices that discounted WATS outbound tariffs in the late 1980s. Because of extensive differences in those discounts across the three large providers, price-cost margins for virtual services varied extensively in 1989 and 1990 (as shown in figure 5-4). Price-cost margins were also ten to fifteen percentage points lower than for WATS services. That would be a difference in margins in keeping with the most profitable price structure of a discriminating monopolist, given that the price elasticity of demand for virtual services is higher (due to the ability of those buyers to self-provide much of that service with their own networks).

FIGURE 5–4
PRICE-COST MARGINS AND MARKET CONCENTRATION—
VIRTUAL NETWORK

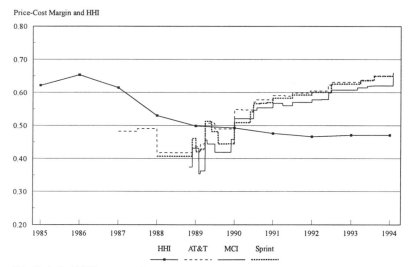

Note: Service for 10,000 hours per month.
Sources: Marginal costs from FCC, Pacific Bell, and AT&T, rates from HTL Telemanagement, Ltd., and market concentration from Multinational Business Services, Inc.

After 1990, margins for AT&T and Sprint were almost identical while those for MCI were lower. Over the first three years of the 1990s, price-cost margins for all three providers increased to levels twice what they were previously; margins for MCI were still lower than for the other two, but that company maintained a roughly constant price differential relative to the others. The HHI decreased from 0.65 to a level of 0.50 by 1989 and stabilized at 0.47 by 1992. Thus, in the 1990s, price-cost margins doubled while the three providers stabilized shares of service revenues.[6]

---

6. Those margin-share relationships are not sensitive to the estimates of marginal cost; for the negative correlation between trend margins and the HHI to have been

Reviewing the behavior of pricing margins across all four sets of markets, one concludes that they increased while concentration stabilized in the first half of the 1990s. When AT&T's share stopped its slide downward, price-cost margins for all three large service providers increased by substantial percentages each year.

PRICE-COST MARGINS IN DISCOUNT PLAN SERVICES

Standard tariffs for message toll services were displaced in part by discount plan tariffs in the first half of the 1990s. At the same time, WATS tariffs for large-volume business subscribers were displaced by contract virtual network service tariffs. The extent to which discounts in the new tariffs reduced the prices subscribers paid is not known, because there is no information as to which tariff—standard or discount—applied for services actually delivered to subscribers. Discount tariffs submitted to the FCC or the state commissions probably applied for a third of WATS services by volume and revenues in the 1990s. No similar estimate can be made of the percentage of volume or revenues of message toll services provided on discount plans.

Even so, the three largest facilities-based carriers offered discount plan message toll services aimed at home and small business subscribers throughout the country. For example, the AT&T True USA Savings plan offered a 20 percent reduction on long-distance charges for customers spending more than $50 per month. The question is what that implied for the "price" of a representative call.

MTS discount calling plans divide into three main classifications.[7] The most common plans in the early 1990s required the

---

reversed, marginal costs would have to have increased by more than 57 percent in 1990 and 75 percent in 1993, relative to marginal costs in 1985. Recall that marginal costs included access charges and operating costs. Leaving aside access charges as reported by the FCC, for the trend in price-cost margins to have been reversed, incremental operating expenses would have to have increased by a factor of four in 1990 and by a factor of five in 1993, relative to 1985, to change the direction of the relationship between concentration and price-cost margins.

7. Appendix 1, Discount Plan Summary, provides detailed information on the most prevalent discount plans of the three large carriers.

customer to pay a monthly fee to receive an amount of "free" calling time during offpeak periods. For example, under AT&T's Reach Out America, a customer paid a fixed fee to receive one hour of calling time to be used during night/weekend hours (calls made during the day were charged the standard MTS rate). Other AT&T plans that fell into that group were: Small Business Option, Block of Time–One-Hour Plan with Evening Option, Block of Time–One-Hour Plan with Evening & Day Option, and Block of Time–Half-Hour Plan. MCI's discount plans that fell into that group were: PrimeTime Plan, PrimeTime–Day Plan, Sure Save Option, Sure Save–Evening & Day Plan, Sure Save–Half-Hour Plan, and Any-Time Plan. Sprint's discount plans in that group were: Sprint Select, Sprint Select–Day Option, Sprint Select–Day Plan, and Sprint Select–Day Plan–Evening/Night Option.

The second set of discount plans consisted of those based on monthly usage levels. For example, under AT&T's True USA Promo, a customer received a 10 percent discount on her monthly long-distance bill between $10 and $24.99, and higher percentage discounts at higher usage levels. The MCI discount plans did not include that type of plan. Sprint had three plans that fell into that group: Dial "1" Usage Discounts, Residential Promo, and Sprint Plus Usage Discounts.

The third classification of discount plans comprised those in which discounts were triggered by selection of a person called. MCI had two plans (Friends & Family I and Friends & Family II) that gave discounts on calls to specific other subscribers. For example, under Friends & Family I, a customer chose a "calling circle" of other MCI customers and received a 20 percent discount on calls to those customers. The AT&T and Sprint discount plans examined here did not include that type of plan.[8]

The price per minute of a representative long-distance call made under any one of those types of discount plan can be determined from (1) the customer's monthly usage level, (2) the distribution of that customer's calls by day, evening, and night/weekend,

---

8. Two plans did not fall into any of the above groups: AT&T's Pro WATS 1 Plan and MCI's EasyRate Option (see individual plan summaries in appendix 1 for more detailed information on all those plans).

(3) the distribution of the customer's calls by mileage, (4) the number of individual calls, and (5) the time length of individual calls.[9] To calculate representative prices for each calling plan, two different distributions of monthly usage levels have been stipulated, that from survey data complied by LINK Resources Corporation (LINK) and that contained in a submission from AT&T in proceedings at the FCC. Based on the LINK data, table 5–5 indicates the percentage of respondents with monthly long-distance bills falling in certain ranges. (For example, 36 percent of AT&T's customers reported monthly long-distance bills of less than $10.99.[10]) Table 5–5 also indicates the distribution of residential customers according to AT&T's submission to the FCC.[11] AT&T's data suggest that a higher percentage of its customers had monthly long-distance bills of less than $10 than the LINK data indicated.

For each of the eleven monthly bill categories provided in the LINK data, standard and discount MTS prices for a representative call have been estimated on the basis of usage rates, time, and mileage distributions assumed in generating the price indexes for standard MTS. The weighted average of those eleven prices, with weights equal to percentages of customers' monthly bills in those classes, yields an index price per call minute for standard versus discount calling plans.[12] In addition to the index prices reported in

9. Calls are assumed to be direct-dialed, not collect, and not to incur any credit card charges.

10. In that survey, some customers reported that they did not know their monthly usage levels. They were assigned on a pro rata basis to the eleven usage categories. The customers' monthly bills were set equal to the midpoints of the ranges shown in table 5–6.

11. According to Mr. Mandl's submission, "a total of over 60% [of its customers spend] $10 or less in calling per month. About a quarter of AT&T's customers make between $10 and $75 in long distance calling per month, [and] less than 5% of AT&T customers make more than $75 in long distance calls per month." Since the stated percentages sum to 90 percent, we must assign the remaining 10 percent of AT&T's customers. To be conservative, they are assigned to the $10 to $75 class, rather than the less than $10 class, since that results in lower prices and price-cost margins. *See* Letter of Alex Mandl, Executive Vice President and Chief Executive Officer of AT&T's Communications Services Group, to the Honorable Reed E. Hundt, Chairman, Federal Communications Commission, Oct. 4, 1994.

12. In some cases, low-volume usage levels caused prices to be higher under discount calling plans than under standard MTS. In those cases the discount prices

this section, appendix 2 (tables A2–6 and A2–7) provides details on a wide range of alternative calling profiles (sixty profiles for residential customers and forty-eight for small-business customers). Calculating prices for discount MTS services with those additional calling profiles ensures that results deriving from the base-case profile are robust: changing assumptions regarding customers' calling profiles does not affect conclusions of the study.

TABLE 5–5			
DISTRIBUTION OF RESIDENTIAL CUSTOMERS			
HAVING MONTHLY BILLS IN THE INDICATED RANGES (%)			
Monthly Bill	AT&T	MCI	Sprint
LINK Data			
Up to $10.99	36	30	27
$11.00 to $14.99	5	4	4
$15.00 to $24.99	17	14	17
$25.00 to $34.99	13	15	15
$35.00 to $49.99	10	14	12
$50.00 to $74.99	9	10	12
$75.00 to $99.99	4	6	5
$100.00 to $149.99	3	2	6
$150.00 to $199.99	1	2	1
$200.00 to $249.99	1	2	1
Over $250.00	1	1	1
AT&T Data			
Up to $10.00	60	n/a	n/a
$10 to $75	35	n/a	n/a
Over $75	5	n/a	n/a

Source: LINK Resources Corp., 1993 HOME MEDIA CONSUMER SURVEY: RESIDENTIAL TELECOMMUNICATIONS 106 (1993); AT&T data as explained in the text.

were excluded from the weighted-average price calculation. Appendix 2 contains further details on the calculation of the weighted-average index prices.

The discount price indexes for Reach Out America[13] (AT&T), Prime Time Day and Friends and Family I (MCI), and Sprint Plus and Sprint Select Day (Sprint) have been used to form a set of offerings on eleven calling patterns. The most striking aspect of that set relates to discount pricing for low-usage customers. Most of those customers could not take advantage of any discount plan to achieve a price per call below the standard price because their monthly bills were below the required minimum. An AT&T submission to the FCC stated that 60 percent (approximately thirty-nine million) of its customers had monthly bills of less than $10, a level that would disqualify all of them from realizing lower prices by signing up for Reach Out America.

Even so, large numbers of subscribers signed on whether they qualified or not. It is instructive to observe what prices small customers paid under carriers' "discount" plans. As shown in figure 5–5, those customers with monthly bills of $5.50 paid more than double the standard price. And those customers who signed on to the most popular MCI plan up to mid-1991 paid more than double the standard MCI tariff price. After 1991, when its Friends and Family I plan was introduced, they received some discount (see figure 5–6).[14] Sprint's customers paid the same as standard MTS rates for its Sprint Plus Usage Discounts, but they paid almost double for its Sprint Select Day plan (see figure 5–7). For most of that period so-called discount plans offered higher prices than standard MTS tariffs to long-distance customers with limited usage rates each month.

For customers with larger monthly bills (for example, equal to the all-sample average bill), there were savings in those years from joining a discount plan.

13. The particular plan was the Block of Time–One-Hour Plan with Day & Evening Option.

14. Friends and Family I produces lower prices because 30 percent of a customer's bill is assumed to be accounted for by calls to individuals in their "calling circle" who are MCI customers. In calculating prices for Friends and Family II, which offers discounts on calls to non-MCI customers in a "calling circle," it is assumed that an additional 50 percent of a customer's calls are made to individuals in their calling circle who are not MCI customers.

FIGURE 5–5

RESIDENTIAL INDEX PRICES FOR AT&T STANDARD SERVICE
AND REACH OUT AMERICA DISCOUNT CALLING PLAN

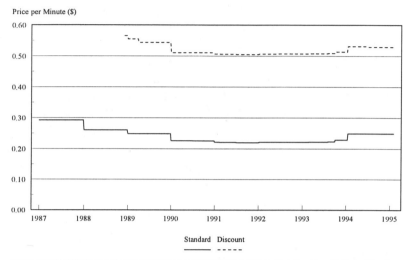

Notes: Monthly bill of $5.50. Discount plan is Reach Out America Block of Time - One-Hour Plan with Day and Evening Option.

FIGURE 5–6

RESIDENTIAL INDEX PRICES FOR MCI STANDARD SERVICE
AND PRIME TIME DAY AND FRIENDS & FAMILY I
DISCOUNT CALLING PLANS

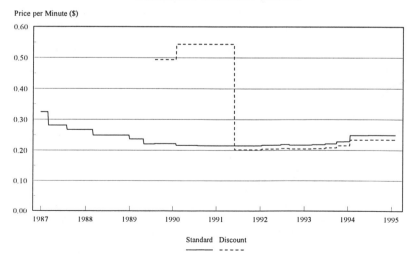

Notes: Monthly bill of $5.50. Discount plan is Prime Time Day (8/1/89 to 5/31/91) and Friends and Family I (6/1/91 to 2/1/95).

FIGURE 5-7

RESIDENTIAL INDEX PRICES FOR SPRINT STANDARD SERVICE
AND SPRINT PLUS USAGE AND SPRINT SELECT DAY
DISCOUNT CALLING PLANS

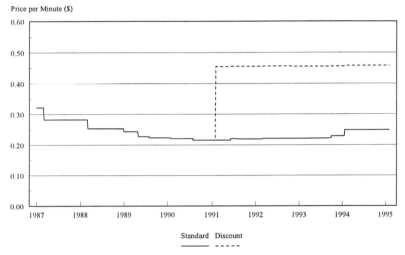

Notes: Monthly bill of $5.50. Discount plan is Sprint Plus Usage Discounts (5/1/89 to 1/31/91) and Sprint Select Day Plan (2/1/91 to 2/1/95).

Figures 5-8 through 5-10 indicate the percentage of the standard price that was saved by being on carrier discount plans. The weighted-average index price for AT&T's Reach Out America plan was approximately 96 percent of the standard MTS index price for the same call (see table 5-6). MCI's customers paid approximately 94 percent of its standard MTS rate (table 5-6), while Sprint's customers received discount rates that were from 94 percent to 77 percent of standard MTS from 1989 to 1994 (table 5-6).

FIGURE 5–8

RESIDENTIAL INDEX PRICES FOR AT&T STANDARD SERVICE
AND REACH OUT AMERICA DISCOUNT CALLING PLAN

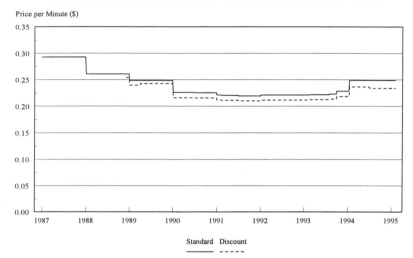

Note: Discount plan is Reach Out America Block of Time - One-Hour Plan with Day and Evening Option.

FIGURE 5–9

RESIDENTIAL INDEX PRICES FOR MCI STANDARD SERVICE
AND PRIME TIME DAY AND FRIENDS & FAMILY I
DISCOUNT CALLING PLANS

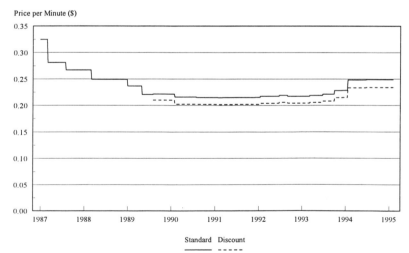

Note: Discount plan is Prime Time Day (8/1/89 to 5/31/91) and Friends and Family I (6/1/91 to 2/1/95).

FIGURE 5–10
RESIDENTIAL INDEX PRICES FOR SPRINT STANDARD SERVICE
AND SPRINT PLUS USAGE AND SPRINT SELECT DAY
DISCOUNT CALLING PLANS

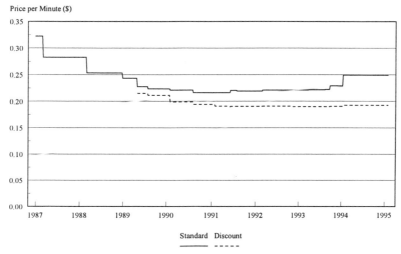

Note: Discount plan is Sprint Plus Usage Discounts (5/1/89 to 1/31/91) and Sprint Select Day Plan (2/1/91 to 2/1/95).

TABLE 5–6 DISCOUNT PLAN PRICES AS A PERCENTAGE OF STANDARD MTS PRICES			
Year	AT&T	MCI	Sprint
1989	96	95	94
1990	96	94	90
1991	96	94	87
1992	96	94	86
1993	96	94	83
1994	94	94	77
Source: As described in the text for price indexes on the representative long-distance call.			

Even though they were discounts, those prices in the discount calling plans offered by AT&T, MCI, and Sprint increased after 1990 and at a faster rate than did prices in standard plans for the same call.[15] Discounting (except for Sprint's) did not decrease prices more over time since discount plan prices were constant or declining percentages of rising standard MTS prices. Thus, as concentration declined, the prices of discount plans show no more evidence of reductions than do those of the standard rates that they discount.

AT&T's price-cost margins on its Reach Out America plan were approximately 97 percent of those on its standard MTS plan (see figure 5–11 and table 5–7).[16] MCI's profit margins for its Prime Time Day and Friends and Family I plans averaged approximately 95 percent of those from offerings under its standard MTS plan (see figure 5–12 and table 5–7). And Sprint's margins earned on its Sprint Plus and Sprint Select discount plans averaged approximately 90 percent of its standard MTS plan (see figure 5–13 and table 5–7). Price-cost margins earned by AT&T, MCI, and Sprint on those discount MTS calling plans increased from 1987 to 1994, even though that period was marked by a substantial decline in market concentration.

That pattern of profit margins, on both standard and discount plans, in the presence of falling market concentration "may have occurred for a variety of reasons."[17] Indeed, there are at least

15. In addition to the index prices calculated on the basis of membership over time in some discount plan, prices were estimated using the extreme assumption that a customer changed plans immediately at zero cost whenever his carrier offered a plan that provided that customer with a lower price. That would result in a theoretical "minimum" index price. As shown in appendix 2, the basic results of the analysis remain unchanged, even under that extreme assumption.

16. AT&T's price-cost margins can also be calculated by using as weights the percentages of customers in the three different monthly bill categories shown in table 5–5. The resulting index prices and price-cost margins using AT&T's data are slightly higher than the prices and margins found using the LINK data. That occurs because AT&T's submission to the FCC reports a higher percentage of customers falling into the less than $10 per month category.

17. Affidavit of B. Douglas Bernheim and Robert D. Willig, *An Analysis of the MFJ Line of Business Restrictions*, United States *v.* Western Elec. Co., Inc. and American Tel. & Tel. Co., Civil Action No. 82-0192 (Dec. 1, 1994).

four reasons why long-distance carriers would offer discounts: (1) to pass on cost savings, (2) to "cheat" on tacitly collusive prices, (3) to provide lower prices specifically to more price-sensitive customers, and (4) to discipline resellers so as to limit their share of markets for MTS services.

FIGURE 5–11

RESIDENTIAL PRICE-COST MARGINS FOR AT&T STANDARD SERVICE AND REACH OUT AMERICA DISCOUNT CALLING PLAN

Price-Cost Margin

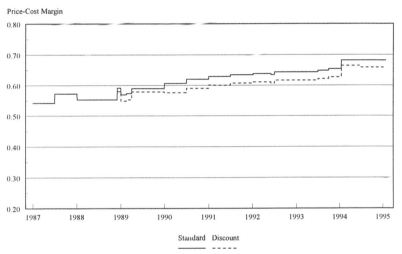

Standard   Discount

Note: Discount plan is Reach Out America Block of Time - One-Hour Plan with Day and Evening Option.

Sources: Marginal costs from FCC and rates from HTL Telemanagement, Ltd.

TABLE 5–7			
DISCOUNT PLAN PRICE-COST MARGINS AS A PERCENTAGE OF STANDARD MTS PLAN PRICE-COST MARGINS			
Year	AT&T	MCI	Sprint
1989	98	95	95
1990	97	96	93
1991	97	96	91
1992	98	96	91
1993	98	97	90
1994	98	97	87
Source: As described in the text.			

FIGURE 5-12

RESIDENTIAL PRICE-COST MARGINS FOR MCI STANDARD
SERVICE AND PRIME TIME DAY AND FRIENDS & FAMILY I
DISCOUNT CALLING PLANS

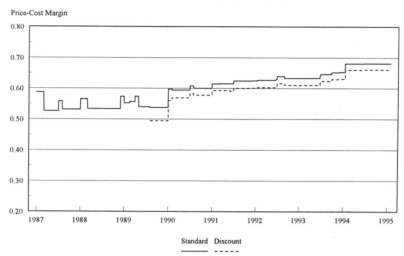

Note: Discount plan is Prime Time Day (8/1/89 to 5/31/91) and Friends and Family I (6/1/91 to 2/1/95).
Sources: Marginal costs from FCC and rates from HTL Telemanagement, Ltd.

FIGURE 5-13

RESIDENTIAL PRICE-COST MARGINS FOR SPRINT STANDARD
SERVICE AND SPRINT PLUS USAGE AND SPRINT SELECT DAY
DISCOUNT CALLING PLANS

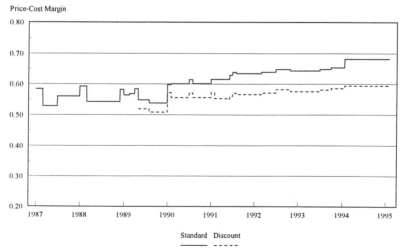

Note: Discount plan is Sprint Plus Usage Discounts (5/1/89 to 1/31/91) and Sprint Select Day Plan (2/1/91 to 2/1/95).
Sources: Marginal costs from FCC and rates from HTL Telemanagement, Ltd.

The first two reasons are scarcely credible. If discount plans passed on cost savings, margins would be the same on standard and discount plans, but they are lower on discount plans. Margins generated by AT&T, MCI, and Sprint for discount services show the same rising trend as for standard MTS service, so that the hypothesis that the discounts were manifestations of "cheating" on tacitly collusive prices would make sense only if "cheating" were being reduced over time. The two remaining explanations for discounts are that prices became discriminatory in favor of more price-sensitive customers or that discounts were an attempt to prevent resellers from capturing MTS market share. The evidence on rising margins does not favor one or the other of those two explanations. Both are consistent with the conclusion that the MTS market's competitiveness lessened in the 1990s with the introduction of discount calling plans.

CALIFORNIA PRICE-COST MARGIN BEHAVIOR

Markets within a state conceivably performed differently as carriers proposed tariffs and service offerings that depended not only on the practices and procedures of the FCC but also on the density of subscribers and distance between metropolitan regions. It is not practically possible to survey and analyze those differences for both business and residence services throughout the country. But the results of the interaction of the three large carriers with the regulatory process in California can serve as the first step in such a survey. The high density of traffic among that state's three large cities should have served as an incentive to increase share growth from reduced profit margins. And the California PUC's required reductions in access charges should have provided the basis for price reductions that themselves could have led to increasing competitiveness in the 1990s.

Prices for representative long-distance calls from California have been estimated on the basis of appropriate adjustments in the assumptions as to calling patterns elsewhere in the country. Marginal costs have been estimated in the same way as for services in other markets, except for intrastate services dependent on within-California access charges, as shown in table 5–8. Thus, marginal costs were at levels approximately half of those for interstate services throughout the 1984 to 1994 period.

Date	Switched Service	Dedicated Service
TABLE 5–8 ESTIMATED MARGINAL COSTS OF A REPRESENTATIVE INTRASTATE LONG-DISTANCE MESSAGE		
	($ per message minute)	
01/01/84	0.212	0.117
07/16/85	0.181	0.102
01/15/86	0.183	0.103
03/15/86	0.179	0.101
03/19/86	0.162	0.092
01/01/87	0.156	0.089
05/01/87	0.134	0.078
06/01/87	0.151	0.087
11/05/87	0.115	0.069
01/01/88	0.127	0.074
06/10/88	0.127	0.075
09/06/88	0.124	0.073
10/01/88	0.124	0.073
01/01/89	0.099	0.060
05/01/89	0.108	0.063
09/01/89	0.110	0.065
01/01/90	0.090	0.055

TABLE 5-8 (CTD.) ESTIMATED MARGINAL COSTS OF A REPRESENTATIVE INTRASTATE LONG-DISTANCE MESSAGE		
	Switched Service	Dedicated Service
Date	($ per message minute)	
06/01/90	0.088	0.053
10/01/90	0.091	0.054
01/01/91	0.083	0.051
06/01/91	0.080	0.049
01/01/92	0.068	0.043
02/01/92	0.068	0.043
09/20/92	0.067	0.042
09/21/92	0.067	0.042
11/01/92	0.067	0.042
12/01/92	0.067	0.042
01/01/93	0.067	0.042
03/06/93	0.067	0.042
08/08/93	0.067	0.042
09/20/93	0.067	0.042
01/01/94	0.066	0.041
Source: As described in the text.		

The resulting price-cost margins on MTS service offerings of AT&T, MCI, and Sprint in California on outbound calls to other states increased over time, as shown in figure 5-14. Initially, they increased and then decreased in a series of steps from 1987 to early 1990, but then increased systematically from mid-1990 to January 1994. The increase in margins in the 1990s was substantial, from five to ten percentage points, even though the HHI declined over that period. In addition, as figure 5-14 illustrates, a pattern evident in many long-distance service markets is repeated here. The individual carrier margins converged over time, and by 1992 changes in margins took place at the same time and to the same percentage point.

FIGURE 5-14

INTERSTATE CALIFORNIA-BASED PRICE-COST MARGINS
AND MARKET CONCENTRATION—MTS

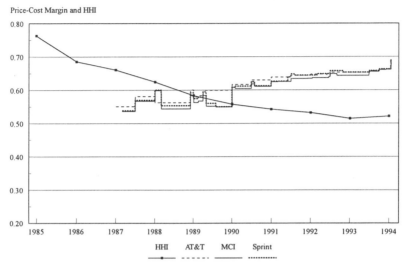

Note: Calling pattern assumption: day =75%, evening = 15%, and night/weekend = 10%.
Sources: Marginal costs from FCC, rates from HTL Telemanagement, Ltd., and market concentration from Multinational Business Services, Inc.

The same three large carriers plus a fringe of smaller carriers and resellers provided interLATA long-distance services within the state. MTS price-cost margins increased despite the fact that the relevant HHI decreased over the entire postdivestiture period (see figure 5-15). The primary difference between interstate and intrastate price-cost margins for MTS services was that interstate margins generally exceeded intrastate margins. That was most likely the result of two factors: (1) intrastate prices for 100-mile calls (the assumed distance) were substantially less than interstate prices for calls traveling between 926 and 3,000 miles (which account for 91 percent of calls in the assumed interstate calling pattern). Second, the marginal costs of those shorter intrastate calls were not substantially lower than the marginal costs of the longer-distance interstate calls. Thus, higher interstate margins indicate that the carriers were able to discriminate against calls traveling long distances, as they did under rate regulation for decades before divestiture.[18] Such price discrimination on the part of interexchange carriers indicates not only that they exercised market power, but also that higher prices on longer-distance services carried forward the rate structure embedded in monopoly services before divestiture.

FIGURE 5–15

CALIFORNIA INTRASTATE PRICE-COST MARGINS
AND MARKET CONCENTRATION—MTS

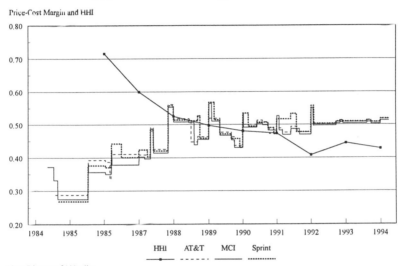

Note: Distance of 100 miles.
Sources: Marginal costs from Pacific Bell, rates from HTL Telemanagement, Ltd., and market concentration from CPUC/Pacific Bell.

18. Given the calling pattern assumptions, AT&T's price for an interstate MTS call equals $0.2462 per minute (as of January 14, 1994), while the marginal cost of interstate switched service equals $0.0766 per minute. For an intrastate MTS call, AT&T's price equals $0.1364 per minute (as of January 1994), while the marginal cost of intrastate switched service equals $0.0658 per minute. Using the economic definition of price discrimination as differences in prices not accountable for by differences in costs, the observed prices and costs demonstrate that AT&T price discriminates against customers making interstate calls. That explains why the price-cost margin for interstate calls, which based on those prices and marginal costs equals 0.69, exceeds the price-cost margin for intrastate calls, which in that instance equals 0.52.

Price-cost margins for California interstate outbound WATS utilizing switched access increased from 1987 to 1993 by 5 percent per year even though the HHI decreased over the same period (as shown in figure 5–16). Margins rose from approximately 45 percent in 1987 to approximately 70 percent for each of the three carriers by 1994. The intrastate price-cost margins for those services followed a similar pattern, although the variation among the three carriers' margins was more substantial than in interstate service (see figure 5–17). Price-cost margins for MCI and Sprint increased from 25 percent in 1987 to 45 percent by 1994, while AT&T's margins fluctuated between 40 and 50 percent. Margins across the three firms changed by the same percentages in 1992, 1993, and 1994, so that margin differences among the firms were exactly maintained. At the same time, the HHI for intrastate service fell to a minimum in 1989 and then fluctuated over a narrow range.

FIGURE 5–16

INTERSTATE CALIFORNIA-BASED PRICE-COST MARGINS AND
MARKET CONCENTRATION—WATS SWITCHED OUTBOUND

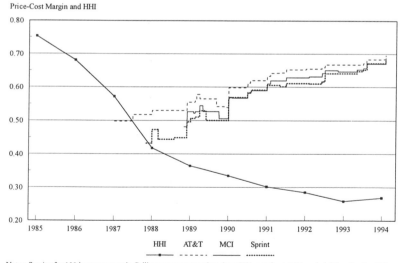

Notes: Service for 100 hours per month. Calling pattern assumption: day =75%, evening = 15%, and night/weekend = 10%.
Sources: Marginal costs from FCC, rates from HTL Telemanagement, Ltd., and market concentration from Multinational Business Services, Inc.

FIGURE 5–17

CALIFORNIA INTRASTATE PRICE-COST MARGINS AND
MARKET CONCENTRATION—WATS SWITCHED OUTBOUND

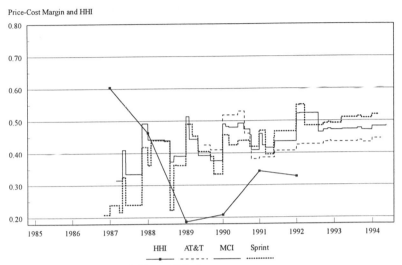

Price-Cost Margin and HHI

Notes: Service for 100 hours per month. Distance of 100 miles.
Sources: Marginal costs from Pacific Bell, rates from HTL Telemanagement, Ltd., and market concentration from CPUC/Pacific Bell.

By 1993, California interstate and intrastate outbound WATS price-cost margins were at the same level as counterpart interstate and intrastate MTS margin series. Since large WATS subscribers generally would be more price-sensitive and would be able to press for margin reductions, that is somewhat surprising. It suggests that even large, sophisticated WATS buyers have been unable to obtain lower prices than those that residential customers pay net of the marginal costs of providing their services. The ability of the three large firms providing service in California to maintain coordinate pricing extends even to markets with large WATS buyers where the temptation would be greatest to engage in price cutting.

Margins for California interstate dedicated outbound WATS (1,000 hours per month) increased from approximately 50 percent in 1987 to 70 percent by 1994 (see figure 5–18). Even though carriers' access costs were less for dedicated outbound services, that did not result in commensurably lower prices.[19] For thirty-six-month as opposed to month-to-month contracts, margins were approximately 70 percent rather than 75 percent by 1994 (compare figure 5–19 with figure 5–16). In both markets, a fifteen-point spread in margins across the three largest service providers from 1987 to 1990 was replaced by essentially identical margins after 1990.

FIGURE 5–18

INTERSTATE CALIFORNIA-BASED PRICE-COST MARGINS AND MARKET CONCENTRATION—WATS DEDICATED OUTBOUND

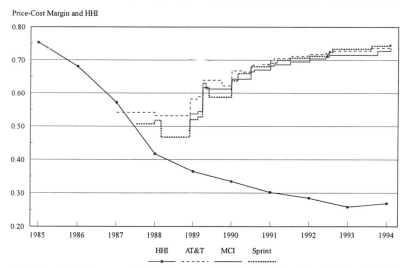

Notes: Service for 1,000 hours per month. Calling pattern assumption: day =75%, evening = 15%, and night/weekend = 10%.
Sources: Marginal costs from FCC/Pacific Bell, rates from HTL Telemanagement, Ltd., and market concentration from Multinational Business Services, Inc.

19. When making comparisons between price-cost margins for switched and dedicated services, it should be recalled that the usage levels differ, being lower for switched than for dedicated. Since the fixed costs of dedicated service are higher than the fixed costs of switched service, dedicated users must maintain a higher monthly usage level to make the dedicated service economic relative to switched service.

FIGURE 5–19

INTERSTATE CALIFORNIA-BASED PRICE-COST MARGINS AND
MARKET CONCENTRATION—WATS DEDICATED OUTBOUND
36-MONTH CONTRACT

Price-Cost Margin and HHI

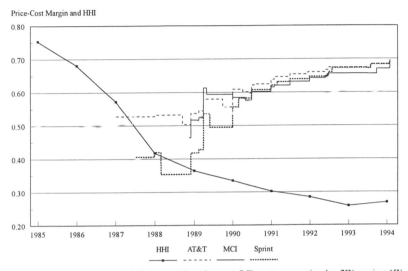

HHI   AT&T   MCI   Sprint

Notes: Service for 1,000 hours per month. Sprint uses a 24-month contract. Calling pattern assumption: day =75%, evening = 15%, and night/weekend = 10%.
Sources: Marginal costs from FCC/Pacific Bell, rates from HTL Telemanagement, Ltd., and market concentration from Multinational Business Services, Inc.

Price-cost margins for California intrastate dedicated out-bound WATS increased for MCI and Sprint from approximately 45 percent in 1989 to 60 percent in 1994 (see figure 5–20). That was the result of MCI and Sprint's margins' moving up to the AT&T margin level, which started in the 50 to 60 percent range. Such convergence reduced the dispersion in those margins substantially after 1989.

Price-cost margins for interstate dedicated outbound WATS in monthly contracts actually exceeded margins in both interstate MTS and interstate outbound services without contract. That held for the respective intrastate services as well—customers entering into contracts for intrastate dedicated outbound WATS services paid higher prices, net of costs, than customers purchasing MTS or the (higher cost) switched outbound WATS services. Those customers demanding dedicated service have been larger volume users than those demanding switched service and should have been able to extract lower prices, net of costs, from the major interexchange carriers by playing one source off against the other. But they did not. Coordination among service providers in setting those margins was extensive, as evidenced in figure 5–20.

FIGURE 5–20

CALIFORNIA INTRASTATE PRICE-COST MARGINS AND
MARKET CONCENTRATION—WATS DEDICATED OUTBOUND

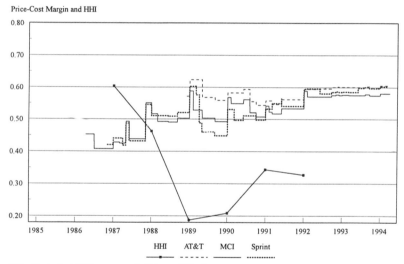

Price-Cost Margin and HHI

Notes: Service for 1,000 hours per month. Distance of 100 miles.
Sources: Marginal costs from Pacific Bell, rates from HTL Telemanagement, Ltd., and market concentration from CPUC/Pacific Bell.

Inbound services showed the same patterns of high and rising margins in California. Interstate switched inbound WATS services generated margins that increased from 45 percent in 1987 to 65 percent by 1994, at a time when concentration in the supply of those services decreased and then leveled off (see figure 5–21). The dispersion in margins among the three large carriers also decreased after 1990, even while AT&T was able to maintain higher margins than MCI and Sprint. Price-cost margins for intrastate WATS inbound service increased for MCI and Sprint from approximately 45 percent in 1988 to 60 percent by 1994 (see figure 5–22). AT&T was able to maintain higher margins than MCI and Sprint, but AT&T's margins also rose, from approximately 63 percent in 1990 to 67 percent of price in 1994. At the same time, AT&T's market share almost halved, from 99 percent in 1986 to 51 percent in 1994. MCI and Sprint's shares respectively rose from 2 and 0 percent in 1987 to 24 and 16 percent in 1994. The HHI fell accordingly, from 0.99 in 1986 to 0.34 in 1994.

Price-cost margins for both interstate and intrastate inbound switched business services were very high, indeed equal to those on MTS services. Customers for inbound switched service, despite their greater volume of use of the service compared with MTS customer volume, were unable to extract lower prices net of costs from the three large interexchange carriers in California.

FIGURE 5–21

INTERSTATE CALIFORNIA-BASED PRICE-COST MARGINS AND MARKET CONCENTRATION—WATS SWITCHED INBOUND

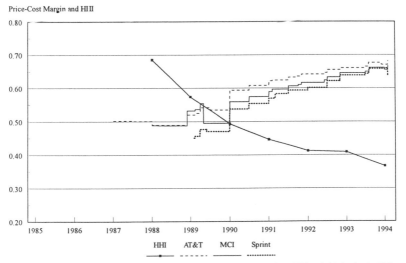

Notes: Service for 100 hours per month. Calling pattern assumption: day =75%, evening = 15%, and night/weekend = 10%.
Sources: Marginal costs from FCC, rates from HTL Telemanagement, Ltd., and market concentration from Multinational Business Services, Inc.

FIGURE 5-22

CALIFORNIA INTRASTATE PRICE-COST MARGINS AND
MARKET CONCENTRATION—WATS SWITCHED INBOUND

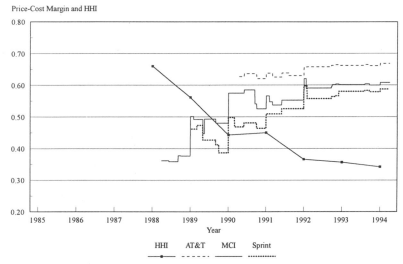

Notes: Service for 100 hours per month. Distance of 100 miles.
Sources: Marginal costs from Pacific Bell, rates from HTL Telemanagement, Ltd., and market concentration from
CPUC/Pacific Bell.

The last important category of service in California was that
in dedicated contracts with large business customers. Margins for
interstate inbound WATS utilizing dedicated access, or so-called
800 service, varied substantially across provider firms before 1990.
But after 1990 margins moved in unison with AT&T's margin,
which was consistently higher than the margins of the other two
providers (see figure 5-23). Before 1990, AT&T dominated service
offerings with first-comer advantages in both technology and marketing. But as MCI gained share in significant steps, the HHI declined from 0.90 to 0.37 (the equivalent of 2.7 equal-sized firms).
With that greatly reduced concentration in supply, supplier price-
cost margins increased from 44 percent for MCI, 39 percent for
Sprint, and 53 percent for AT&T to approximately 70 percent of
price for all three service providers.

FIGURE 5–23

INTERSTATE CALIFORNIA-BASED PRICE-COST MARGINS AND
MARKET CONCENTRATION—WATS DEDICATED INBOUND

Price-Cost Margin and HHI

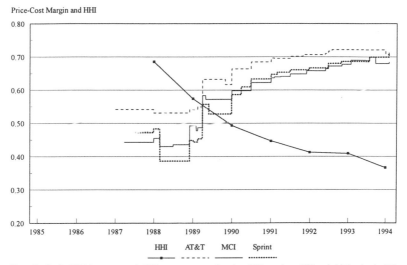

HHI   AT&T   MCI   Sprint

Notes: Service for 1,000 hours per month. Calling pattern assumption: day =75%, evening = 15%, and night/weekend = 10%.
Sources: Marginal costs from FCC/Pacific Bell, rates from HTL Telemanagement, Ltd., and market concentration from Pacific Bell.

Price-cost margins for intrastate inbound WATS dedicated contracts exhibited substantial variation among the firms before 1992, especially in comparison with the interstate margins for the same services (see figure 5–24). Price-cost margins increased after 1989, but only by five percentage points, with most of the increase occurring after 1992. The important change was that those margins for the three carriers converged: Sprint was able to match AT&T's margin, while MCI's margin remained lower, but by only half the previous difference by 1993. Those margins exceeded the MTS margins at that time. Business subscribers to inbound WATS services were as unsuccessful as those for outbound WATS services in securing substantial price discounts net of cost discounts.

FIGURE 5–24

CALIFORNIA INTRASTATE PRICE-COST MARGINS AND
MARKET CONCENTRATION—WATS DEDICATED INBOUND

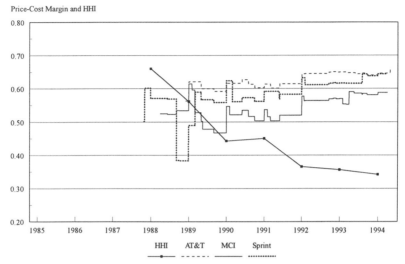

Notes: Service for 1,000 hours per month. Distance of 100 miles.
Sources: Marginal costs from Pacific Bell, rates from HTL Telemanagement, Ltd., and market concentration from CPUC/Pacific Bell.

All those price-cost margins have been based on assumed calling patterns representative of a customer located in the 415 area code (San Francisco) making calls to interstate locations in each area code outside California with equal probability. Intrastate calling patterns were for a customer also located in the 415 area but making calls to points 100 miles distant with the same time-of-day usage, mileage distribution, and monthly calling volume as the interstate customer. One could ask whether the observed pattern of rising margins is specific to those calls only. To respond to that query, the time-of-day usage levels can be varied for interstate calls according to the alternatives shown in table 5–9. With respect to mileage distributions, intrastate calls can be assumed to travel 25, 200, or 300 miles, in addition to the base case of 100 miles. Monthly calling volumes can be varied for inbound and outbound WATS services from 25 to 500 hours per month for switched services and from 500 to 5,000 hours per month for dedicated services.

TABLE 5–9 CALLING PATTERN ASSUMPTIONS FOR SENSITIVITY ANALYSIS				
Time-of-Day Distribution				
	Alternative Distributions: Assumption Sets			
Time of Day	1	2	3	4
Day	65%	75%	80%	85%
Evening	20%	10%	10%	10%
Night/Weekend	15%	15%	10%	5%
Source: As described in the text.				

Reestimated prices with all combinations of those assumptions result in a pattern of price-cost margins that does not differ from that derived from the original set of assumptions. Interstate prices calculated according to those alternative time-of-day calling patterns changed only slightly, so that the price-cost margins increased to and above the 0.5 level over the decade (as shown in appendix 2). Also, those prices did not change as a result of varying the mileage assumptions—at least not enough to change price-cost margins (see appendix 2). Margins were lower because of new mileage assumptions for MTS services, at 25 miles rather than at 200 or 300 miles from 1985 to 1990. All three margin series were, however, in the range of 0.45 to 0.52 by 1994. Finally, prices corresponding to different monthly usage levels did not change enough to cause price-cost margins for WATS services to take on a different pattern over time. Those margins were not different from the margins for the base-case assumptions either at the beginning or toward the end of the time period.[20]

20. Appendix 2 contains price-cost margins based on cost estimates provided in testimony by AT&T. *See* Direct Testimony of John Sumpter on Behalf of AT&T Communications of California, Inc., Application of AT&T Comm. of California, Inc. (U 5002 C) for Authority to Provide Intrastate AT&T 800 READYLINE Service, June 18, 1990. AT&T's cost estimates are somewhat higher than the marginal costs used here because they include such nonmarginal expenses as billing, compensation, and marketing. As a result, the price-cost margins are lower. The overall

But discount calling plans in California did offer substantial new options for MTS customers in the 1990s. The plans offered by AT&T, MCI, and Sprint fell into the same three classifications as those for interLATA customers throughout the rest of the country. The largest set of discount plans was based on the customer's paying a monthly fee and receiving a block of "free" calling time to be used only during specific time periods, while the second set of plans was based on monthly usage levels. The third set of discount plans, based on who was called, included only MCI's two plans (Friends & Family I and Friends & Family II) that gave discounts to a specific calling circle of other MCI subscribers.

Price-cost margins based on MTS discount prices for AT&T and MCI remained stable after 1990, while Sprint's margins increased during that period (see figure 5–25). The approximately 60 percent level of those margins in discount plans compares with the 65 percent level that the carriers earned on provision of standard MTS by 1994 (see figure 5–14). The margins earned by AT&T, MCI, and Sprint in discount MTS calling plans remained stable or increased slightly from 1987 to 1994, even though that period was marked by a substantial decline in market concentration. Increased competitiveness did not emerge, even in the discounting process inherent in those plans. Carriers did not use discount prices to undertake price-cut initiatives to increase their individual market shares, given that profit-margins for discount MTS calling plans remained constant or increased from 1987 to 1994. Discount plans did not break down and depart from pricing over time for standard MTS services.

Thus, neither standard nor discount pricing strategies of the three large carriers made markets in California for long-distance message toll services "competitive" in the postdivestiture decade. The same can be concluded with respect to business services. Large-volume business subscribers on discount plans paid prices that generated the same margins as on nondiscount plans.[21] With respect to tailored discount tariffs, versions of FCC Tariff 12 for

pattern of rising margins in the presence of falling market concentration remains, however.

21. See figures 5–18 and 5–19 for outbound WATS discount price-cost margins, and figures 5–23 and 5–24 for inbound WATS margins on discount plans.

the largest business customers, AT&T entered into fewer than 200 contracts that generated revenues accounting for approximately 3 percent of total revenues. Those contracts turned out to be no more "competitive" than other plans. In all those markets, as carriers' shares of sales in various markets equalized, the price-cost margins on those and standard plans in those markets increased.

FIGURE 5–25

INTERSTATE CALIFORNIA-BASED PRICE-COST MARGINS
ON DISCOUNT PLANS FOR MTS

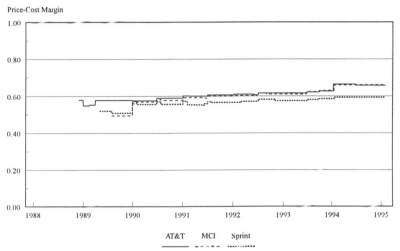

Notes: AT&T discount plan is Reach Out America Block of Time - One-Hour Plan with Day and Evening Option, MCI discount plan is Prime Time Day (8/1/89 to 5/31/91) and Friends and Family I (6/1/91 to 2/1/95), and Sprint discount plan is Sprint Plus Usage Discounts (5/1/89 to 1/31/91) and Sprint Select Day Plan (2/1/91 to 2/1/95).
Sources: Marginal costs from FCC and rates from HTL Telemanagement, Ltd.

TESTING CHANGES IN PRICE-COST
MARGINS FOR COMPETITIVENESS

A procedure for estimating the extent of interfirm pricing competition can be undertaken on the basis of the estimated price-cost margins in those different residential and business markets nationally and in California. The procedure consists of estimating a linear relationship between margins and concentration while holding market-related factors constant. The hypothesis is that price-cost margins for nationwide interLATA services have been determined by the "toughness" of competition as defined by the structure and conduct in those markets (as in the previous chapter). The data comprise 159 observations, at the firm level, on price-cost margins and the HHIs for AT&T, MCI, and Sprint on MTS, outbound WATS (switched, dedicated, and dedicated with thirty-six-month contracts), inbound WATS (switched inbound and dedicated inbound), and virtual network services. Market shares for each company in each service market have been estimated and binary variables created to identify each market and each carrier.

The first model is static, which implies that the margin outcome in any one period did not differ from outcomes in other periods. Price-cost margins are regressed on the market HHI, individual market share, the carrier-specific binary variable, and binary variables for individual markets. MTS services for AT&T serve as the base case against which the binary variables (0, 1) of other carriers and services were measured.

The second model is dynamic, which implies that a margin outcome in one period affects outcomes in subsequent periods. In the current context, the dynamic model assumes that any year's price-cost margin influences future price-cost margins. The price-cost margins are regressed on the HHI, market share, the carrier-specific binary variable, the market-specific binary variable, and the prior year's price-cost margin. As in the static model, the MTS service offering of AT&T provides a base case against which other carriers and services are measured.

The market share variable is included in both the static and dynamic model estimations to test for the robustness of the HHI-measured concentration as a determinant of price-cost margins. Prior research by David Ravenscraft suggests that if regressions based on industry-level data (that is, data in which observations at the level of the firm are aggregated to the industry-level) show a positive relationship between concentration and profitability, that relationship can switch to negative when firm-level market shares are included.[22] That possibility can serve as a hypothesis as to behavior in those markets—that AT&T's share, not the marketwide

---

22. David J. Ravenscraft, *Structure-Profit Relationships at the Line of Business and Industry Level*, 65 REV. ECON. & STAT. 22 (1983).

HHI, determines price-cost margins.

The inclusion of the prior year's price-cost margins in the dynamic regression tests whether there is persistence in price-cost margins over time. A finding of persistence would be evidence against the hypothesis of emerging competition because it counters the argument that high margins draw entry and generate price-cost discounting initiatives to gain market share.

The estimated regression results for the static model are shown in table 5–10. The *R*-square coefficient indicates that over 80 percent of the variance in price-cost margins is explained by that in the independent variables. The coefficient for market share is positive and has a *t*-statistic of 2.34, indicating significance at the 2 percent confidence level so that an increase in a carrier's price-cost margin is associated with an increase in that carrier's share. Contrary to Ravenscraft's findings, the inclusion of firm market shares changes neither the sign nor the significance of the coefficient estimate for the HHI. Pricing margins are inversely related to the HHI, the coefficient of which is statistically significant, so we must reject the hypothesis that long-distance service markets became more competitive as the HHI declined from 1987 to 1994.

To illustrate the pattern established by the estimated regression for the static model, consider a service with a price-cost margin of 0.40. An increase in a carrier's market share from 40 percent to 60 percent resulted in an increase in the price-cost margin to 0.41, while a decrease in the HHI from 0.60 to 0.40 resulted in an increase in the price-cost margin from 0.40 to 0.52. Determinants of change in the HHI were clearly much more important in setting margins; as firms became more equal in shares, margins increased.

Coefficients for the variables for specific service markets can be interpreted as indicating the level of margins to be associated with each service when we hold the HHI and market shares fixed. For example, the negative and significant coefficients for the three outbound WATS services (switched, dedicated, and dedicated with thirty-six-month contracts) indicate that the carriers had lower price-cost margins for those services than for MTS.

TABLE 5-10
PRICE-COST MARGINS AS A FUNCTION OF CONCENTRATION,
MARKET SHARE, CARRIER, AND TYPE OF SERVICE

Dependent Variable: Weighted Price-Cost Margin Explanatory Variables:	Parameter Estimate	Standard Error	t for Null Hypothesis: Parameter$=0$	Significance Level
Intercept	1.015	0.032	31.58	0.0001
MCI	−0.017	0.012	−1.35	0.1806
Sprint	−0.021	0.013	−1.63	0.1057
Dedicated Inbound	−0.118	0.015	−7.80	0.0001
Dedicated Outbound	−0.270	0.019	−14.57	0.0001
Dedicated Outbound, Contract	−0.346	0.018	−18.76	0.0001
Switched Inbound	−0.036	0.015	−2.32	0.0215
Switched Outbound	−0.175	0.018	−9.46	0.0001
Virtual Network	−0.326	0.016	−20.86	0.0001
HHI	−0.601	0.048	−12.47	0.0001
Market Share	0.055	0.024	2.34	0.0209

Notes: $R^2 = 0.82$; number of observations $= 159$.
Source: As described in the text.

Such lower margins for outbound WATS relative to MTS can be explained by characteristics of demand—unlike residential and small business customers, large business customers with outbound WATS contracts could economically build private networks, and that ability to self-provide selected long-distance services increases the elasticity of demand for those services. Price-cost margins set in a coordinated set of strategies across companies should be inversely related to the elasticity of demand. The negative value for that binary variable for low price-cost margins supports the hypothesis of tacit collusion.

Although the coefficients for the inbound WATS services are both significantly negative, their magnitudes are smaller. That may be due to the large subscribers' inability to self-provide inbound services. But also, until recently, the inability of 800 customers to take their 800 numbers with them when changing carriers made it less likely that carriers in the early period would have been able to increase market shares by discounting price, even if they wanted to at the initial stage of market development. The negative and significant coefficient for virtual network services is consistent with large business customers' having more elastic demands than MTS customers. Coefficients for the carrier-specific binary variables are negative but not significant. The hypothesis that price-cost margins were the same can be disproved for the three large long-distance service providers.

The regression results for the dynamic model are shown in table 5–11. The *R*-square of 0.97 indicates that the equation variables explain over 95 percent of the variance in price-cost margins. The variable for the prior year's price-cost margin has a positive and statistically significant coefficient, which indicates that there is persistence in margin levels; high price-cost margins in one year have a positive impact on price-cost margins in the next year. That persistence, as indicated, argues against there having been any outbreak of competition in price-cost margins in the interLATA market from 1984 to 1994. The coefficient estimate for the HHI is negative and significant, which indicates that price-cost margins increased when concentration declined. But the inclusion of the prior year's price-cost margins results in a reduction in the magnitude of the effect of the HHI on price-cost margins. Again, that inverse relationship between market concentration and profitability is the opposite of what one would expect if the share-increasing strategies of the smaller long-distance carriers drove down price-cost margins. But the persistence in margin levels makes the effects of declining concentration on higher margins less pronounced. The inclusion of the prior year's price-cost margin resulted in a significant reduction in the magnitude and the significance of the market-share coefficient. Market share is still positive, but it is no longer statistically significant.

As was the case in the static regression, the service-specific binary variables are generally negative and significant, which indicates that price-cost margins have been lower in business services where demands conceivably have been more elastic.

TABLE 5–11

PRICE-COST MARGIN AS A FUNCTION OF LAGGED
PRICE-COST MARGIN, CONCENTRATION, MARKET SHARE,
CARRIER, AND TYPE OF SERVICE

Dependent Variable: Weighted Price-Cost Margin Explanatory Variables:	Parameter Estimate	Standard Error	t for Null Hypothesis: Parameter=0	Significance Level
Intercept	0.180	0.046	3.88	0.0002
Lagged Price-Cost Margin	0.875	0.036	24.54	0.0001
MCI	0.003	0.005	0.62	0.5390
Sprint	0.007	0.005	1.27	0.2074
Dedicated Inbound	−0.002	0.008	−0.19	0.8472
Dedicated Outbound	−0.038	0.016	−2.34	0.0210
Dedicated Outbound, Contract	−0.051	0.018	−2.75	0.0068
Switched Inbound	−0.003	0.007	−0.41	0.6861
Switched Outbound	−0.028	0.014	−2.05	0.0421
Virtual Network	−0.029	0.014	−2.04	0.0438
HHI	−0.150	0.047	−3.18	0.0019
Market Share	0.005	0.011	0.45	0.6521

Notes: R^2 = 0.97; number of observations = 138.
Source: As described in the text.

The direct measure of the extent of firm-cooperative interaction on prices is the component term in price-cost margins due to conjectural variation. This hypothesis, developed in the last chapter, has focused on the carrier's margin—that is, $(p - mc)/p = ms(1 + v)/e$, where ms is that carrier's market share and v is the conjectural variation term that approximates that carrier's extent of interfirm price coordination. With $v = 0$, there is no coordination, and price-cost margins depend only on firm shares and the market demand elasticity. With $v < 0$, the initiative generates a response in the opposite direction; changes in sales levels by firms result in price-cost margins' being driven down, ultimately to marginal costs as in competitive markets (where $v = -1$ or all output initiatives are matched by other providers with the same magnitude in the opposite direction). But $v > 0$ implies coordinated changes in sales levels in the same direction that increase margins toward monopoly levels (ultimately, where $ms = 0.50$, then $v = 1$ implies the monopoly price level for the three firms).

From that database, it is possible to estimate conjectural variation terms for AT&T, MCI, and Sprint.[23] Annual data on prices, marginal costs, and market shares of the individual carriers are taken from sources described earlier in this chapter; what is still needed is an estimate of market demand elasticity. On the basis of the econometric evidence provided elsewhere, the long-run demand elasticity for MTS is set equal to -0.75,[24] and for WATS is set at -0.83. To derive average estimates for interexchange carriers' conjectural variations, individual v are calculated for all domestic MTS, outbound WATS, inbound WATS, and virtual network services offered by the carriers for each year from 1988 to 1994. Those computations yield samples of thirty-three observations of v for AT&T and MCI and thirty-two for Sprint.[25]

---

23. To complete the estimation procedure, we redefine a firm's conjectural variation to equal [(price − marginal cost) (demand elasticity) / (price) (market share)] minus one. That equation formulation is presented in J. Brander & A. Zhang, *Market Conduct in the Airline Industry: An Empirical Investigation*, 21 RAND J. ECON. 56 (1990).

24. *See* LESTER D. TAYLOR, TELECOMMUNICATIONS DEMAND IN THEORY AND PRACTICE ch. 6 (Kluwer Academic Publishers 1994). The WATS demand elasticity is from Blaine E. Davis, Gerald J. Caccappolo & Muhammed Ali Chaudry, *An Econometric Planning Model for American Telephone and Telegraph Company*, 4 BELL J. ECON. & MGMT. SCIENCE 29 (1973). *See also* James M. Griffen & Bruce L. Egan, *Demand System Estimation in the Presence of Multi-Block Tariffs: A Telecommunications Example,* 67 REV. ECON. & STAT. 520 (1985).

25. For example, one observation is for AT&T's provision of MTS in 1988, while a second observation is for provision of virtual network services in 1988, and so forth.

Average conjectural variations for each carrier (with 95 percent confidence intervals) are shown in table 5–12.[26] The AT&T estimated v indicates a minimal response in MCI and Sprint's sales levels in particular products; specifically, the hypothesis of no response ($v = 0$) cannot be rejected. MCI and Sprint's conjectural responses to changes in sales levels are large and positive, however. AT&T's conjectural variation implies that if the firm were to decrease its sales level, MCI and Sprint would increase their combined sales levels by 7 percent of that level. The conjectural variation term is negative, and therefore not collusive, and is too small to indicate that AT&T would expect a competitive response. But conjectural variation terms for both MCI and Sprint imply that any restriction in the sales of one of them would be more than responded to by a larger restriction from rivals. MCI's conjectural variation indicates that if it were to decrease its sales level, it could anticipate that AT&T and Sprint would decrease their combined sales by 1.53 times that level, which would result in a commensurately higher market price than could be achieved by a single firm's restricting supply.

Together, those estimates of conjectural variation imply that AT&T acts to restrict supply and increase its price while assuming that the supply of the other two large carriers is fixed. The other two large carriers use that condition to decrease their sales levels by disproportionate amounts, which implies that they seek even higher prices. Their coordination takes levels of price-cost margins toward higher levels than would result from independent price setting.

---

26. Additional computations were undertaken based on the assumption that MCI and Sprint nonaccess costs at the margin were twice those of AT&T. The average levels of v decreased by 0.23 and 0.29 for MCI and Sprint, respectively. Computations were made assuming that MTS and WATS price elasticities were the same. Those resulted in decreases of v of 0.12, 0.37, and 0.39 for AT&T, MCI, and Sprint, respectively. If both extreme assumptions were to hold, the estimate of average v for AT&T would still not differ from zero, nor for MCI and Sprint would it be less than one.

TABLE 5–12 CONJECTURAL VARIATIONS FOR AT&T, MCI, AND SPRINT— SENSITIVITY RUN 2		
Carrier	Average	95 Percent Confidence Interval
AT&T	−0.07	(−0.17, 0.02)
MCI	1.91	(1.63, 2.18)
Sprint	2.54	(2.31, 2.78)
Source: As described in the text.		

PRICE-COST MARGINS ON SERVICES
IN INTERNATIONAL MARKETS

The potentially most profitable markets, given the opportunity to set noncompetitive prices, would have been those for outbound services from the United States to the major foreign capitals. The distance and densities are large so that marginal costs should have been lower than on many domestic servcies. Prices set collectively on calls to the largest cities the farthest from New York City, by using noncompetitive mileage factors, would generate high profits.

Carriers' prices per minute for standard international and discount international MTS and WATS services have been estimated from FCC tariffs for AT&T, MCI, and Sprint for the 1990s. Prices for representative outbound international calls from the United States depend on (1) local time in the foreign country receiving the call with respect to U.S. Eastern Standard Time (EST) and (2) the specification of the destination country. Carriers have had in place three price categories: standard, discount, and economy from most to least expensive. An example of the pricing categories for calls from the United States to the United Kingdom appears in table 5–13; if local time in the United States is between 7 A.M. and 1

P.M. EST, then an outbound call to the United Kingdom is charged according to the standard time rate. Because of the five-hour time difference between the U.S. East Coast and the United Kingdom, a call made during the standard period arrives between noon and 6 P.M. local time in the United Kingdom. The other extreme is local time after midnight in the United States, when calls reach London in the morning at the lowest or economy rate.

TABLE 5–13 PRICING CATEGORIES FOR CALLS FROM THE UNITED STATES TO THE UNITED KINGDOM			
	Standard	Discount	Economy
Local Time in Eastern Standard Time Zone	7 A.M. to 1 P.M.	1 P.M. to 6 P.M.	6 P.M. to 7 A.M.
Local Time in United Kingdom	12 M. to 6 P.M.	6 P.M. to 11 P.M.	11 P.M. to 12 M.
Source: As explained in the text.			

For each of eight foreign countries, assumptions have been made regarding the percentage of IMTS and IWATS calls in each of the three price categories,[27] on the basis of the likely times in which residential customers would make MTS calls and business customers would make WATS calls. For example, for standard and discount MTS from the United States to the United Kingdom, calls have been assumed to be distributed so that 30 percent were made during the standard period, 50 percent during the discount period, and 20 percent during the economy period. Two further assumptions as to the percentage of calls during the three time periods have been made for each type of service for each of the eight country pairs.[28]

27. Details of the calling-pattern assumptions are shown in tables A3–1 and A3–2 of appendix 3.

28. As shown in appendix 3, conclusions regarding the extent of competition in

Prices for discount services are assumed to vary according to the number of minutes per call with discounts for more minutes of use. Prices for MTS discount plans have been estimated by assuming a monthly usage level of fifty minutes of international calls.[29] WATS prices have been based on an assumed usage level of 200 hours per month.[30]

As an example of standard MTS prices, consider the prices for calls from the United States to the United Kingdom in figure 5–26. In 1993 prices charged by AT&T, MCI, and Sprint for standard MTS service were essentially identical at $0.89 per minute. Standard MTS prices for the other country pairs were also identical across the three carriers, with the exceptions of Italy and the Dominican Republic, where prices differed across companies and also increased more rapidly for all three companies.

With respect to discount MTS plans, AT&T offered Reach Out–World for international callers in which customers paid a $3.00 monthly usage charge to be entitled to lower rates on calls to any international direct-dial country during certain times of the day.[31] MCI offered discounted international rates to its customers through its MCI Friends Around the World AnyTime plan. Participation in that plan also required a $3.00 monthly fee to be able to use a choice of discount options.[32]

---

those international markets are not sensitive to those assumptions.

29. In addition, two other usage levels (30 minutes and 100 minutes per month) were used to calculate the prices of international discount IMTS services (see appendix 3).

30. An alternative usage level of 1,000 hours of IWATS calls per month was also used (see appendix 3).

31. The discount MTS plans offered by AT&T, MCI, and Sprint used somewhat different time periods for calculating rates than did their standard plans. For example, the companies considered weekends offpeak in discount but not in standard plans.

32. Customers could either designate three international phone numbers eligible for a 25 percent discount or select one international country and receive a 20 percent discount for calls to that country. Customers could change the three eligible phone numbers or the country chosen as many times as they wished, but no more than once per monthly billing cycle. Discounts applied to the first $500 of international calls per month. Usage in excess of $500 was billed at full international IMTS rates.

FIGURE 5–26

STANDARD IMTS INDEX PRICES FOR LONG-DISTANCE CALLS
FROM THE UNITED STATES TO THE UNITED KINGDOM

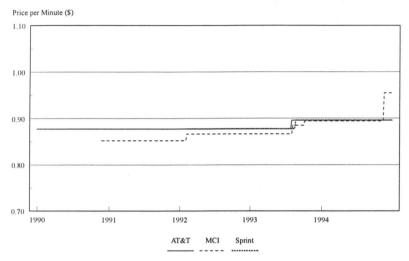

Note: Time of day based on 30% standard, 50% discount, and 20% economy.

Sprint offered an international plan known as Sprint World that provided discounted rates for calls during offpeak periods, once again for a monthly fee of $3.00. Those discount prices followed standard prices, given that they were quoted as percentages off standard tariffs (see figures 5–27 and 5–28). The discounts actually offered by the carriers are shown in table 5–14 for 1994; they ranged from 76 percent to 95 percent of standard prices. When one carrier's discount was larger, the others offered larger percentage reductions.[33]

Given that the discounts were convergent, the prices resulting were almost identical across carriers by the mid-1990s. They also became more similar across country pairs; the pairs in which carriers offered larger discounts were those in which prices for standard services were higher. For example, standard prices for calls to Canada exceeded those for Mexico and the Dominican Republic, but the discounts shown in table 5–14 were larger for Canada than for Mexico and the Dominican Republic.

33. There are two exceptions. Sprint offered a smaller discount for calls to the United Kingdom than did AT&T and MCI, and AT&T offered a smaller discount for calls to Germany than did MCI and Sprint.

FIGURE 5–27

DISCOUNT IMTS INDEX PRICES FOR LONG-DISTANCE CALLS
FROM THE UNITED STATES TO THE UNITED KINGDOM

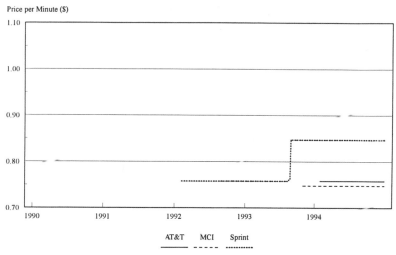

Notes: Prices based on 50 minutes per month. Time of day based on 30% standard, 50% discount, and 20% economy.

FIGURE 5–28

IWATS INDEX PRICES FOR LONG-DISTANCE CALLS
FROM THE UNITED STATES TO THE UNITED KINGDOM

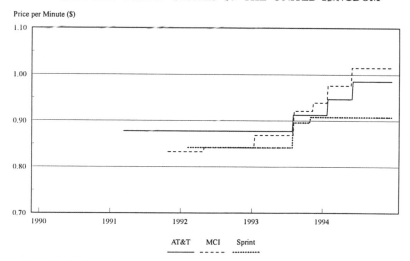

Notes: Prices based on 200 hours per month. Time of day based on 60% standard, 20% discount, and 20% economy.

TABLE 5–14 DISCOUNT PRICES AS A PERCENTAGE OF STANDARD MTS PRICES FOR 1994 (PERCENTAGE)			
Country	AT&T	MCI	Sprint
Canada	85	82	88
Mexico	95	93	95
United Kingdom	85	84	95
Germany	90	77	77
France	80	79	81
Italy	80	77	78
Japan	76	76	77
Dominican Republic	88	89	n/a
Source: As explained in the text.			

WATS prices changed over time with MTS prices. For example, for calls to the United Kingdom, all three carriers had similar price changes from 1991 to 1994 (as in figure 5–8). Those price increases exceeded increases in standard and discount MTS prices. Outbound WATS prices increased from $0.11 to $0.18 per minute for the United States to the United Kingdom during that period, as they did for the other country pairs.

The next step in estimating carriers' price-cost margins on international services is to determine marginal costs. The marginal costs of outbound U.S. international calls have three components: originating access costs, network transport costs, and settlement costs. Originating access costs are charges of local exchange companies for transporting the call from the customer's location to the interexchange carrier's point of presence. For example, for a switched call from San Francisco to London, the long-distance carrier must pay an originating access charge to Pacific Telesis for transporting the call from the customer's location to the long-distance carrier's point of presence. Network costs are those that the interexchange carrier incurs for transporting the call on its system from the point of presence to the foreign carrier's terminating gateway. For calls from the United

States to the United Kingdom, those costs would be for transport and switching from the San Francisco point of presence to British Telephone's gateway at the midpoint of the Atlantic Ocean. Those costs have been assumed to remain constant at $0.02 per conversation minute from 1990 to 1994. The third component, international settlement costs, consists of the charges the originating interexchange carrier pays the foreign carrier for transporting and switching the call from the international gateway to the destination location. Settlement costs, which include profit margins for the recipient foreign carrier, have been high and have been decreasing. For example, settlement costs for calls from the United States to the United Kingdom fell from $0.53 to $0.305 per minute, or as much as 50 percent,[34] from 1990 to 1994.

In addition to paying settlement costs to foreign carriers for outbound calls, domestic carriers receive settlement payments from foreign carriers for calls terminating in the United States. Under the settlements process, AT&T or MCI's net settlement costs equal the difference between payments to and from foreign carriers. Assuming that those net settlement payments determine a carrier's marginal costs, then any increase in a carrier's outbound minutes to a particular foreign country, all else constant, could reduce or increase the carrier's marginal costs (since inbound traffic minutes are allocated according to outbound market share). Carriers' marginal costs for net and gross settlement payments are shown in table 5–15 for calls from the United States to the United Kingdom. As is apparent, net settlement payments resulted in low and falling marginal costs because of the high relative level and growth in U.S. outbound over inbound traffic.[35] Because net settlement payments more accurately represented the cash flow results for the outbound carrier from both outbound and inbound international traffic flows, marginal costs based on net settlement rates were used to calculate price-cost margins.

---

34. Those costs represent the amount paid by a U.S. carrier to a foreign carrier for terminating a call originating in the United States. The foreign carrier also pays one-half the accounting rate to U.S. carriers for calls originating in their countries (termed the "accounting rate").

35. FCC data on net settlement payments were available through 1993. Here 1994 marginal costs were assumed to be equal to 1993 costs, which is conservative (resulting in lower profit margins), given that marginal costs generally declined over that period.

TABLE 5–15

MARGINAL COST OF INTERNATIONAL TELECOMMUNICATIONS
SERVICE FROM THE UNITED STATES TO THE UNITED KINGDOM
(PRICE PER MINUTE ($))

Date	All Carriers[1]	AT&T[2]	MCI[2]	Sprint[2]
1990	0.588	0.200	0.151	0.099
1991	0.541	0.208	0.236	0.136
1992	0.425	0.176	0.169	0.160
1993	0.359	0.178	0.140	0.146
1994	0.359	0.178	0.140	0.146

[1] Marginal costs based on gross settlement payments.
[2] Marginal costs based on net settlement payments.
Source: As explained in the text.

Price-cost margins for standard services across the eight largest country pair markets in general were high, and they increased substantially in the first half of the 1990s. Figure 5–29 shows the margins for outbound service from the United States to the United Kingdom. Company margins are shown by year and market for outbound service to Canada, Mexico, Germany, France, Italy, Japan, and the Dominican Republic in appendix 4. Margins to most of those countries were in excess of 0.70 by 1994, the exceptions being Mexico, Italy (for AT&T and Sprint), and the Dominican Republic. At the same time, price-cost margins for discount services in outbound U.S. international markets were also stable or increasing over the period. The margins for discount services paralleled those for standard MTS service, because discount prices are percentages off standard prices. (Those margins are shown by country and year in appendix 4.) Price-cost margins for standard and discount MTS were at the same level for service to Canada, the United Kingdom, and Japan. Margins were up to 10 percent lower for discount service to Mexico, Germany, Italy, France, and the Dominican Republic. Except for service to Germany and the Dominican Republic, margins on discount plans increased from 1990 to 1994. Given that limited range, discount plans did not generally lead carriers to compete on margins.

FIGURE 5-29

IMTS PRICE-COST MARGINS AND MARKET CONCENTRATION
FOR INTERNATIONAL LONG-DISTANCE CALLS FROM
THE UNITED STATES TO THE UNITED KINGDOM

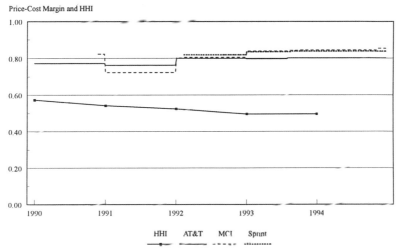

Price-Cost Margin and HHI

Notes: Marginal costs based on net settlement payments. Time of day based on 30% standard, 50% discount, and 20% economy.

Sources: Marginal costs from FCC and WEFA, rates from HTL Telemanagement, Ltd., and market concentration from FCC.

Price-cost margins for outbound WATS services also increased from 1991 to 1994, despite declines in concentration in the sales revenues of the three large outbound service providers. Margins in most international markets exceeded 70 percent by 1994. Only margins on services to Mexico and Italy (for AT&T and Sprint), however, were as low as 60 percent and, for the Dominican Republic, even lower at 50 percent of price. Margins to those three countries were lower because of larger net settlement payments that resulted from higher charges on terminating calls—charges, in effect, that resulted in high profit margins for the receiving foreign carrier. Since margins for outbound WATS were the same as for standard MTS calls, the data offer no evidence that markets for outbound WATS were any more competitive than were markets for MTS services.

What can one conclude from the pricing behavior and changes in shares in outbound international markets? Essentially, changes in price-cost margins of the three large service providers in individual country-pair markets were in the opposite direction from those expected from declines in the HHI in those markets over time. In five of the country-pair markets (Germany, Japan, France, the Dominican Republic, and Italy), the HHI fell from one in 1990 to values from 0.42 to 0.56 by 1994 (see table 5–16). Price-cost margins did not decline, but rather were constant or increasing in that period. Further, there was no systematic relationship between (lower) HHIs and (lower) margins across country-pair markets. For example, the HHI in Mexico exceeded that in Canada, but price-cost margins in Mexico were lower than in Canada. The highest margins were on service to France and Japan, but the highest concentration was on service to Germany and Italy.

Comparisons between domestic and foreign markets are even more striking. MTS and WATS margins in the eight country-pair markets exceeded those in domestic markets for comparable services. MTS margins for AT&T, MCI, and Sprint service to foreign countries were approximately 10 percent higher than for domestic service except in Mexico, the Dominican Republic, and Italy, where the receiving foreign carrier took part of the margin. Those MTS and WATS margins also exceeded levels found in concentrated manufacturing industries in the United States. In a sample of 284 U.S. industries in 1981, the average price-cost margin was 27.5 percent, or less than half the value found for most of those standard or discount international markets.[36] In addition, for the group of industries in that sample having the highest market concentration (the top four firms accounting for at least 81 percent of sales), the average price-cost margin was 33 percent or still less than half that in most of those international markets.

36. I. Domowitz, R. Hubbard & B. Petersen, *Business Cycles and the Relationship Between Concentration and Price-Cost Margins*, 17 RAND J. ECON. 1 (1986).

TABLE 5–16				
HHIs and Standard MTS Price-Cost Margins (1994)				
		Price-Cost Margins		
Country	HHI	AT&T	MCI	Sprint
Canada	0.42	0.80	0.74	0.71
Mexico	0.55	0.45	0.58	0.60
United Kingdom	0.50	0.80	0.84	0.84
Germany	0.56	0.70	0.72	0.75
Japan	0.43	0.87	0.82	0.84
France	0.49	0.90	0.76	0.74
Dominican Republic	0.52	0.50	0.40	0.41
Italy	0.56	0.58	0.58	0.81
Source: As described in the text.				

Tests for Competitiveness in International Markets

The price-cost margin equation fitted to the interLATA data can be adapted for data on international long-distance services. A data set of eighty-nine observations has been developed on price-cost margins, market shares, and HHIs for international outbound MTS services provided by AT&T, MCI, and Sprint for the years 1991 through 1994. The country-pair markets for which there are data in that sample include those between the United States and Canada, the Dominican Republic, France, Germany, Italy, Japan, Mexico, and the United Kingdom.

As in the analysis of interLATA price-cost margins, both static and dynamic models have been estimated. For the static model, international price-cost margins have been regressed on the HHI, market shares, carrier-specific binary variables, and country-specific binary variables. AT&T's service to Canada is the base case against which carrier and country variables have been measured. For the dynamic model, price-cost margins have been regressed on the HHI, market share, price-cost margins lagged by one year, carrier-specific binary variables, and binary variables for individual countries.

The static regression equation, based on eighty-nine observations, has an *R*-square coefficient of 0.84, indicating that the equation variables explained more than 80 percent of the variance in price-cost margins. The equation price-cost margins (as in table 5–17) are inversely related to the HHI, although the coefficient of the HHI is significant only at the 10 percent confidence level.

TABLE 5–17

PRICE-COST MARGIN FOR INTERNATIONAL MTS AS A FUNCTION OF CONCENTRATION, MARKET SHARE, CARRIER, AND COUNTRY

Dependent Variable: Weighted Average Price-Cost Margin Explanatory Variables:	Parameter Estimate	Standard Error	*t* for Null Hypothesis: Parameter=0	Significance Level
Intercept	1.346	0.122	11.04	0.0001
MCI	−0.334	0.082	−4.06	0.0001
Sprint	−0.398	0.099	−4.03	0.0001
Mexico	−0.147	0.038	−3.86	0.0002
Dominican Republic	−0.296	0.039	−7.55	0.0001
Japan	−0.118	0.031	3.86	0.0002
France	−0.070	0.032	2.21	0.0300
Germany	0.013	0.041	0.32	0.7516
Italy	−0.100	0.039	−2.60	0.0113
United Kingdom	−0.101	0.033	3.09	0.0028
HHI	−0.325	0.182	−1.78	0.0784
Market Share	0.694	0.161	−4.31	0.0001

Notes: $R^2 = 0.84$; number of observations = 89.
Source: As described in the text.

Price-cost margins are inversely related to market share for the individual carrier. Contrary to the analysis of interLATA price-cost margins, the coefficients for carrier-specific binary variables are negative and significant, which indicates that MCI and Sprint had lower price-cost margins than AT&T had. Price-cost margins are significantly lower for service to Italy, Mexico, and the Dominican Republic than for service to Canada. In contrast, price-cost margins are significantly higher for service to Japan and the United Kingdom. Coefficients for the remaining countries were not significantly different from zero.

The dynamic equation, based on sixty-six observations, had an R-square of 0.89, indicating that the equation variables explained almost 90 percent of the variation in price-cost margins (see table 5–18). As in the domestic dynamic model, the coefficient for the prior year's price-cost margin is positive and significant, which indicates the persistence of profits in contradiction to a hypothesis that there was an emergence of competition during that period. Although the HHI coefficient is negative, it is not statistically significant. Because of the significance of the persistence term and the insignificance of concentration changes, we must reject the hypothesis that international MTS service has been in the process of becoming more competitive.

The coefficients of the carrier-specific binary variables in that regression confirm the findings from the static regression. Significantly negative coefficient estimates for MCI and Sprint indicate that they had lower price-cost margins than had AT&T. But those estimates are of a smaller magnitude and lower significance level than the estimates in the static model. For example, the coefficient for Sprint in the static model is -0.398, significant at the 0.01 percent confidence level. In the dynamic model, the Sprint coefficient is -0.368, significant only at the 0.4 percent confidence level. In both models the two nondominant long-distance carriers have lower price-cost margins than AT&T, while all margins are at or above those in domestic service markets.

The coefficient estimates for country-specific binary variables also confirm the findings from the static regression model. Again, the coefficients were of a lower magnitude and significance than their counterparts in the static model. For example, the coefficient in table 5–17 for Italy is -0.100 and is significant at the 1 percent confidence

Table 5–18 PRICE-COST MARGIN FOR INTERNATIONAL MTS AS A FUNCTION OF LAGGED PRICE-COST MARGIN, CONCENTRATION, MARKET SHARE, CARRIER, AND COUNTRY				
Dependent Variable: Weighted Average Price-Cost Margin Explanatory Variables:	Parameter Estimate	Standard Error	*t* for Null Hypothesis: Parameter=0	Significance Level
Intercept	1.000	0.194	5.15	0.0001
Lagged Price-Cost Margin	0.274	0.109	2.51	0.0152
MCI	−0.320	0.100	−3.20	0.0023
Sprint	−0.368	0.122	−3.01	0.0040
Mexico	−0.127	0.052	−2.44	0.0179
Dominican Republic	−0.231	0.058	−3.99	0.0002
Japan	0.076	0.033	2.29	0.0264
France	0.050	0.036	1.40	0.1679
Germany	−0.023	0.053	−0.43	0.6696
Italy	−0.047	0.052	−0.92	0.3631
United Kingdom	0.068	0.039	1.77	0.0833
HHI	−0.038	0.289	−0.13	0.8970
Market Share	−0.670	0.213	−3.15	0.0027
Notes: $R^2 = 0.89$; number of observations = 65. Source: As described in the text.				

level, while in the dynamic model in table 5–18 the coefficient is 0.068 and not significant at any standard confidence level. Still, the dynamic model shows that price-cost margins are significantly lower for service to Mexico and the Dominican Republic than for service to Canada and that price-cost margins are significantly higher for service to Japan. The pattern follows that of country-to-country revenue settlement payments—those with Mexico equal 51.3 cents per minute and to the Dominican Republic equal 63.0 cents per minute, both more than twice those to France and Japan (at 24.0 cents and 24.9 cents, respectively). That pattern is as if the first two countries were imposing a tax on the profit margins of the outbound U.S. carriers.[37]

CONCLUSION

Competitiveness in price formation where seller concentration is declining is by definition marked by prices and hence profit margins that decline. But any lack of competitiveness also depends on whether the individual carrier can engage in coordinated pricing decisions with other carriers. If carriers are able to set their own prices based on their own demand functions, given that those functions are stable, then price-cost margins have to be above competitive levels. If conditions for coordination develop during periods when there are substantial declines in the concentration of market shares, then price-cost margins could increase rather than decline. Margins could even increase substantially as shares change in a fixed sequence. In fact, price-cost margins in long-distance telephone markets increased when concentration decreased in the late 1980s, and they increased more rapidly when concentration stabilized or decreased less rapidly in the first half of the 1990s. That reversal of the structure-performance relationship took place in message toll and all the business service markets nationally. The reversal was more pronounced in California, with a turnaround and sharp increase of margins in the early 1990s that resulted in standard plan levels of 75 percent of prices on interstate calls and 55 percent of prices on the shorter distance intrastate calls. Discount plans resulted in margins 5 percent less. While that relationship could not be documented in international outbound markets, because

---

37. Estimates for the conjectural variation parameter v have been compiled for all MTS and WATS country pair markets from 1991 to 1994. The average estimates are -0.318 for AT&T, 1.427 for MCI, and 4.443 for Sprint. While the values for AT&T and Sprint are larger, in absolute terms, the interpretation is the same at this stage of development of the analysis.

tariff prices are available only for the 1990s, price-cost margins on outbound calls were highest to foreign countries for which service was least concentrated and for which concentration was declining. Price-cost margins were highest for the longest distance service and for service for which the receiving country set lower charges for terminating calls. The construction of price offerings that the three large long-distance service providers filed with the FCC for calls originating from New York City was tacitly collusive whether the calls terminated in Sacramento or Tokyo.

In the early part of the ten years after divestiture, AT&T set relatively high prices in markets in which its shares exceeded 90 percent. It probably earned higher profits by maintaining high prices on services to that large customer base than by reducing prices in an effort to slow the erosion of its shares. But by 1990, AT&T's then-reduced shares provided an increased threat of credible price reductions. The importance to AT&T of maintaining high prices for existing customers had diminished, while the importance of reducing prices to profit from adding customers had increased. At the same time, MCI and Sprint's larger market shares provided more incentive for those companies to match AT&T's prices, since the cuts they would make otherwise would leave their relatively new but established customer base less profitable. Thus, emerging coordination provided the basis for each carrier's setting higher price-cost margins in long-distance markets in the 1990s.

That price-cost margins increased in all major long-distance service markets confounds propositions about increasing "competitiveness." Changes in regulation—the setting of uniform access charges and the establishment of price-cap regulation—made regularization of price formation possible in the tariff submissions of the three carriers. The dynamic behavior of margins in the early 1990s provides evidence that the three major carriers were able to establish coordinated strategies over that period in place of competition.

Could the pattern of rising price-cost margins herein identified have resulted from the process of estimating price-cost margins? Of course, all estimates may contain error. But the question is whether prices and costs could have been so misestimated that the underlying time series of margins was constant rather than increasing. The answer as to prices is that they could not have been incorrect to the extent and direction identified, given that they were taken directly from company tariffs. With respect to marginal costs, the amount of additional misspecified cost in operations, exclusive of access costs, necessary to correct hypothetical error would increase from the specified level of $0.01 per minute from 1987 to 1989 to almost $0.04 per minute in 1994. The increases in marginal costs caused by adding the "additional charge" would be 40 percent. To produce a declining price-cost margin series, the additional costs would have to be even greater. Also, even with the additional costs, the price-cost margin would remain constant at approximately 0.57—much higher than in other concentrated industries. To reduce the level of the price-cost margin to 0.35 (a value associated with highly concentrated industries), another $0.06 to $0.07 per minute would have to be added to the "additional costs" and would result in total "additional costs" of approximately $0.08 to $0.10 per minute.

Then, could marketing costs, particularly those associated with the widely publicized MTS discount plans, have been those costs incorrectly left out of the analysis? They could not, at least analytically, since they are not marginal costs (and are determined by the price-cost margin).[38] AT&T's total marketing expenses have been only one-half the required addition or one-third the amount needed to reduce the price-cost margin to 0.35; for example, they were approximately $0.025 per minute in 1993.

From another point of view, AT&T's total marketing expenses increased by $0.0026 per minute from 1990 to 1993. But that is less than one-tenth the amount of the increase in additional costs necessary to keep the price-cost margin constant over that period. Price-cost margins have more likely increased.

Thus, this analysis has centered on comparisons of changes in market sales concentration with changes in carriers' price-cost margins. For findings of increased competitiveness, margins should have decreased when concentration declined, or when concentration reached and then stabilized at levels below those associated with the presence of second or third equal-sized sources of service. But that did not take place in the ten years since industry restructuring. To

---

38. Robert Dorfman & Peter O. Steiner, *Optimal Advertising and Optimal Quality*, 44 Am. Econ. Rev. 835 (1954).

the contrary, margins have increased, particularly during and after concentration stabilized at those lower levels. Reduced competitiveness has been the result.

6

Prospects for Competition under Telecommunications Regulatory Reform

THE CHALLENGE THAT has been facing regulators and anti-trust officials since 1984 has been to effect policies that will cause competition to emerge in long-distance telephony. Those policies, if successful, would cause profit margins to fall by half or more and largely eliminate the rationale for regulation of long-distance markets. Numerous responses to the challenge, the most recent being the Telecommunications Act of 1996, seek to activate the transformation to competitive markets. But none of the earlier responses has produced results that measure against a standard for a finding of open and pervasive competition.

The results of the first decade since divestiture imply that direct regulatory management of prices and services does not work. To be effective, new policies would instead focus on entry, principally of the existing operating companies into markets for interLATA long-distance services in their respective regions, and of foreign carriers into outbound U.S. service markets. That entry is precisely what the Modification of Final Judgment had outright prevented and what the recent federal legislation would subject to difficult and costly preconditions.

The new policy embodied in the Telecommunications Act of 1996 is found in the centrally featured "checklist" for competitive "safeguards." A Bell operating company's entry into in-region interLATA services is forbidden until regulatory authorities deem the operating company's local loop to be competitive against the safeguards checklist. The rationale for requiring that precondition is that a Bell operating company, by entering the market for interLATA transport within its region, will leverage its monopoly power in local exchange to gain control of the interLATA market. To adherents to that view, it would not suffice to rely, as antitrust and regulatory policies do in virtually every other product market in the economy, on the threat of antitrust litigation for treble damages to address a resulting injury to competition. Rather, to forestall any such potential injury to competition, the Bell operating company must be prevented from entering the interLATA market before regulators have concluded that there could be no future injury.

What has resulted is regulation's rendition of *Waiting for Godot*. The great wait for competition in long-distance telephony now has to be focused on that being realized first in local telephony. Such a prolonged process is an unnecessary burden on consumers and a charade. Consumers lose because Bell operating company entry into interLATA markets has a low probability of causing competitive harm and a high probability of producing lower prices. The checklist is a charade because complying is sufficiently complicated to require years of litigation before the FCC and the state public utilities commissions. The ultimate explanation for such a process must be based on the incentives facing those agencies—by checking off Bell operating company performance against the list, they would put themselves out of business. It would be naive to expect regulators to hasten the demise of their own bureaucracies by determining soon that the day had arrived when their oversight should end.

The incumbent interexchange carriers contributed to the development of that approach. They opposed the entry of any of the Bell operating companies or their spinoffs into interLATA markets. They fought Ameritech's requests to the antitrust court for a waiver to the divestiture decree that would have allowed it to enter the interLATA market on a limited basis. And they impeded AirTouch's efforts to enter the California interLATA market following its divestiture as an independent wireless entity by a Bell operating company.

Those carriers attempted to apply early versions of the checklist. When applying to state public utilities commissions to open local exchange and local toll markets to their entry, they demanded resale of the Bell operating companies' local exchange services and unbundled sale of basic service elements, according to pricing principles that imply an operating company subsidy. In short, they thoroughly litigated every step in competitive entry to delay that entry as long as possible.

How policy changes that generate entry, on a timely schedule, would affect the competitiveness of long-distance markets is the subject of this chapter. The various preconditions for a Bell operating company's entry into interLATA service in the new Telecommunications Act are of central concern. It is now clear that it will be most difficult for that type of company to establish as an evidentiary matter in a regulatory proceeding that it can meet "checklist" conditions in a timely way. The likely focus of the most intense litigation between the Bell operating companies and the interexchange carriers will be on qualifications for passing the checklist. Not being able to pass makes it unlikely that the Bell operating companies will be able to enter so as to establish a semblance of effective competition in interLATA markets before the turn of the century.

REGIONAL BELL OPERATING COMPANY
ENTRY INTO INTERLATA SERVICE MARKETS

The logic of the antitrust court's ban on the Bell operating companies' being able to enter interLATA markets is misguided. Even if one assumes that a Bell operating company has the potential after entry to engage in anticompetitive behavior in long-distance markets, it does not follow that antitrust policy should preempt that entry.

Substantive antitrust policy seeks to (1) prevent anticompetitive conduct that is injurious to consumers, (2) enhance competitive behavior that otherwise is mischaracterized as anticompetitive and therefore injurious to consumers, and (3) hold down costs of litigating claims under any imposed rule. By broadening the definition of what is anticompetitive, antitrust policy implementation decreases the extent of competitive behavior in (2) and increases litigation costs in (3). Forestalling behavior that could become anticompetitive in its "incipiency" has that potential. If the probability of failing to recognize anticompetitive and therefore injurious behavior is small, then antitrust officials should not apply an incipiency standard that prevents a firm from engaging in entry that also enhances competition. The combined benefits of (1) and (2) would be higher from instead penalizing transgressors after the fact.[1] As a respected appellate judge put it, "Especially when the prevalence of the conduct the law seeks to deter is low, simpler rules are preferable."[2] To that assessment one should add that more *permissive* rules on entry by themselves have merit because they more likely result in the elimination of structures and conditions that offer the potential for anticompetitive practices.[3]

1. *See* Paul L. Joskow & Alvin K. Klevorick, *A Framework for Analyzing Predatory Pricing Policy*, 89 YALE L.J. 213, 223 (1979); *see also* J. Gregory Sidak, *Debunking Predatory Innovation*, 83 COLUM. L. REV. 1121, 1144–45 (1983); Frank H. Easterbrook, *Predatory Strategies and Counterstrategies*, 48 U. CHI. L. REV. 263, 318–19 (1981); Richard L. Schmalensee, *On the Use of Economic Models in Antitrust: The* ReaLemon *Case*, 127 U. PA. L. REV. 994, 1018–19 n.98 (1979).

2. Northeastern Tel. Co. *v.* American Tel. & Tel. Co., 651 F.2d 76, 88 (2d Cir. 1981) (Kaufman, J.), *cert. denied*, 455 U.S. 943 (1982).

3. William J. Baumol and J. Gregory Sidak have made an analogous argument with respect to the Modification of Final Judgment's prohibition on Bell operating companies' entry into manufacturing and with respect to the statutory ban on a telephone company's providing video programming within its area of local exchange operations:

> To maximize social welfare, government policy on entry in telecommunications should aim to minimize the *sum* of welfare losses from predation and from new products forgone, rather than minimizing only the former without regard for the magnitude of the latter. The policy imperative should be to minimize the combined damage attributable to monopoly and regulation, while awaiting the advent of effectively competitive or contestable markets in local telephony.

WILLIAM J. BAUMOL & J. GREGORY SIDAK, TOWARD COMPETITION IN LOCAL TELEPHONY 132 (MIT Press & AEI Press 1994) (emphasis in original). "The same argument applies to a Bell operating company's entry into video programming in the geographic area where it provides telephone service—in contrast to mere common carriage of such programming in its service area, which is not forbidden by regulation or statute." *Id. See also* Kenneth J. Arrow, Dennis W. Carlton & Hal S. Sider, *The Competitive Effects of Line-of-Business Restrictions in Telecommunications*, 16 MANAGERIAL & DECISION ECON. 301, 305 (1995) ("The goal of public policy in telecommunications should not be simply to minimize potential regulatory problems

That calculus applies to the ban on operating company entry into interLATA services. The gains from competition in interLATA services could be substantial, and there is some probability that such gains will actually accrue. On the other side, the probability of anticompetitive conduct by an operating company in long-distance markets and the magnitude of competitive harm that would result are unknown. In addition, the costs of the regulatory machinery to operate the entry-forestalling system could consume a disproportionate share of any net welfare benefits sought for consumers.[4]

THE "COMPETITIVENESS" BENEFITS FROM BELL OPERATING COMPANY ENTRY INTO INTERLATA SERVICE MARKETS

The outbreak of competition from Bell operating company entry is likely for sound analytical reasons. The entrants necessarily would reduce long-distance rates, because doing so would increase their earnings from providing increased access to the other incumbent carriers. David Sibley and Dennis Weisman have demonstrated that a Bell operating company would have an incentive to promote higher volumes of message service because doing so would expand its sale of access to the interexchange carriers.[5] To the extent that the

but instead to maximize net benefits to society.").

4. Building on important contributions by William J. Baumol and Robert H. Bork, two respected experts on predation have incisively observed:

> Perhaps one of the most efficient methods for disadvantaging existing and prospective competitors that is available to an incumbent firm is through the strategic use (or abuse) of the political and legal process. Disadvantages inflicted upon the existing rival and the entry barriers created by means of such strategies are frequently more permanent than those that could be generated through more standard means.

Janusz A. Ordover & Garth Saloner, *Predation, Monopolization, and Antitrust, in* 1 HANDBOOK OF INDUSTRIAL ORGANIZATION 537, 573 (Richard Schmalensee & Robert D. Willig eds., North-Holland 1989). *See also* ROBERT H. BORK, THE ANTITRUST PARADOX: A POLICY AT WAR WITH ITSELF 347–64 (Basic Books 1978; Free Press rev. ed. 1993); William J. Baumol & Janusz A. Ordover, *Use of Antitrust to Subvert Competition,* 28 J.L. & ECON. 247 (1985).

5. DAVID S. SIBLEY & DENNIS L. WEISMAN, COMPETITIVE INCENTIVES OF

access charge exceeded access marginal cost, the operating company would have a compensatory source of earnings to cancel out lower earnings from lower MTS and WATS prices. Thus, *relative to incumbents in a given interLATA market,* the Bell operating company would be willing to accept a lower profit margin on its sale of services. Permitting that carrier to enter would conceivably reduce prices, which would make markets more competitive.

The aggregate monetary value of such lower prices from operating company entry can be estimated by using two different methods. The first method uses the historical responses of interexchange carriers to changes in rivals' output strategies to determine how those firms likely would respond to such entry. It is assumed that they would respond to subsequent changes in outputs in either a noncooperative or a cooperative process of interaction. The former assumption does not change incumbent interactions—the established carriers continue to tacitly collude. The latter assumption is conservative in that it produces a low estimate of the gains to consumers because operating company entry does not change the tacitly collusive behavior of all firms. The second method assumes that all carriers act noncooperatively and break down the cooperation that existed as a result of a Bell operating company's entry.

It is important to note first the effects on prices of barriers to entry.[6] An interexchange carrier's investments in a fiber-optic network are largely sunk—the firm cannot recoup those costs if it leaves a market or region of the country. AT&T, MCI, and Sprint have large investments in fiber-optic networks, and their sunk costs create a barrier to new firm entry. Indeed, since the divestiture of AT&T in 1984, no new facilities-based carrier has entered the long-distance market on a nationwide basis, on the scale of Sprint, despite the fact that the size of the market has increased by more than 50 percent.[7]

VERTICALLY INTEGRATED LOCAL EXCHANGE CARRIERS (University of Texas Working Paper, Aug. 9, 1995).

6. *See* JEAN TIROLE, THE THEORY OF INDUSTRIAL ORGANIZATION ch. 8 (MIT Press 1988).

7. FCC, STATISTICS OF COMMUNICATIONS COMMON CARRIERS, 1993/1994 EDITION table 8.7 (reporting the number of intrastate and interstate toll dial equipment minutes).

Even so, the established operating companies are positioned to enter long-distance markets, because they have sunk the required network costs in facilities that provide in-region local toll services. Allowing them to enter would create an additional facilities-based carrier in each of the seven Bell operating company regions that form a network potentially larger than MCI or Sprint's.

The assumption is that allowing such entry would result in the addition of one new national carrier with capacity equivalent to the second largest incumbent carrier. Then what would be the likely competitive result? To answer that question, we must have two additional pieces of information: the likely long-distance market share of the operating company in its region and the price response of existing interexchange carriers to new entry.

Market shares of the operating companies in interLATA long-distance service have been estimated in market research studies undertaken in Maryland, Michigan, Florida, as well as other states. Estimates from a California study are used here because of the importance of that market and because of the detailed analysis undertaken of price-cost margins in that state in chapter 5. On the basis of a survey of its residential customers, Pacific Telesis has estimated that its interLATA share after entry would be approximately 34 percent (see table 6–1).[8] Most of that share would come from AT&T, as its share fell from 65 to 46 percent. MCI and Sprint would have similar, albeit smaller, declines in share. The likely ability of Pacific Telesis to gain market share at the expense of existing interexchange carriers follows from its brand-name identification with consumers and its large, established network facilities.

The price responses to entry cannot be known but rather have to be assumed. A first assumption would be that interfirm coordination on pricing would continue—so that there would be no response. But an increase in the number of large, facilities-based

---

8. This share assumes that interLATA relief is granted at the same time as interexchange carriers obtain equal access (that is, presubscription) for their intraLATA toll services. If presubscription were granted before interLATA relief, Bell operating companies' likely long-distance market shares would decline. *See* discussion *infra* and Paul W. MacAvoy, Declaration in Support of Pacific Telesis, Dkt. No. I.87-11-033 (Cal. Pub. Util. Comm'n, filed July 31, 1995).

competitors in interLATA markets would make the process of establishing tacit collusion more difficult; in fact, not only would a fourth full-scale supplier operate in each local market, but in seven regions of the country that supplier would be a different entity. The extent to which the large interexchange carriers could threaten price cuts to punish discounters diminishes as the number of equal-sized alternative carriers increases; the impact of responsive cuts to "cheating" decreases as the number of firms increases.[9] The entry of the operating companies and their ability to capture one-third of interLATA long-distance markets could have a disruptive effect on the pattern of current coordinated price-setting behavior of the three large interexchange carriers.[10]

TABLE 6–1 CARRIERS' INTERLATA MARKET SHARES FOR RESIDENTIAL SERVICE (PERCENTAGE)		
	Market Shares without Entry	Market Shares with Bell Operating Company Entry
Pacific Telesis	n/a	34
AT&T	65	46
MCI	18	13
Sprint	13	8
Sources: Market shares without entry come from CALIFORNIA PUBLIC UTILITIES COMMISSION, COMMISSION ADVISORY AND COMPLIANCE DIVISION, REPORT ON 1991 CALIFORNIA INTEREXCHANGE MARKET MONITORING PLAN, ex. 5 (Dec. 1993). Market shares with entry come from a Pacific Telesis internal study. For detail please contact the author.		

The resulting price cuts from granting interLATA entry rights to operating companies likely would be substantial. So would the gains for subscribers in dollars of cost savings. Residential and

---

9. Daniel Orr & Paul W. MacAvoy, *Price Strategies to Promote Cartel Stability*, 32 ECONOMICA 186 (1965).

10. InterLATA relief would promote competition in intraLATA markets as well, because Bell operating companies could offer "one-stop-shopping" for all toll calls on a presubscribed basis. The interexchange carriers would be forced to market their services without a bundling advantage.

business customers spent approximately $61.5 billion on interLATA calls (both intrastate and interstate) in 1993.[11] Because the volume of their business was so large, even small reductions in prices caused by entry of new facilities-based carriers would generate substantial gains to consumers. Their gains would equal (1) the reduced payments required to purchase the existing volume of service and (2) the additional value net of cost derived by consumers who purchase increased levels of service at lower prices. Those two sources appear in figure 6–1, where the rectangle *A* equals the dollar value of reduced payments on the existing level of service and the triangle *B* equals the dollar value of increased purchases. The sum of *A* and *B* is the gain for consumers caused by the price reduction. To estimate areas *A* and *B*, the prices and quantities must be determined before and after the price reduction caused by entry. The interaction process will be examined for continuation of tacit collusion and for a "breakdown" to noncooperative behavior.

FIGURE 6–1
GAIN IN CONSUMERS' SURPLUS
RESULTING FROM INTERLATA RELIEF

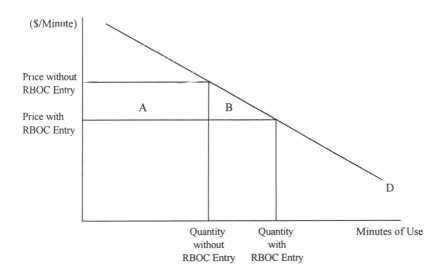

11. FCC, STATISTICS OF COMMUNICATIONS COMMON CARRIERS, 1993/1994 EDITION table 1.4.

Consumer Gains from Entry Assuming That Incumbent Carriers Maintain Tacitly Collusive Pricing

The gains resulting from Bell operating company entry into the long-distance market can be estimated in a five-part procedure. In the first step the entrant's long-distance market share is taken from the survey work conducted by Pacific Telesis. That market share and the predicted shares for the interexchange carriers are shown in table 6–1; they are used to calculate the postentry HHI, given operating company shares region by region. The second step is to use that HHI in conjunction with an assumed demand elasticity of -0.75 and the conjectural variation to estimate postentry price-cost margins.[12] That postentry price-cost margin equals 0.49. When the operating company is assumed to act noncooperatively, the postentry price falls by 47 percent. In contrast, when the operating company is assumed to act collusively, the resulting postentry price falls by 9 percent. The third step takes that margin resulting from entry by the operating company, and the marginal cost for message toll service, shown in table 5–4 to equal $0.077 per message minute, to calculate the postentry price of message toll service.

In the fourth step the percentage decrease in the postentry price is used in conjunction with the assumed demand elasticity to calculate the increase in demand stimulated by the entry. When the

12. The formula for calculating the price-cost margin is as follows:

$$L_i = \sum_{i=1}^{n} s_i L_i = \frac{HHI + \sum_{i=1}^{n} \lambda_i s_i^2}{e}$$

where

L	=	the industry average price-cost margin
HHI	=	the Herfindahl-Hirschman index
s	=	market share
λ	=	conjectural variation
e	=	demand elasticity.

See S. MARTIN, ADVANCED INDUSTRIAL ECONOMICS (Blackwell 1993) ch. 2 at 167.

entrant is assumed to act as a noncooperator, the resulting post-entry quantity demanded increases by 6 percent.

In the final step consumers' gain is calculated by using all pre- and postentry prices and quantities demanded. That gain equals areas *A* and *B* in figure 6-1, as shown in table 6-2.[13]

TABLE 6-2 CONSUMER GAINS FROM BELL OPERATING COMPANY ENTRY ASSUMING AT&T, MCI, AND SPRINT MAINTAIN THEIR TACITLY COLLUSIVE PRICING STRATEGIES	
Entrant Assumed to Act Noncooperatively	Entrant Assumed to Cooperate Tacitly in Pricing
$24.4 billion annually	$4.8 billion annually
$305.6 billion present value	$59.9 billion present value

Consumer Gains from Entry Assuming That All Carriers Set Prices Noncooperatively

Rather than the interexchange carriers' maintaining their historical pricing behavior, in response to entry all carriers could behave noncooperatively. The resulting gains to consumers would equal approximately $24 billion annually or $300 billion in present value (see table 6-3).[14] The resulting welfare benefit to consumers closely approximates that, assuming that only the operating companies act noncooperatively. That occurs because the industry-average price-cost margin is weighted by carriers' market shares. Since AT&T and the operating companies account for a combined 80 percent of the market, and their conjectural variations are at or near the noncooperative response, the resulting benefits are the same.

Together, those results demonstrate that consumers would reap large gains from entry into the interLATA market. The operat-

13. The present value is evaluated in perpetuity with all future, annual consumer benefits discounted at the social rate of discount of 8 percent.

14. On the basis of that assumption, the welfare gain was derived by using the five-step process described previously.

ing companies are positioned to enter long-distance markets and either set prices independently or totally disrupt the current tacitly collusive price structure. But those gains would be diminished if current interexchange carriers were allowed to offer intraLATA toll service on an equal-access (that is, presubscribed) basis before the Bell operating companies were allowed to enter the interLATA market.

TABLE 6–3 CONSUMER GAINS FROM ENTRY ASSUMING ALL CARRIERS ACT AS COMPETITORS
$24.1 billion annually or $300.7 billion present value

BENEFITS VERSUS COSTS: THE ANTICIPATED
HARM TO COMPETITION FROM ENTRY INTO
INTERLATA SERVICE MARKETS

The operating companies' entry into interLATA service markets carries with it the threat of leveraging from a bottleneck facility to fragile competitive markets. The antitrust concern is that the bottleneck's owner, by restricting the availability of local exchange service, can prevent or destroy competition among the incumbent providers of long-distance services; by so doing, the bottleneck's owner is thought to make a second monopoly for itself in long-distance service markets.

The antitrust consent decree reified the belief that it was better to reduce the probability of bottleneck leveraging to zero and thereby prevent any competition from the owner of the bottleneck than it was to allow the bottleneck owner to enter and then observe whether leveraging was sufficient to prosecute that owner for violating the antitrust laws. By adopting a policy that prevented leveraging in its incipiency, the Justice Department improved the appearance of its win-loss record. It could avoid the embarrassment of bringing a case against an operating company if it simply forbade that company to enter the interLATA market.

There is, of course, a net loss to consumers from the Department of Justice's prophylaxis against monopoly leveraging. There would be no price reductions resulting from competitive incursions by the operating companies, from which would be subtracted the costs of a successful leveraging strategy perpetrated on all or some long-distance markets. But such costs are extremely problematical. There appears never to have been a case against a firm that successfully leveraged a second monopoly from a bottleneck facility. Robert Bork dispelled much of the theory of bottleneck monopoly by showing that in most instances two monopolies were not better than one: A firm could get all its market returns from the first monopoly.[15] In long-distance markets an attempt to leverage from a bottleneck in local exchange to a second monopoly in long-distance service would not increase profits because the two services are used in fixed proportions—a minute of (bottleneck) local access is necessary to originate a minute of interLATA transport and exchange service. An increase in the Bell operating company's price for access would reduce, in that exact amount, the price that consumers would pay for the rest of the long-distance service. Nothing would be gained from charging a second monopoly price for long-distance service.

The Department of Justice sees an exception to such a theory of futility. Because the price of the bottleneck facility is regulated, the Bell operating company cannot extract its full monopoly rent in that price. Thus, it has an incentive to leverage around regulation; and if regulation is ineffective in detecting the leveraging, the operating company would have the opportunity to take that rent in higher long-distance prices instead. But market power is not fungible, so that the operating company cannot transfer from local exchange to the interLATA markets. The contrary argument is surprisingly pedestrian for a theory that has motivated the Department of Justice's industrial policy for telecommunications: manipulation of cost accounting supposedly enables the operating company to mischaracterize the costs of long-distance service provision as arising from its regulated local exchange and access activities. Those artificially understated costs of long-distance service provision

---

15. BORK, *supra* note 4, at 372–73.

enable the operating company to underprice efficient rivals in interLATA markets. Thus, that company is allowed to price predatorily in the competitive market and pass some or all of its current profit sacrifice on to consumers of the locally regulated bottleneck services in higher cost-determined local exchange rates.

That scenario of cross-subsidy and predatory pricing is not credible for several reasons. First, even the myopic regulator that such a theory assumes to exist must be expected to see such an artifice over time. In fact, contrary to the assumption of regulatory ineptitude, since the Bell System's divestiture, state and federal regulators have implemented sophisticated cost allocation procedures and have had the opportunity to apply them to a number of unregulated activities that the operating companies have been allowed to undertake. They can detect cross-subsidy and below-cost pricing.

Second, the transition from rate-of-return to price cap regulation has attenuated and perhaps eliminated altogether any hypothetical benefit to the operating company from passing through to regulated businesses the costs incurred in unregulated markets. The reason is straightforward: price caps on regulated local services in general are not set based on cost of service, so that any surreptitious pass-through of costs is not possible. In practice, some caps have been related to some costs; but as experts on predation have observed, "the spread of price-cap regulation means that if there ever was a possibility of financing losses incurred in predatory pricing in the interLATA market by raising local rates, it is rapidly disappearing."[16] Although not all states have adopted price-cap regulation to date, there is a consistent trend in that direction,[17] to an extent sufficient to render the general argument that there is a regulatory incentive for predation in long-distance incorrect under current conditions.[18]

16. Susan Gates, Paul Milgrom & John Roberts, *Deterring Predation in Telecommunications: Are Line-of-Business Restraints Needed?*, 16 MANAGERIAL & DECISION ECON. 427, 435 (1995).

17. *See* DAVID E. M. SAPPINGTON & DENNIS WEISMAN, DESIGNING INCENTIVE REGULATION FOR THE TELECOMMUNICATIONS INDUSTRY (MIT Press & AEI Press 1996).

18. Moreover, the 1995 proposed federal bills for "reform" would abolish rate-of-return regulation. *See* H.R. 1555, 104th Cong., 1st Sess. (1995) (proposed 47

Third, the existence of seven Bell operating companies (and an eighth local carrier of comparable size, GTE) enables regulators to "benchmark" the costs of any given Bell operating company for purposes of detecting cost misallocation.[19] In each of seven regions of the country, the three major interexchange carriers would face a Bell operating company as a facilities-based competitor. In any given region, the interexchange carriers would be able to compare the operating company's costs of providing local telephone service with the costs for the same services in six other regions. The interexchange carriers could therefore watch for aberrant cost levels in local service that would be consistent with subsidization costs of the operating company's interLATA services.

Fourth, the actual experience of the Bell operating companies in markets outside local exchange does not support the conclusion that cost misallocation and predation have resulted. For example, Jerry Hausman has noted, "No claims have been brought against a BOC that it has cross-subsidized its intraLATA long-distance service."[20] Similarly, econometric analysis by Richard Higgins supports the conclusion that anticompetitive cross-subsidization did not occur after Bell operating companies were allowed to provide limited "corridor" interLATA service around New York City and Philadelphia, nor have the seven Bell operating companies resorted to cross-subsidization to reduce competition in the markets for cellular telephony, paging, pay telephones, customer premises equipment, or videotext gateway services.[21] Similarly, GTE's supply of interexchange service did not result in cross-subsidization or exclusionary conduct even though the company was simultaneously a local exchange carrier.[22]

U.S.C. § 248(b)); S. 652, § 301(A)(3), 104th Cong., 1st Sess. (1995).

19. Paul S. Brandon & Richard L. Schmalensee, *The Benefits of Releasing the Bell Companies from the Interexchange Restrictions*, 16 MANAGERIAL & DECISION ECON. 349, 357 (1995).

20. Jerry A. Hausman, *Competition in Long-Distance and Telecommunications Equipment Markets: Effects of the MFJ*, 16 MANAGERIAL & DECISION ECON. 365, 373–74 (1995).

21. Affidavit of Richard S. Higgins, Motion of Bell Atlantic Corporation, BellSouth Corporation, NYNEX Corporation, and Southwestern Bell Corporation to Vacate the Decree, United States *v.* Western Elec. Co., No. 82-0192 (filed D.D.C. July 6, 1994).

22. *Id. See also* MICHAEL K. KELLOGG, JOHN THORNE & PETER W. HUBER,

Fifth, a campaign of predatory pricing in the interLATA market could not produce a monopoly. Even if a Bell operating company could bankrupt one or more of the three major interexchange carriers, that carrier's fiber optic capacity would remain intact for another firm to purchase. Given the long useful life of optical fiber, any network "darkened" by hypothetical predation would be relit by a new entrant if the predator were to attempt to recoup profits lost in predation by raising prices after the bankruptcy.[23]

Finally, the fulcrum on which the Bell operating company's lever must operate—a monopoly in local access and transport—is evidently declining. Local entry has occurred most noticeably in those services that make positive contributions to margin, such as interstate access and intraLATA toll. Comprehensive entry of those carriers has been understandably much slower into services that make negative contributions to margin, as is the case in rural markets for residential local exchange service. But even wireline services in such markets are going to be vulnerable to competition from wireless technologies.[24] In the meantime, however, a monopoly over unprofitable services that regulators require the operating company to provide is no fulcrum for leveraging market power. The operating company has no ability to raise price to generate profits on long-distance service because competitors have targeted those subscribers who would make gains from leverage attractive.

THE AMERITECH PROPOSAL

In March 1993 Ameritech requested approvals from the FCC and a temporary waiver from the Bell System antitrust decree judgment court to offer interLATA service.[25] In return for being granted the opportunity to provide in-region interLATA services on a trial

FEDERAL TELECOMMUNICATIONS LAW 420–21 (Little, Brown & Co. 1992).

23. Gates, Milgrom & Roberts, *supra* note 16, at 435.

24. *See, e.g.*, Daniel F. Spulber, *Deregulating Telecommunications*, 12 YALE J. ON REG. 25 (1995).

25. Petition of Ameritech for Declaratory Ruling and Related Waivers to Establish a New Regulatory Model for the Ameritech Region (filed before the FCC Mar. 1, 1993).

basis, Ameritech would support all actions sought before state and federal regulators, and before the judgment court, to open local markets within its region to other carriers.

The Ameritech plan assumed a significance that transcended the issue of competition in long-distance service in the Great Lakes region. The plan demonstrated how many concessions an operating company would have to make to receive authorization to provide interLATA service. Ameritech first proposed its plan to the Antitrust Division of the Department of Justice in December 1993.[26] The Antitrust Division, whose support would have increased the likelihood that the judgment court would grant Ameritech's waiver request, considered the proposal with maximum delay and then so constricted the scope of the trial that it could not produce results that would help answer questions about the competitive effects of entry.

In July 1994 four other Bell operating companies filed a motion to vacate the entire consent decree—an action that signaled that they would pursue a unified strategy to secure the judgment court's approval to enter interLATA markets.[27] Pacific Telesis followed in 1994 with its own motion to vacate the decree's interLATA ban to the extent that it affected California.[28] While four of those operating companies took polite exception to the Ameritech plan, one of them excoriated it on grounds that its implementation would result in "a massive shift of power from state and federal regulators, and the decree court, to the Department of Justice."[29]

The Ameritech plan indeed offered limited prospects for establishing an operating company competitor in long-distance services in the Great Lakes region. Originally, Ameritech proposed to offer interLATA services originating or terminating anywhere in

26. AMERITECH CORP., 1993 SEC FORM 10-K, at 9 (1994).

27. Motion of Bell Atlantic Corporation, BellSouth Corporation, NYNEX Corporation, and Southwestern Bell Corporation to Vacate the Decree, United States *v.* Western Elec. Co., No. 82-0192 (D.D.C. filed July 6, 1994).

28. Motion of Pacific Telesis Group to Vacate the Decree, United States *v.* Western Elec. Co., No. 82-0192 (D.D.C. filed 1994).

29. *Ameritech Open Market Plan Attacked by Other RHCs*, COMMON CARRIER WK., May 8, 1995 (*quoting* memorandum circulated to other Bell operating companies by Southwestern Bell Corp. Vice President Thomas Barry).

its region (comprising Indiana, Illinois, Michigan, Ohio, and Wisconsin). Following the filing of opposition comments by the interexchange carriers and negotiations with the Antitrust Division, Ameritech in April 1995 acquiesced to a revised proposal to *resell* interLATA services originating or terminating *only in the Grand Rapids, Michigan, LATA and a portion of the Chicago LATA*.[30] Ameritech would be prohibited from using its own facilities to provide interLATA transport.

The Antitrust Division did not so much constrict the scope of the plan as denude it of policy significance. That was so since the plan could not have been undertaken over any reasonable time horizon. Before Ameritech could have commenced interLATA service, it would have had to satisfy an eight-part test on conditions for opening its local markets and it would have had to file with the Antitrust Division a ten-part "compliance plan" that certified the finding that, among other things, "actual competition (including facilities-based competition) in local exchange telecommunications exists in the Trial Territory."[31] Even without considering the inevitable delay of litigation to follow on those aspects of the plan before the decree court,[32] completion of those steps would have taken so many years that there would not likely have been empirical evidence on the effects on prices and outputs of a local Bell operating company's entry into interLATA markets.

There was still the second question, What would have been required? The criterion by which one would have expected the Antitrust Division in the first instance, and the decree court in the second, to evaluate Ameritech's waiver request was section VIII(C) of the AT&T consent decree.[33] That section provided:

---

30. Proposed Order to Permit an Interexchange Trial by Ameritech Submitted by the Department of Justice, United States *v.* Western Elec. Co., No. 82-0192 (D.D.C. filed Apr. 3, 1995).

31. *Id.* at ¶ 11(b)(i).

32. Paul H. Rubin & Hashem Dezhbakhsh, *Costs of Delay and Rent-Seeking Under the Modification of Final Judgment*, 16 MANAGERIAL & DECISION ECON. 385 (1995).

33. United States *v.* American Tel. & Tel. Co., 552 F. Supp. 226 (D.D.C. 1982).

> The restrictions imposed upon the separated BOCs
> by virtue of [the line-of-business restrictions con-
> tained in] section II(D) shall be removed upon a
> showing by the petitioning Bell Operating Company
> that there is no substantial possibility that it could
> use its monopoly power to impede competition in
> the market it seeks to enter.[34]

By its direct language, section VIII(C) would have required that the
decision to grant Ameritech's waiver request rest on a finding of
whether Ameritech's *probable conduct* in interLATA markets would
have impeded competition in those markets. But to avoid having to
make that finding, the Antitrust Division employed the legerdemain
of basing its proposed order not on section VIII(C), but on section
VII of the decree.[35] Nothing in section VIII(C) suggested that its
logic would have failed to apply if the Antitrust Division had characterized the waiver request as a "temporary" lifting of the line-of-
business restriction. But, more conveniently, section VII said nothing about evaluating the probable effect on competition in the markets that the operating company sought to enter. Indeed, by its plain
language, section VII was nothing more than legal boilerplate concerning the ability of the decree court to retain jurisdiction for the
purposes of construing, carrying out, modifying, or enforcing the
decree, or punishing violations of it.[36] But to say that the decree

---

34. *Id. See* KELLOGG, THORNE & HUBER, *supra* note 22, at 370–99; United
States *v.* Western Elec. Co., 900 F.2d 283 (D.C. Cir. 1990).

35. Ameritech Proposed Order at 1.

36. Section VII provided in its entirety:

> Jurisdiction is retained by this Court for the purpose of enabling
> any of the parties to the Modification of Final Judgment, or, after
> the reorganization specified in section I, a BOC to apply to this
> Court at any time for such further orders or directions as may be
> necessary or appropriate for the construction or carrying out of
> this Modification of Final Judgment, for the modification of any
> of the provisions hereof, for the enforcement of compliance
> herewith, and for the punishment of any violation hereof.

United States *v.* American Tel. & Tel. Co., 552 F. Supp. 226 (D.D.C. 1982).

court had retained jurisdiction over Ameritech to consider its interLATA proposal (a proposition never in dispute) in no way answered the question of what the legal test should have been for evaluating the relevant economic effects of that proposal. Section VII did not enunciate an operative test in the way that section VIII(C) did. In that respect, section VII was described as a more lenient "public interest" standard for modification of the decree when the waiver request was "uncontested"—that is, when it was supported by AT&T and the Department of Justice,[37] as had been the case with the revised version of the Ameritech proposal ultimately filed with the decree court.

And how would one define the public interest for purposes of section VII? In an attempt to keep section VII from becoming amorphous, the U.S. Court of Appeals for the D.C. Circuit in 1990 held that "the appropriate question under section VII is whether the proposed modification would be *certain* to lessen competition in the relevant market,"[38] and it rejected the possibility that an incipiency theory based on leveraging could satisfy that test.[39] Moreover, the D.C. Circuit defined market power as the Bell operating company's "ability to raise prices or restrict output *in the market it seeks to enter.*"[40] Thus, the D.C. Circuit established that section VII should have been applied in the same manner as section VIII(C), except that a denial of the proposed entry by the Bell operating company had to be based on a finding that a lessening of competition in the market to be entered would have been "certain" rather than "substantially possible."

Nonetheless, in Ameritech's case the Antitrust Division turned the supposedly more lenient section VII standard into one more demanding than section VIII(C). In so doing, the Antitrust Division swept under the rug the question of the competitiveness of interLATA services in the Great Lakes region.

The division's requirement that Ameritech offer interLATA services only on a resale basis was especially ominous. It is widely

37. KELLOGG, THORNE & HUBER, *supra* note 22, at 386–94.
38. United States *v.* Western Elec. Co., 900 F.2d 283, 308 (D.C. Cir. 1990) (emphasis added).
39. *Id.* at 296.
40. *Id.* (emphasis added).

recognized that a Bell operating company could initiate interLATA service within its operating region with small incremental investment, given that it already provides *intra*LATA toll service over its own facilities.[41] In effect, a Bell operating company would connect in series its contiguous intraLATA networks to provide continuous interLATA transport across its region. But that operating company would have no cost advantage in reselling the capacity of an interexchange carrier. It could charge a price that, by definition, was no lower than the bulk price at which the facilities-based carrier would sell it such capacity. Ameritech could only be as price competitive in its sale of interLATA services as AT&T, MCI, and Sprint permitted.

The situation would be considerably different if Ameritech were allowed to use its own facilities to provide interLATA services within-region. Ameritech's price floor would no longer be what the interexchange carriers permitted, but rather the incremental cost to Ameritech of modifying and using its existing toll network to carry calls among the various LATAs in its region. Ameritech is the single company capable of providing interLATA competition in the Great Lakes region, for it is the only firm that has a full-scale fiber-optic network traversing that region that does not now supply interexchange services.

The perversity of the Antitrust Division's response to the original Ameritech proposal becomes apparent. By rejecting Ameritech's original proposal to permit its facilities-based provision of interLATA services within-region, the division shielded AT&T, MCI, and Sprint from the one carrier possessing the resources necessary to give those companies a run for market share. How an antitrust authority charged with protecting consumer welfare, by expanding competitive opportunity, could produce so convoluted a result is mystifying.

The Antitrust Division squeezed the competitive vitality out of the Ameritech plan. In its original form, the plan would have yielded insights on the pricing significance in interLATA markets of economies between Ameritech's production of local exchange services and in-region interLATA services. In its constricted form, the

41. *See, e.g.*, Brandon & Schmalensee, *supra* note 19, at 349–50, 353.

plan would reveal nothing about system cost differences and their competitive ramifications. Rather, the plan at most would provide an indication of the market value of a Bell operating company's trademarks in interLATA resale services—hardly an issue that would go to the heart of market "competitiveness." Further, the constricted plan would prohibit, at the Antitrust Division's insistence, Ameritech's joint marketing of local services and interLATA resale services. Thus, even with respect to the experiment that the Antitrust Division consented to support, it made sure to destroy any opportunity for consumers to reap the benefits of Ameritech's economies of scope in marketing. All that, of course, the Antitrust Division did to protect consumers from the risk that Ameritech would monopolize the interLATA long-distance markets in the Great Lakes region.

THE AIRTOUCH INITIATIVE

The restrictive nature of the Department of Justice's response to the Ameritech proposal was matched, at least, by that in its treatment of AirTouch as a potential long-distance competitor. The Pacific Telesis Group, the Bell operating company serving California and Nevada, decided in December 1992 to spin off its wireless and other unregulated activities from its regulated local exchange operations. The share distribution to shareholders created two completely separate and independently managed corporations.[42] The new wireless company is now known as AirTouch Communications.

Pacific Telesis intended the spinoff to exempt AirTouch from the restrictions that the consent decree placed on Bell operating companies. Pacific Telesis wrote in 1993 that it "expected that the spin-off [would] eliminate many of the financial, legal and regulatory constraints that have impeded the Corporation's efforts to grow and compete, including, for the wireless businesses, those restraints established as part of the Consent Decree."[43] Sam Ginn, the chairman of AirTouch and the former chairman of Pacific Telesis, subsequently explained that the burden of complying with the

---

42. PACIFIC TELESIS GROUP, 1992 FORM 10-K, at 4-10 (1993).
43. *Id.* at 5 (1993), *quoted in* BAUMOL & SIDAK, *supra* note 3, at 19.

consent decree had foreclosed attractive business opportunities.[44] One example that he gave was the following:

> [Before the spinoff, Pacific Telesis] bought a cellular company in Michigan that covered the southern half of Michigan and the northern half of Ohio. At the time of the acquisition, the [acquired] company provided long-distance service to its customers. To satisfy the line of business restrictions of the consent decree, we had to rearrange the [acquired] company's entire network, take down all of the long-distance connections, and inform our customers that we didn't provide that service anymore. Even if one were to assume that a bottleneck exists in the local exchange, which I do not believe applies in California, what in the world did that have to do with a market in another location? Moreover, if there was a dominant player in the Michigan and Ohio market at the time, it was Ameritech, not PacTel.[45]

By ridding itself of such regulatory constraints, Pacific Telesis could provide its stockholders with opportunities to use its knowledge of technologies to build wireless long-distance systems for entry into new markets. As William J. Baumol and J. Gregory Sidak noted in 1994, "PacTel Wireless could quickly, if imperfectly, replicate the AT&T-McCaw merger by acquiring or merging with one of AT&T's competitors in the interexchange market—MCI, Sprint, or LDDS."[46]

In April 1994 the Pacific Telesis Group formally divested AirTouch. The two companies have since then separately traded and have shared no directors, officers, employees, assets, or control. The directors of Pacific Telesis reiterated that AirTouch would be "freed from the line-of-business restrictions imposed [upon the Bell

---

44. Sam Ginn, *Restructuring the Wireless Industry and the Information Skyway*, 4 J. ECON. & MGMT. STRATEGY 139 (1995).

45. *Id*. at 142.

46. BAUMOL & SIDAK, *supra* note 3, at 19.

operating company] at divestiture."[47] As such it would be able to enhance its cellular services by integrating with interexchange long-distance wired services and to pursue satellite-based long-distance communications as well.[48] Within one year of completing the transaction, however, AirTouch found itself unable to pursue that strategy.

On August 15, 1994, MCI complained to the Department of Justice that AirTouch was still bound by the consent decree and had failed to obtain a waiver before providing interexchange services.[49] On January 11, 1995, the Department of Justice informed AirTouch that it was a "successor" to a Bell operating company, as defined in the decree, and was consequently subject to the decree's interLATA entry restrictions.[50] AirTouch filed a motion with the judgment court seeking a declaratory judgment to the effect that it was not subject to the decree.[51] The Department of Justice opposed AirTouch's motion.[52] As of the passage of the Telecommunications Act of 1996, the court had not ruled on the motion. Before the passage of the new act, AirTouch had agreed not to extend its business activities to areas prohibited to Bell operating companies under the decree.[53] In effect, the Department of Justice had succeeded in impeding the competitive entry of AirTouch into interLATA long-distance markets.

The irony in the Department of Justice's position becomes apparent upon comparing it with the department's policy on the same matters with AT&T. Divested of its local monopolies, AT&T was free to enter all other markets while the Bell operating companies remained restricted to their local exchange businesses. Under the department's interpretation, AirTouch, although severed completely from the operations of its former parent, a Bell operating

47. PACIFIC TELESIS GROUP, 1993 ANNUAL REPORT 2 (1994).

48. *Id.* at 21.

49. Letter from Anthony C. Epstein, Jenner & Block, to Richard Liebeskind, Assistant Chief, Communications and Finance Section, Antitrust Division, U.S. Department of Justice (Aug. 15, 1994).

50. AIRTOUCH COMMUNICATIONS, INC., 1994 SEC FORM 10-K, at 23 (1995).

51. *Id.* at 23.

52. *Justice Dept. Seeks Limits on AirTouch*, N.Y. TIMES, Mar. 14, 1995, at D10.

53. AIRTOUCH COMMUNICATIONS, INC., 1994 ANNUAL REPORT 23 (1995).

company, would remain similarly restricted. To bring the policy full circle, AT&T, the erstwhile parent of all entities subject to the decree, provides both wireless local exchange and cellular long-distance service through its recent acquisition of McCaw, the nation's largest cellular operator. Yet the Department of Justice argued that the decree, implemented to enhance competition, prevented independent AirTouch from competing against AT&T-McCaw in providing cellular long-distance service.

One can only ask whether the department, misled by bottleneck arguments, had become lost. There was no bottleneck rationale for placing control over the wireless local exchange. In most markets the FCC has licensed two cellular operators and, in 1995, issued two additional licenses for each market for the technically more advanced personal communications services, which will increase the number of wireless operators in most markets to four. Eventually, there will be eight wireless network operators in every market in the country. The judgment court, however, had identified a new rationale for control with respect to cellular operators.

On April 28, 1995, the court ruled that the Bell operating companies could offer interLATA service on a resale basis to their cellular customers if they met certain safeguards against potential discrimination.[54] It conceded that cellular operators did not themselves maintain control over an "essential facility" that would give rise to potential discrimination against competitors in an adjacent market such as interexchange service. Rather, the court identified the Bell operating companies' "mobile bottleneck" as the reason for concern, given that they have nearly complete control over interexchange services between mobile telephone switching offices and the long-distance carriers. Because those connections apply for nearly all cellular long-distance calls, the Bell operating companies have "the ability to control a part of virtually every interexchange cellular call, just as the landline bottleneck (monopoly control over the wire-based local exchange) gives those companies similar, albeit more complex, control over every wired interexchange call."[55] By pointing to the potential anticompetitive significance of the mobile

---

54. United States *v.* Western Elec. Co., 890 F. Supp. 1 (D.D.C. 1995).
55. *Id.* at 8.

link to the landlines' bottleneck and by establishing safeguards to prevent abuse, the court implemented the policy of incipiency once again.

Whether or not one agrees with the court's reasoning, it is certain that AirTouch does not control a landline bottleneck; it was divested from Pacific Telesis. Thus, AirTouch should not have been subject to the decree, and it should not have needed a conditional waiver to provide cellular long-distance service. Yet to spend a year litigating the question epitomizes the most salient characteristic of the consent decree oversight process: a regulatory regime of litigation delay that prevents entry into markets lacking competitive prices and service offerings.

ACHIEVING COMPETITION IN INTERLATA SERVICES BY LEGISLATIVE REFORM

Another route to develop competition in long-distance services is the passing of federal telecommunications legislation that would promote the entry of the operating companies into the interLATA markets. In light of the excess capacity that exists in long-distance service provision, it is unlikely that any firm would enter the interLATA market by constructing new facilities. The incumbent operating companies, however, have the capacity to provide interLATA services within their respective regions in existing facilities for providing intraLATA services. The question is whether "reform" legislation could address that most likely class of potential entrants in ways that would inject price competition into long-distance service markets.

Unfortunately, the 1995 experience with such legislation provides a negative answer to that question. The Telecommunications Act of 1996, of massive scale and detail, calls for a total restructuring of telecommunications by developing cross-entry of all types of carriers into each others' markets. But when dealing with entry into long-distance services, the legislation squandered the opportunity to create real interLATA competition over any reasonable time horizon. Instead, the act creates a new regulatory regime that could delay a Bell operating company's entry into interLATA services longer than the waiver process under section VIII(C) of the consent decree.

The act allows a Bell operating company to offer long-distance service outside its own service region immediately "after the date of enactment."[56] But the company may provide interLATA service in its own region only after the FCC verifies that the company has met certain competitive conditions.

That distinction was a late addition in the House and Senate conference formulating the act. Earlier versions of the House and Senate bills made no such distinction between long-distance services offered in-region and those offered out-of-region. As a concession to the established interexchange carriers, the distinction is notable. The operating companies' home regions are where they might be reasonably expected to present the sharpest challenge to the current long-distance carriers; by preventing the companies from entering markets in those regions, the act dilutes the potential deregulatory benefits from facilities-based entry. Moreover, despite the operating companies' current availability, they must wait for the FCC to write more than eighty rules after deciding issues as vital as how new rivals for local phone service will pay the operating companies for interconnection and issues as mundane as how rivals will obtain physical access to local service tandems.[57] But in general those conditions require that the operating company promote entry of the long-distance carriers into their local service markets before they are allowed access to long-distance markets. One section of the new act amends Title II of the Communications Act of 1934 to add specific interconnection requirements that must be implemented before the FCC authorizes an operating company to provide in-region interLATA services. That authorization would be forthcoming upon the successful fulfillment of the following: an in-region test and a "competitive checklist."[58] All conditions must be satisfied for an operating company to gain the FCC's permission to provide such services.

Though daunting for its technicality, the checklist of the Telecommunications Act of 1996 is reproduced herein in its entirety

---

56. Telecommunications Act of 1996, Pub. L. 104-104, 110 Stat. 56 (Feb. 8, 1996) [hereinafter Telecommunications Act].

57. Bryan Gruley & Albert R. Karr, *Bill's Passage Represents Will of Both Parties*, WALL ST. J., Feb. 2, 1996, at B1, B2.

58. Telecommunications Act § 271(c).

to indicate the economic, legal, and engineering complexities that the operating companies face in their quest to enter interexchange markets. The requirements are as follows:[59]

> (A) Presence of a facilities-based competitor.—A Bell operating company meets the requirements of this subparagraph if it has entered into one or more binding agreements that have been approved under section 252 specifying the terms and conditions under which the Bell operating company is providing access and interconnection to its network facilities for the network facilities of one or more unaffiliated competing providers of telephone exchange service (as defined in section 3(47)(A), but excluding exchange access) to residential and business subscribers. For the purpose of this subparagraph, such telephone exchange service may be offered by such competing providers either exclusively over their own telephone exchange service facilities or predominantly over their own telephone exchange service facilities in combination with the resale of the telecommunications services of another carrier. For the purpose of this subparagraph, services provided pursuant to subpart K of part 22 of the Commission's regulations (47 C.F.R. 22.901 et seq.) shall not be considered to be telephone exchange services.

> (B) Failure to request access.—A Bell operating company meets the requirements of this subparagraph if, after 10 months after the date of enactment of the Telecommunications Act of 1996, no such provider has requested the access and interconnection described in subparagraph (A) before the date which is 3 months before the date the company makes its application under subsection (d)(1), and a statement of the terms and conditions that the company generally offers to provide such access and interconnection has been approved or permitted to take effect by the State commission under section 252(f). For purposes of this

59. *Id.*

subparagraph, a Bell operating company shall be considered not to have received any request for access and interconnection if the State commission of such State certifies that the only provider or providers making such a request have (i) failed to negotiate in good faith as required by section 252, or (ii) violated the terms of an agreement approved under section 252 by the provider's failure to comply, within a reasonable period of time, with the implementation schedule contained in such agreement.

(2) Specific interconnection requirements.——

(A) Agreement required.—A Bell operating company meets the requirements of this paragraph if, within the State for which the authorization is sought—

(i)(I) such company is providing access and interconnection pursuant to one or more agreements described in paragraph (1)(A), or

(II) such company is generally offering access and interconnection pursuant to a statement described in paragraph (1)(B), and

(ii) such access and interconnection meets the requirements of subparagraph (B) of this paragraph.

(B) Competitive checklist.—Access or interconnection provided or generally offered by a Bell operating company to other telecommunications carriers meets the requirements of this subparagraph if such access and interconnection includes each of the following:

(i) Interconnection in accordance with the requirements of sections 251(c)(2) and 252(d)(1).

(ii) Nondiscriminatory access to network elements in accordance with the requirements of sections 251(c)(3) and 252(d)(1).

(iii) Nondiscriminatory access to the poles, ducts, conduits, and rights-of-way owned or controlled by the Bell operating company at just and reasonable rates in accordance with the requirements of section 224.

(iv) Local loop transmission from the central office to the customer's premises, unbundled from local switching or other services.

(v) Local transport from the trunk side of a wireline local exchange carrier switch unbundled from switching or other services.

(vi) Local switching unbundled from transport, local loop transmission, or other services.

(vii) Nondiscriminatory access to—

(I) 911 and E911 services;

(II) directory assistance services to allow the other carrier's customers to obtain telephone numbers; and

(III) operator call completion services.

(viii) White pages directory listings for customers of the other carrier's telephone exchange service.

(ix) Until the date by which telecommunications numbering administration guidelines, plan, or rules are established, nondiscriminatory access to telephone numbers for assignment to the other carrier's telephone exchange service customers. After that date, compliance with such guidelines, plan, or rules.

(x) Nondiscriminatory access to databases and associated signaling necessary for call routing and completion.

(xi) Until the date by which the Commission issues regulations pursuant to section 251 to require number portability, interim telecommunications number portability through remote call forwarding, direct inward dialing trunks, or other comparable arrangements, with as little impairment of functioning, quality, reliability, and convenience as possible. After that date, full compliance with such regulations.

(xii) Nondiscriminatory access to such services or information as are necessary to allow the requesting carrier to implement local dialing parity in accordance with the requirements of section 251(b)(3).

(xiii) Reciprocal compensation arrangements in accordance with the requirements of section 252(d)(2).

(xiv) Telecommunications services are available for resale in accordance with the requirements of sections 251(c)(4) and 252(d)(3).

The various elements of that checklist would, at a minimum, provide rich new material for litigation to delay entry into interLATA exchange markets. But some elements of the list are more important than others—more likely to be so important strategically that the operating company is inhibited from entering long-distance markets. The impression is that there are three "deal-breaking" requirements likely to arise: (1) access to an operating company's unique resources; (2) use of the operating company's facilities for independent network access by the other carrier; and (3) pricing of those types of access.

Access to Operating Company Resources: Databases and Signaling

Characteristic of strategically important requirements, one section specifies that the operating company provide "[n]ondiscriminatory access to databases and associated signaling necessary for call routing and completion." That obligation for technical "access" in fact has far-reaching strategic consequences. A telephone call involves two connections, to a voice path and a control path. The control path is a high-speed network with physical links that contain information concerning whether the number dialed is busy, how the call should be billed, and how the call should be routed. The voice path carries the actual telephone conversation and converges with the control path at the end-office switch.

That checklist requirement obligates a Bell operating company to provide its control paths to other carriers. That would imply that other carriers have control of the intelligence in the company's Signaling System 7 (SS7) network,[60] which would allow remote control of a call through someone else's facilities. With SS7, moreover, control of a local call can reside in two alternative places: the switch and a service control point involved in real time in the processing of calls. There would also be a handing over of non-real-time components of local telephone service—namely, the service management system, which involves hooking up customers, and the service creation environment, which actually creates new services.

Such a requirement would confront the operating company with significant risks concerning network reliability and cost recovery. Because of reduced control over the reliability and quality of network operation, the customer may correctly or incorrectly impute to the operating company the responsibility for unsatisfactory service. The Bell operating company's provision of that access to its signaling system also raises issues in revenue generation—if the operating company were to price at incremental cost, it would fail to recover hundreds of millions of dollars of fixed costs in the software embedded in SS7 systems.

But the strategic issues are more critical. With unbundled access to signaling, a Bell operating company could lose all its local toll traffic. AT&T, for instance, could purchase the trigger that is activated as soon as the customer's telephone is taken off the hook. From that point in time AT&T would control the call; the operating company would provide access but would neither select the carrier nor route the call. AT&T itself would become the only carrier of

---

60. *See* Bell Communications Research, BOC Notes on the LEC Networks, 1994 6-255 to 6-288 (1994).

the call and could even prevent the customer from using dialing codes to connect to another interexchange carrier. In essence, AT&T could establish itself as the bottleneck by itself deploying SS7 technologies of the operating companies.

The requirement of unbundled access to signaling thus poses an issue over which the operating company and the interexchange carrier will likely reach an impasse. The interexchange carrier can keep the operating company from entering interLATA services by making demands that the operating company price access to those elements at the (zero) marginal costs. The operating company will have to deny such demands, because the software implementation interexchange carrier's access to signaling gives it the means to capture the local toll markets without investing substantial resources.

Access to a Bell Operating Company's Resources: Network Access

Implementation of the checklist also requires the operating company to provide "interconnection services" to other carriers in local exchange service markets *à la carte*. Interconnection services include switched local access and other functions used to terminate a local call on the terminating carrier's network. The other functions are local loop transmission, local transmission, and access to poles, conduits, and rights-of-way.

Given that the Bell operating company is required to offer those network elements on an unbundled basis, the relevant question is, What advantage does that provide the entering interexchange carrier? The answer to that question is straightforward: mandatory provision of interconnection services allows the entrant to configure selectively its service territory and thus to limit its facilities to serve only customers generating higher profit margins. Such a strategy is feasible only if the entrant is able to terminate calls throughout the service territory of the operating company. Mandated interconnection provides that capability.

The incumbent local exchange company will have to maintain its complete local network, while the entrant serves just the high-profit "midtown" network. But, in addition, the incumbent is required to ascertain that those two networks are interconnected.

That checklist requirement guarantees that the operating company will not have the same subscriber mix but rather have fewer high-profit subscribers.

Whether the interconnection requirement is a burden on the operating company is a pricing issue. Entrants will argue for "cost-based" prices such as those set equal to the long-run incremental cost of access.[61] But incremental cost pricing of access would prevent the operating company from recovering its fixed network costs as well as earnings to provide service as the carrier of last resort.

The incumbent carriers have proposed to set access prices equal to long-run incremental costs plus a markup to cover joint and common costs. In practice, that or any other markup is likely to be the source of intense debate. But given that the goal is to conform to the checklist, incremental cost pricing could become the ransom for which the operating company obtains the right to provide long-distance service.

Access to a Bell Operating Company's Resources:
Interconnection and Unbundled Access

Critical to meeting the checklist requirements is the demonstration that there is interconnection and unbundled access to the basic elements of local service. More specifically, the operating company's network functions have to be priced on an unbundled basis to other

---

61. In fact, in California's local exchange competition proceedings, MCI has argued that interconnection services be priced to recover only their direct economic costs. On MCI's behalf, Nina Cornell has stated:

> It is appropriate for the incumbent LECs [Bell operating companies] and competitive local carriers both to recover their direct costs and profits only from retail customers because carriers go into business to supply retail services, not interconnection services. The need to supply and to use interconnection services is a consequence of the need to interconnect networks, and, while necessary, should not be the source of recovery of indirect costs or profits.

Phase II Testimony of Dr. Nina Cornell, on Behalf of MCI Telecommunications Corporation, Before the Public Utilities Commission of the State of California, at 44, Dkt. Nos. R.95-4-043, I.95-04-044 (Oct. 10, 1995).

carriers entering local service markets so that other carriers cannot claim that those prices constitute barriers to entry. Given that a regulatory authority sets prices, the authority decision or review of tariffs must result in prices high enough to cause the facilities to be used efficiently, but low enough that they be used.

Congress or the FCC must mandate that the state regulatory agencies price access to the local exchange and access to the local exchange carrier's unbundled basic service elements according to the efficient component-pricing rule.[62] That rule would price access at long-run incremental cost plus opportunity costs, equal to the contribution of margin necessary globally to cover joint and common costs. Such a rule satisfies two economic criteria. The first is productive or technical efficiency, requiring that the total costs of providing any given set of services should be no greater than the minimum attainable. The second criterion is efficiency in exchange, such that the allocation of products should leave an individual better off without making another worse off.

The rule is being considered in Illinois,[63] Michigan,[64] and California,[65] and it may have been considered in Maryland.[66] Each of the commissions in those states has been pressured by the interexchange carriers to consider other rules that would force the operating company to sell interconnection for less or at a level that fails to contribute to the recovery of joint and common costs. The experience in setting prices in Michigan indicates the process to come in all the states in which entry by the Bell operating company into interLATA services will be subject to the checklist process. In

---

62. BAUMOL & SIDAK, *supra* note 3, at 93–116; William J. Baumol & J. Gregory Sidak, *The Pricing of Inputs Sold to Competitors*, 14 YALE J. ON REG. 171 (1994).

63. Dkt. No. 95-048 (Ill. Commerce Comm'n Nov. 3, 1995).

64. In the Matter, on the Commission's Own Motion, to Establish Permanent Interconnection Arrangements Between Basic Local Exchange Services, Case U-10860 (Mich. Pub. Serv. Comm'n 1995).

65. Order Instituting Rulemaking on the Commission's Own Motion into Competition for Local Exchange Service, R.95-04-043, I.95-04-044 (1995); Alternative Regulatory Framework for Local Exchange Carriers, Invest. No. 87-11-033, 33 C.P.U.C.2d 43, 107 P.U.R.4th 1 (Cal. Pub. Util. Comm'n 1989).

66. MFS Intelenet of Md., Inc., Case No. 8584, Order No. 71155, 152 P.U.R.4th 102 (Md. Pub. Serv. Comm'n 1994).

late 1995 the Michigan Public Service Commission presided over Ameritech's request for approval to provide interLATA service under conditions similar to those in the Telecommunications Act of 1996. Ameritech had to have the public service commission's certification, which required that structural conditions in markets for local services be free of barriers to entry created by Ameritech. In effect, finding those conditions called for answering the question, How much of a discount on retail prices would Ameritech tolerate in setting its wholesale rates for long-distance carriers entering local service markets, given that Ameritech had to show the FCC that "competition" exists in its local exchange markets?

The voluminous testimony of economists and engineers presenting arguments for various wholesale rate discounts provides an answer. For a reseller that takes basic exchange services at wholesale from Ameritech, the marginal cost of self-providing retail services cannot exceed 10 percent of the retail price. But the discount sought by the interexchange carriers is in the range of 20 to 30 percent. Such a discount would produce a 60 percent profit margin on retailing, roughly equal to the profit margin that AT&T, MCI, and Sprint realize on interLATA services. And why should long-distance carriers enter local markets unless entry would yield margins comparable to those already achieved in the tacitly collusive interLATA markets? By waiting for the answer, the interexchange carriers determine the timing of Ameritech's entry into their interLATA markets. The experiment in Michigan has been intended to demonstrate how an operating company becomes a competitive long-distance carrier, in both local toll and interLATA toll markets. But the experiment has not done that and has instead shown that the regulatory litigation of prices has become the means by which to prevent both local and long-distance entry.

CONCLUSION

Basic change in regulatory policy should be able to further the development of open and competitive markets in long-distance telephone services. Those policies calling for change had been embedded in the waiver process of the judgment court, which so resisted change that it gave the impression of complete inactivity. Now the legislative reform initiative in the Telecommunications Act of

1996 promises basic movement of the barriers to new long-distance market competition. But the act does not appear to be able to deliver on its promise, given the way the legislation structures the regulation of entry of potential competitors into long-distance service markets. Perhaps AT&T, MCI, and Sprint will compete more in television advertising of "discount" plans with famous actresses. But those advertisements do not imply that the carriers cut each other's prices to gain market share in the way that the trucking companies and airlines did when they were deregulated in the late 1970s. There has been no concrete proposal to deregulate telecommunications because policy makers have placed virtually no weight on the benefits to consumers from interLATA competition by the Bell operating companies. The objective instead of both old waiver and new checklist policy has been to prevent the Bell operating companies' supposed incipient monopolization of the interLATA market.

The wrong objective leads to the wrong process, by which the entrant into long-distance markets seeks to qualify on a checklist of conditions in local exchange markets. In reality that company could spend years trying to satisfy the requirements of the list in proceedings not different from those that considered Ameritech's restructuring or AirTouch's introduction of long-distance wireless services. Such an approach by its nature stimulates protracted litigation that will ensure that the operating companies will not enter interLATA markets on a timely basis.

One can even envision a scenario in the implementation of the new legislation in which competition in interLATA services diminishes. AT&T currently has a significant first-mover advantage in bundling the local exchange services in its McCaw cellular service offerings with AT&T wireline long-distance services. If AT&T can implement such an "end-to-end" strategy over the near term, and if it adds enhanced services to those offerings, then high-volume subscribers would not want another carrier. In the meantime, MCI's wireless plans would be incomplete, and Sprint's personal communications services network would not yet be operational.

Under those circumstances, the Bell operating companies would be the only carriers able to respond strategically to AT&T—but, of course, they cannot because of the new legislation's impediments to their rapid entry into interLATA markets. To be sure, the new legislation grants "relief" to the Bell operating companies to offer interLATA services in conjunction with their wireless services. But the extent to which the checklist has to be worked over before the Bell operating companies can offer even that service is not now predictable. And, given the checklist, AT&T, by participating in the proceedings before each state public utility commission as a potential entrant-reseller of retail local services, can ensure that a Bell operating company's qualifying according to the list will be quite protracted. Thus, even though an operating company in principle should be able to bundle local and long-distance services, it too could be left far behind.

The past experience in the waiver proceedings and in the 1995 and 1996 legislative "reform" process provides an indication of how policy intended to make telecommunications competitive is vulnerable to strategic delay. The incumbent long-distance carriers can for the foreseeable future forestall the Bell operating companies' competitive entry into interLATA markets. The conclusion to be drawn from such a state of affairs is that antitrust and regulatory policies bar effective competition that would follow from inducing entry into long-distance markets. The failure of antitrust and regulation to make long-distance markets competitive continues to the continuing detriment of consumers seeking prices in line with costs of providing service.

Appendix 1

Discount Plan Summary

SUMMARIES OF THE VARIOUS DISCOUNT PLANS of AT&T, MCI, and Sprint follow.

TABLE A1–1 SUMMARY OF AT&T DISCOUNT PLANS			
Plan Name	Start Date	End Date	Plan Description
Pro WATS 1	01/01/88	12/31/99	For a monthly fee of $5, a customer receives a 10% discount on all dial station calls made during any time period day, evening, night/weekend, or holiday. There is a nonrecurring service order charge of $10 per order. [08/03/94]
Small Business Option	06/04/91	12/31/99	For a monthly fee of $22.50, a customer receives 100 minutes of interstate dial station calls (regardless of the time of day or distance of the call). That monthly fee must be paid whether or not the customer uses the 100 minutes of calling time. Interstate calls made in addition to the initial 100 minutes will be billed at $0.225 per minute. A condition of the plan is that a customer may only subscribe to one interstate optional calling plan at a time. The customer will also receive a discount on his interstate bill equal to 10% of his total intrastate dial station calls (already discounted under AT&T's State Calling Plan) made during the same billing period. There is a nonrecurring service order charge of $5 per order. [08/03/94]

TABLE A1–1 (CTD.) SUMMARY OF AT&T DISCOUNT PLANS			
Plan Name	Start Date	End Date	Plan Description
Block of Time–One–Hour Plan (i.e., Reach Out America "ROA")	07/01/87	12/31/99	For a monthly fee of $7.50, a customer receives one hour of calling time during the night/weekend time period (Mon.– Fri., 5 P.M. to 8 A.M., Sat. & Sun. all day). This monthly fee must be paid whether or not the customer uses the one hour of night/weekend calling time. This plan applies only to customers who are not also subscribing to the evening and/or day options. Calls made during other time periods will be billed at the appropriate specified rates. The charge for all calls made in excess of the initial one hour during the night/weekend time period will be $0.10 for each additional minute. In addition, an ROA customer receives a 5% discount on international dial calls, which would otherwise be charged at international standard, and receives a 5% discount on his total intrastate dial station charges excluding those calls already discounted under another plan. There is a nonrecurring service order charge of $5 per order. [08/03/94]

TABLE A1–1 (CTD.)			
SUMMARY OF AT&T DISCOUNT PLANS			
Plan Name	Start Date	End Date	Plan Description
Block of Time–One-Hour Plan with Evening Option (ROA)	07/01/87	12/31/99	For a set monthly fee of $7.80, a customer receives all of the discounts under the One-Hour Plan but in addition receives a discount on calls made during the evening time period (Sun.–Fri., 5 P.M. to 10 P.M., holidays that fall on Mon.–Fri., 8 A.M. to 5 P.M.). This monthly fee must be paid whether or not the customer uses the one hour of night/weekend calling time. Charges for any calls made during the evening time period will first be determined under the appropriate rate schedule and then that total will be discounted by 40%. The Evening Option discount does not apply to any calls made during the night/weekend or day time periods. There is a nonrecurring service order charge of $5 per order. [08/03/94]
Block of Time–One-Hour Plan with Evening & Day Option (ROA)	12/01/88	12/31/99	For a set monthly fee of $8.70, a customer receives all the discounts under the One-Hour Plan with Evening Option but in addition receives a discount on calls made during the day time period (Mon.–Fri., 8 A.M. to 5 P.M.) excluding holidays. This monthly fee must be paid whether or not the customer uses the one hour of night/weekend calling time. Charges for any calls made during the day time period will be first determined under the appropriate rate schedule and then that total will be discounted by 10%. This plan is only available to customers who have already subscribed to the One-Hour Plan with Evening Option. There is a nonrecurring service order charge of $5 per order. [08/03/94]

TABLE A1–1 (CTD.) SUMMARY OF AT&T DISCOUNT PLANS			
Plan Name	Start Date	End Date	Plan Description
Block of Time–Half-Hour Plan (ROA)	10/30/89	12/31/99	For a monthly fee of $4, a customer receives one-half hour of calling time during the night/weekend time period (Sun.–Fri., 10 P.M. to 8 A.M., Sat. all day, and Sun. until 5 P.M.). This monthly fee must be paid whether or not the customer uses the one-half hour of night/weekend calling time. The charge for all calls in excess of the initial one-half hour during the night/weekend time period is $0.12 for each additional minute. The customer also receives a 20% discount on calls made during the evening time period (Mon.–Fri., 5 P.M. to 10 P.M., and holidays, 8 A.M. to 5 P.M.). All other calls will be billed at the appropriate rates. There is a nonrecurring service order charge of $5 per order. [08/03/94]

TABLE A1-1 (CTD.) SUMMARY OF AT&T DISCOUNT PLANS			
Plan Name	Start Date	End Date	Plan Description
True USA Promo	01/10/94	01/09/96	Under this LDMTS basic schedule discount promotion, a customer enrolled in this promotion received a discount based on "combined monthly usage" (CMU) and "eligible LDMTS usage" based on the following schedule: CMU between $10 and $24.99 received a 20% discount; CMU between $25 and $74.99 received a 20% discount; and CMU greater than $75 received a 30% discount. The above discounts were applied to the eligible LDMTS usage when CMU was in the specified range. Under this plan, CMU was defined as: "a Customer's billed usage and service charges . . ., for a monthly billing period for the combined total of domestic and international Dial Station calls, domestic and international CIID/891 Card Calls . . ., domestic and international Operator Handled Calls, AT&T DIRECTory LINK Service calls, AT&T SelectCall Service calls and AT&T EasyReach Service calls." "Eligible LDMTS usage is defined as Combined Monthly Usage minus any international call usage." Eligible LDMTS usage included intrastate calls unless they were already similarly discounted under an AT&T intrastate tariff. [08/03/94]

TABLE A1–2 SUMMARY OF MCI DISCOUNT PLANS			
Plan Name	Start Date	End Date	Plan Description
Prime Time	05/08/89	12/31/99	For a monthly fee of $7.45, a customer receives one hour of calling time during the evening and night/weekend time periods (Mon.–Fri., 5 P.M. to 8 A.M., all day Sat., and Sun. until 5 P.M., and from 11 P.M. Sun. to 8 A.M. Mon.). This monthly fee must be paid whether or not the customer uses the one hour of evening and night/weekend calling time. The charge for calls made in addition to the initial one hour of calling time during these time periods is $0.11 per minute. Any calls made outside this time period will be billed at the appropriate specified rate. But for an additional monthly fee of $1.25, all calls made outside the evening and night/weekend time period will receive a 10% discount. In addition, MCI also offers for an additional monthly fee of $2 an 800 number with a 4-digit security code with which the customer can receive incoming calls during the evening and night/weekend time period at an hourly rate of $6.30. "Both inbound and outbound usage will apply to the customer's first hour's charge." A customer may combine all the above options; however, the total monthly fee is not eligible for the Friends and Family discount. [08/19/94]

	Start	End	
TABLE A1–2 (CTD.) SUMMARY OF MCI DISCOUNT PLANS			
Plan Name	Date	Date	Plan Description
Prime Time– Day (DayTime Savings Option)	05/08/89	12/31/99	For a monthly fee of $12, a customer receives one hour of domestic long-distance calling from 9 A.M. to 5 P.M., Mon.–Fri. This monthly fee must be paid whether or not the customer uses the one hour of specified calling time. The charge for any additional minutes in excess of the initial hour made during this time period will be $0.20 per minute. All other calls will be billed at the appropriate specified rate. For an additional monthly fee of $2, all calls made outside the above specified time period will receive a 10% discount. [08/19/94]
Sure Save ("Sure Save One-Hour Option")	02/18/92	12/31/99	For a monthly fee of $7.45, a customer receives one hour of domestic long-distance calls placed between 12 A.M. to 8 A.M. and 5 P.M. to midnight, Mon.–Fri., and all day Sat. and Sun. This monthly fee must be paid whether or not the customer uses the one hour of specified calling time. The charge for any calls made in excess of the initial one hour of calls during these time periods is $6 per hour (and is prorated accordingly). All other calls will be billed at the appropriate specified rate. In addition, customers are eligible for a 5% discount on intrastate or international calls unless they are enrolled in the Friends Around the World plan (which is the only Premier plan in which a customer may be concurrently enrolled). [08/01/94]

TABLE A1–2 (CTD.) SUMMARY OF MCI DISCOUNT PLANS			
Plan Name	Start Date	End Date	Plan Description
Sure Save– Evening & Day Option	02/18/92	12/31/99	For a monthly fee of $8.65, a customer receives one hour of domestic long-distance calls placed between midnight and 8 A.M. and 5 P.M. and midnight, Mon.–Fri., all day Sat., and Sun. until 5 P.M. and 10 P.M. to midnight. This monthly fee must be paid whether or not the customer uses the one hour of specified calling time. The charge for calls in excess of the initial hour during the above time periods will be $0.10 for each additional minute. In addition to the above discounts, a customer receives a 40% discount on calls made between 5 P.M. and 10 P.M., Sun.–Fri., and a 10% discount on calls made between 8 A.M. and 5 P.M., Mon.–Fri. [08/01/94]
Sure Save– Half-Hour Plan	02/18/92	12/31/99	For a monthly fee of $3.95, a customer receives 30 minutes of domestic long-distance calls from midnight to 8 A.M. and 10 P.M. to 12 A.M., Mon.–Fri., all day Sat., and Sun. until 5 P.M. and 10 P.M. to midnight. This monthly fee must be paid whether or not the customer uses the 30 minutes of specified calling time. The charge for calls made during the above time periods in excess of the initial 30 minutes will be $0.12 per minute. In addition, the customer receives a 20% discount on calls made between 5 P.M. and 10 P.M., Sun.–Fri., as well as a 5% discount on intrastate or international calls under the same provisions as the Sure Save One-Hour Plan. [08/05/94]

	Start	End	
	Start	**End**	
Plan Name	Date	Date	Plan Description
EasyRate Option	01/01/93	12/31/99	For a monthly fee of $3, a customer pays $0.23 for calls made Mon.–Fri., 8 A.M. to 5 P.M., and $0.12 per minute for all other calls. This plan may be combined with MCI's Around the World or Friends Around the World AnyTime Plans. [08/01/94]
AnyTime	06/01/92	12/31/99	For a monthly fee of $9.90, a customer receives one hour of domestic long-distance calls made at "AnyTime." This monthly fee must be paid whether or not the customer uses the one hour of calling time. "Additional minutes of business day calling are available for $0.20 per minute. Additional evening and Night/Weekend calling are available for $0.11 per minute." In addition, the customer receives a 5% discount on intrastate and international calls. [08/01/94]

TABLE A1–2 (CTD.)
SUMMARY OF MCI DISCOUNT PLANS

TABLE A1–2 (CTD.) SUMMARY OF MCI DISCOUNT PLANS			
Plan Name	Start Date	End Date	Plan Description
Friends & Family I	04/01/91	12/31/99	Under this plan a customer forms a "Calling Circle" and receives a 20% discount ("Friends & Family Discount") on all "qualified" domestic interstate and international calls. A "Calling Circle is a group of up to 21 U.S. telephone numbers, including the number of the Subscriber, which numbers are presubscribed to MCI, except those domestic telephone numbers nominated for inclusion in their Calling Circle which are not presubscribed to MCI, and three telephone numbers in international locations served by MCI." To be "qualified," calls need to meet one of the following criteria: "direct-dialed calls from the Subscriber to a Member of his or her Circle; or his or her designated international telephone number(s); operator-assisted calls from the Subscriber to a Member which are billed to the Subscriber's account; collect calls placed to the Subscriber by a Member; third party calls made to a Member and billed to Subscriber's account; direct-dialed calls placed to a Member by someone using a 7-digit access code and the Subscriber's 5-digit authorization code; calls placed to a Subscriber's Personal 800 number; and calls placed to a Subscriber's Private 800 number." "For Subscribers enrolled in a domestic Premier Calling Plan, if specific plan rates apply, the F&F Discount will be applied to the call usage and surcharge as determined by these plan rates. If plan discounts are applied, the F&F Discount will be applied against the call usage charges and surcharges prior to the application of any plan discount." [05/04/94]

TABLE A1–2 (CTD.) SUMMARY OF MCI DISCOUNT PLANS			
Plan Name	Start Date	End Date	Plan Description
Friends & Family II	06/07/94	12/31/99	For a monthly fee of $3, a customer receives (in lieu of his F&F I discount) a 40% discount on "qualifying" domestic long-distance calls to members of his Calling Circle who are also MCI customers and a 20% discount on "qualifying" calls to members of his Calling Circle who are not MCI customers. This monthly fee must be paid whether or not the customer takes advantage of the above discounts. See MCI F&F I for a description of the "qualifying calls" applicable under this plan (with the exception of the subscriber's personal 800 or private 800 numbers, which are not included). But under this plan (and included in the monthly fee) a subscriber will receive a new personal 800 Plan R number (see details in tariff for further information). [01/06/95]

TABLE A1–3 SUMMARY OF SPRINT DISCOUNT PLANS			
Plan Name	Start Date	End Date	Plan Description
Dial "1" Usage Discounts	08/01/86	02/28/91	Under this plan, a customer was charged for calls based on time of day and distance. Rates charged for calls were determined under the appropriate rate schedule. The time periods for this plan were divided into day (Mon.–Fri., 8:00 A.M. to 5:00 P.M.), evening (Sun.–Fri. 5:00 P.M. to 11:00 P.M.), and night/weekend (all other times). The customer received a discount on U.S. domestic calls based on usage levels and time periods. The customer was given a 1% "usage discount" on monthly totals above $25 for U.S. domestic calls placed in the D/E/N/W time periods. Note: The "usage discount" varied by time period, usage level, and percent discounted during the life of the plan. [09/01/90]
Sprint Select– Evening/ Night/ Weekend Plan	09/01/90	12/31/99	For a monthly fee of $7.50, a customer receives one hour of domestic direct-dial calls placed during the evening/night/weekend time period (all hours excluding Mon.–Fri., 8 A.M. to 5 P.M.). This monthly fee must be paid whether or not the customer uses the one hour of specified calling time. Any calls in excess of the initial hour will be charged at a set "additional hourly rate" of $6.50 (or appropriate prorated amount). Any calls placed during the day time period (Mon.–Fri., 8:00 A.M. to 5:00 P.M.) will be charged at rates set forth in the appropriate schedule. In addition, the customer receives a discount on his interstate bill equal to 5% of his intrastate direct-dial charges on the same bill, excluding intrastate calls that may be discounted under another calling plan. [08/03/92]

TABLE A1–3 (CTD.) SUMMARY OF SPRINT DISCOUNT PLANS			
Plan Name	Start Date	End Date	Plan Description
Sprint Select–Day Option	09/01/90	12/31/99	For a monthly fee of $8.10, a customer receives all the discounts under the Sprint Select plan and in addition receives a 10% discount on direct-dial calls placed during the day time period. This monthly fee must be paid whether or not the customer uses the one hour of specified calling time. [08/03/92]
Sprint Select–Day Plan	02/01/91	12/31/99	For a monthly fee of $11.95, a customer receives one hour of domestic direct-dial calls placed during the day time period (Mon.–Fri., 8 A.M. to 5 P.M.). This monthly fee must be paid whether or not the customer uses the one hour of day calling time. The charges for calls made in excess of the initial hour of specified calling time will be $11.80 per hour (or an appropriate prorated amount). Any calls placed in other time periods will be charged at rates set forth in the appropriate schedule. In addition, the customer receives a discount on his interstate bill equal to 5% of his intrastate direct-dial charges on the same bill, excluding intrastate calls that may be discounted under another calling plan. [06/01/91]
Sprint Select–Day Plan–EN Option	02/01/91	12/31/99	For a monthly fee of $12, a customer receives all the discounts under the Sprint Select–Day Plan and in addition receives a 10% discount on direct dial calls placed during the evening/night/weekend time periods. [06/01/91]

TABLE A1–3 (CTD.) SUMMARY OF SPRINT DISCOUNT PLANS			
Plan Name	Start Date	End Date	Plan Description
Residential Promo	06/28/94	01/06/96	Under this plan a customer received a discount based on his total monthly usage of "domestic, FONCARD, and/or operator service" calls. To be eligible for this plan, the customer could be enrolled in any other Sprint calling plans. A customer received: a 20% discount if his monthly calls totaled $30–$74.99; a 30% discount for calls totaling $75–$149.99; and 35% discount if the monthly total was $150 or more. International calls could contribute toward the monthly total but were exempt from the discount. [02/14/95]
Sprint Plus Usage Discounts	05/01/89	12/31/99	Under this plan a customer receives a discount on his monthly bill on the basis of the volume of calls and the time period during which calls are made. The time periods are divided into day (Mon.–Fri., 8 A.M. to 5 P.M.) and evening/night/weekend (all other times). The customer receives a 10% discount on calls made during the day when the total of day calls is $20 or more. The customer receives the following discounts based on the monthly total of evening/night/weekend calls: a 20% discount for totals between $20 and $99.99; a 25% discount for totals between $100 and $199.99; and a 30% discount if the total is greater than $200. Charges for calls are determined under the appropriate rate schedule, based on time period and distance. [08/03/92]

Appendix 2

Sensitivity Analysis of Prices and
Price-Cost Margins of Discount Calling Plans

THE INDEX PRICES as presented in the text depend on assumptions regarding the types of calls customers make. This appendix reports prices and price-cost margins based on alternative assumptions regarding customers' calls. There are two sets of sensitivity estimations. The first uses the distribution of types of calls as assumed in the text but reports a different index price calculated by using the extreme assumption that a customer changes plans immediately whenever a carrier offers a plan with a lower price. That assumption implies a price index that would be a minimum for each carrier.

The second set of estimations does not use the eleven classifications in the text but rather replaces them with different assumptions regarding (1) monthly usage levels, (2) the time of day calls are made, and (3) the distance calls travel. A total of sixty different types of calls are considered for residential customers, and an additional forty-eight different types are considered for small-business customers.

Theoretical Minimum Index Prices and
Margins Using Eleven Types of Calls

The minimum index prices for AT&T, MCI, and Sprint are based on the same eleven types of calls as in chapter 5. Those prices appear in figures A2–1 to A2–3. The theoretical minimum prices for AT&T and MCI are approximately $0.03 to $0.04 per minute lower for 1994 than those estimated for the MTS discount plans, and $0.05 to $0.06 less than standard MTS prices. Those minimum prices remained approximately the same since 1991. Sprint's minimum prices were identical to the prices of its well-known discount plans until mid-1994 (approximately $0.06 less than its standard MTS service), and its theoretical minimum prices also remained approximately constant from 1991 through 1994.

FIGURE A2-1
RESIDENTIAL INDEX PRICES FOR AT&T STANDARD SERVICE,
REACH OUT AMERICA DISCOUNT CALLING PLAN,
AND THEORETICAL MINIMUM PRICE PLAN

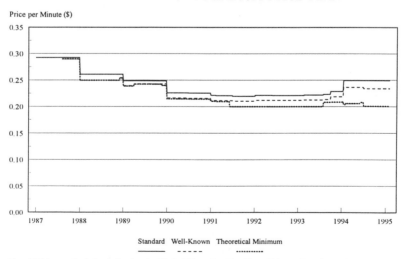

Note: Well-known plan is Reach Out America Block of Time - One-Hour Plan with Day and Evening Option.

FIGURE A2-2
RESIDENTIAL INDEX PRICES FOR MCI STANDARD SERVICE, PRIME TIME DAY AND FRIENDS & FAMILY I DISCOUNT CALLING PLANS, AND THEORETICAL MINIMUM PRICE PLAN

Note: Well-known plan is Prime Time Day (8/1/89 to 5/31/91) and Friends and Family I (6/1/91 to 2/1/95).

FIGURE A2-3
RESIDENTIAL INDEX PRICES FOR SPRINT STANDARD SERVICE, SPRINT PLUS USAGE AND SPRINT SELECT DAY DISCOUNT CALLING PLANS, AND THEORETICAL MINIMUM PRICE PLAN

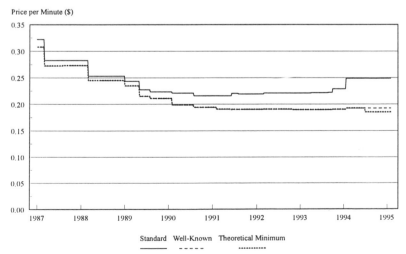

Note: Well-known plan is Sprint Plus Usage Discounts (5/1/89 to 1/31/91) and Sprint Select Day Plan (2/1/91 to 2/1/95).

With those theoretical minimum prices, price-cost margins
for AT&T, MCI, and Sprint were calculated (see figures A2–4 to
A2–6). Margins for the theoretical minimum prices generally followed the same pattern as those for the well-known plans. AT&T's
margin on its theoretical minimum price plan increased gradually
from 1987 to 1994, to a level of 0.63 or 91 percent of the margin
on standard MTS. MCI and Sprint's margins on their theoretical
minimum price services also increased from 1987 to 1994; they rose
to a level of 0.60 or 87 percent of their standard MTS margins.
Thus, margins calculated on the basis of the carriers' theoretical
minimum prices did not decline in the 1990s.

FIGURE A2–4

RESIDENTIAL PRICE-COST MARGINS FOR AT&T STANDARD
SERVICE, REACH OUT AMERICA DISCOUNT CALLING PLAN,
AND THEORETICAL MINIMUM PRICE PLAN

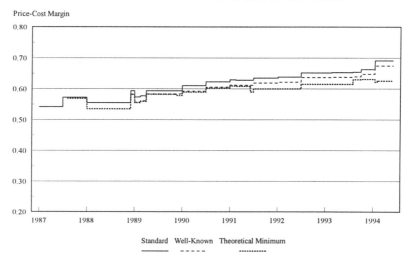

Note: Well-known plan is Reach Out America Block of Time - One-Hour Plan with Day and Evening Option.
Sources: Marginal costs from FCC and rates from HTL Telemanagement, Ltd.

FIGURE A2–5

RESIDENTIAL PRICE-COST MARGINS FOR MCI STANDARD SERVICE, PRIME TIME DAY AND FRIENDS & FAMILY I DISCOUNT CALLING PLANS, AND THEORETICAL MINIMUM PRICE PLAN

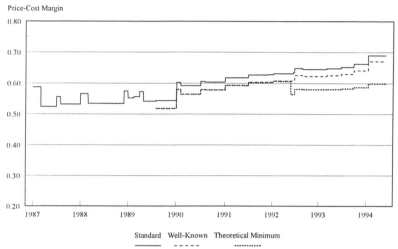

Note: Well-known plan is Prime Time Day (8/1/89 to 5/31/91) and Friends and Family I (6/1/91 to 2/1/95).
Sources: Marginal costs from FCC and rates from HTL Telemanagement, Ltd.

FIGURE A2–6

RESIDENTIAL PRICE-COST MARGINS FOR SPRINT STANDARD SERVICE, SPRINT PLUS USAGE AND SPRINT SELECT DAY DISCOUNT CALLING PLANS, AND THEORETICAL MINIMUM PRICE PLAN

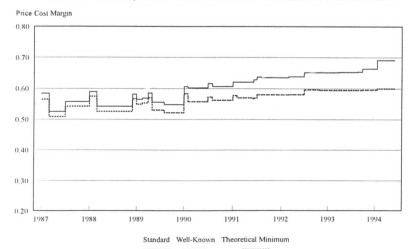

Note: Well-known plan is Sprint Plus Usage Discounts (5/1/89 to 1/31/91) and Sprint Select Day Plan (2/1/91 to 2/1/95).
Sources: Marginal costs from FCC and rates from HTL Telemanagement, Ltd.

*Prices and Margins Based
on Alternative Types of Calls*

This section of the appendix reports prices and margins based on types of calls that differ from the eleven types used previously. Those alternative types are based on different assumptions regarding monthly usage levels, time-of-day calling, and mileage distributions. A total of sixty different types of calls are considered for residential customers and forty-eight different types for small-business customers.

The alternative monthly usage levels for residential and small-business customers appear in table A2-1. Residential usage levels range from 50 to 1,000 minutes per month, while small-business usage levels range from 250 to 1,500 minutes per month. The different usage levels were selected to span the likely usage levels of residential and small-business customers using MTS discount plans.

TABLE A2-1
MONTHLY MINUTES OF USE FOR
RESIDENTIAL AND SMALL-BUSINESS CUSTOMERS

Usage Levels	Residential	Small Business
One	50	250
Two	125	500
Three	250	1,000
Four	500	1,500
Five	1,000	N.A.

The distributions of the number of calls made by residential customers appear in table A2-2. In distribution 1, for example, residential customers make 21 percent of their calls during the day, 31 percent during the evening, and approximately one-half during the night-weekend period.

TABLE A2–2
TIME-OF-DAY CALLING DISTRIBUTION
FOR RESIDENTIAL CUSTOMERS
(PERCENTAGE OF NUMBER OF MESSAGES)

Time-of-Day Distribution	Day	Evening	Night-Weekend
Distribution 1	21	31	49
Distribution 2	40	32	28
Distribution 3	62	31	7

The distributions of the number of calls made by small-business customers appear in table A2–3. As reflected in the table, small-business customers make a higher percentage of their calls during the day than do residential customers.

TABLE A2–3
TIME-OF-DAY CALLING DISTRIBUTION
FOR SMALL-BUSINESS CUSTOMERS
(PERCENTAGE OF NUMBER OF MESSAGES)

Time-of-Day	Day	Evening	Night-Weekend
Distribution 1	75	10	5
Distribution 2	85	10	5
Distribution 3	95	5	0

Mileage distributions for residential and small-business customers appear in table A2–4. Distributions 1 and 3 are distributed according to a normal curve with average calling distances of approximately 350 and 600 miles, respectively. Distribution 2 is the one used in the text, while the fourth distribution is the mirror image of the second. The mileage distributions are selected to span the likely range of calls made by residential and small-business customers.

TABLE A2–4

MILEAGE DISTRIBUTIONS OF CALLS FOR
RESIDENTIAL AND SMALL-BUSINESS CUSTOMERS
(PERCENTAGES OF CALLS MADE WITHIN SPECIFIED DISTANCES)

Mileage	Distribution			
	1	2	3	4
0–55	17	6	14	17
56–292	19	8	14	33
293–430	29	6	22	30
431–925	15	30	22	6
926–1,910	13	33	19	8
1,911–3,000	7	17	8	6

In sum, residential customer calls have five different classes of monthly usage levels, three different classes of time-of-day distributions, and four different classes of mileage distributions that result in a distribution of sixty calls (that is, five times three times four). Small-business customers have four different classes of monthly usage levels, three different classes of time-of-day distributions, and four different classes of mileage distributions that result in forty-eight calls (four times three times four). Table A2–5 summarizes those distributions.

TABLE A2–5
NUMBER OF TYPES OF CALLS FOR
RESIDENTIAL AND SMALL-BUSINESS CUSTOMERS

	Number of Different Monthly Usage Levels	Number of Different Time-of-Day Distributions	Number of Different Mileage Distributions	Total Number of Calling Profiles
Residential Customers	5	3	4	60
Small-Business Customers	4	3	4	48

An example of how to calculate the index price of a calling plan follows from considering profile 1 in table A2–6, which shows a residential customer making 250 minutes of calls per month.[1] The minutes and number of different calls are distributed as shown for the day, evening, and night-weekend periods. Calls are made according to mileage distribution 1. Given those parameters, the carrier's FCC tariff specifies the rate charged for each type of call. By summing up the charges for all types, we obtain the customer's monthly bill according to that plan, as well as the price per minute (obtained by dividing the monthly bill by 250 minutes). Repeating that process for all sixty calling profiles yields sixty monthly bills and sixty prices per minute. The simple average of those sixty prices per minute equals the index price per minute for the calling plan that month.[2] Table A2–7 uses similar calculations for small-business customers.

1. Tables A2–6 and A2–7 provide detailed information on the sixty types of residential calls and the forty-eight types of small-business calls.
2. The program used here calculates prices on the basis of monthly usage levels, with updates to tariff data made on a weekly basis. So, for example, if a tariff changes more than once in a month, the prices are adjusted to take account of the changes.

Prices for standard and theoretical minimum price plans offered by AT&T for residential and small-business customers appear in figures A2–7 and A2–8. The index of theoretical minimum prices for residential customers remained at approximately $0.15 per minute for the period since 1991, while the price of standard MTS was $0.02 to $0.03 higher. AT&T theoretically offered increasing discounts from its standard MTS, but since that price increased over time, the theoretical minimum price remained approximately constant. AT&T's index prices calculated on the basis of the forty-eight small-business profiles show a similar pattern to those of residential prices, with the exception that index prices for the small-business profiles exceeded those of the residential profiles because the former assumed that a higher percentage of calls was placed during the day. Similar behavior was observed for both MCI and Sprint, as evidenced by the data in figures A2–9, A2–10, A2–11, and A2–12. And further comparison of price-cost margins with theoretical minimum prices yields yet more evidence of that discrepancy, as figures A2–13 through A2–18 indicate. Price-cost margins rose, as theoretical minimum prices plans for all three carriers stabilized over time.

Table A2-6
Summary of Residential Calling Profiles

Profile	Total Minutes	Average Monthly Bill	Call Distribution (based on minutes) (%)			Call Distribution (based on calls) (%)			Mileage Distribution
			Day	Even.	NWE	Day	Even.	NWE	
1	250	$ 50	31.6	38.4	30.0	40.3	31.9	27.7	Assumption 1
2	500	$100	31.6	38.4	30.0	40.3	31.9	27.7	Assumption 1
3	1,000	$200	31.6	38.4	30.0	40.3	31.9	27.7	Assumption 1
4	125	$ 25	31.6	38.4	30.0	40.3	31.9	27.7	Assumption 1
5	50	$ 10	31.6	38.4	30.0	40.3	31.9	27.7	Assumption 1
6	250	$ 50	31.6	38.4	30.0	40.3	31.9	27.7	Assumption 2
7	500	$100	31.6	38.4	30.0	40.3	31.9	27.7	Assumption 2
8	1,000	$200	31.6	38.4	30.0	40.3	31.9	27.7	Assumption 2
9	125	$ 25	31.5	38.4	30.0	40.3	31.9	27.7	Assumption 2
10	50	$ 10	31.6	33.4	30.0	40.3	31.9	27.7	Assumption 2
11	250	$ 50	31.6	38.4	30.0	40.3	31.9	27.7	Assumption 3
12	500	$100	31.6	38.4	30.0	40.3	31.9	27.7	Assumption 3
13	1,000	$200	31.6	38.4	30.0	40.3	31.9	27.7	Assumption 3
14	125	$ 25	31.6	38.4	30.0	40.3	31.9	27.7	Assumption 3
15	50	$ 10	31.6	38.4	30.0	40.3	31.9	27.7	Assumption 3
16	250	$ 50	31.6	38.4	30.0	40.3	31.9	27.7	Assumption 4
17	500	$100	31.6	38.4	30.0	40.3	31.9	27.7	Assumption 4
18	1,000	$200	31.6	38.4	30.0	40.3	31.9	27.7	Assumption 4
19	125	$ 25	31.6	38.4	30.0	40.3	31.9	27.7	Assumption 4
20	50	$ 10	31.6	38.4	30.0	40.3	31.9	27.7	Assumption 4

TABLE A2-6 (CTD.)
SUMMARY OF RESIDENTIAL CALLING PROFILES

Profile	Total Minutes	Average Monthly Bill	Call Distribution (based on minutes) (%)			Call Distribution (based on calls) (%)			Mileage Distribution
			Day	Even.	NWE	Day	Even.	NWE	
21	250	$ 50	51.6	38.4	10.0	61.6	31.5	6.8	Assumption 1
22	500	$100	51.6	38.4	10.0	61.6	31.5	6.8	Assumption 1
23	1,000	$200	51.6	38.4	10.0	61.6	31.5	6.8	Assumption 1
24	125	$ 25	51.6	38.4	10.0	61.6	31.5	6.8	Assumption 1
25	50	$ 10	51.6	38.4	10.0	61.6	31.5	6.8	Assumption 1
26	250	$ 50	51.6	38.4	10.0	61.6	31.5	6.8	Assumption 2
27	500	$100	51.6	38.4	10.0	61.6	31.5	6.8	Assumption 2
28	1,000	$200	51.6	38.4	10.0	61.6	31.5	6.8	Assumption 2
29	125	$ 25	51.6	38.4	10.0	61.6	31.5	6.8	Assumption 2
30	50	$ 10	51.6	38.4	10.0	61.6	31.5	6.8	Assumption 2
31	250	$ 50	51.6	38.4	10.0	61.6	31.5	6.8	Assumption 3
32	500	$100	51.6	38.4	10.0	61.6	31.5	6.8	Assumption 3
33	1,000	$200	51.6	38.4	10.0	61.6	31.5	6.8	Assumption 3
34	125	$ 25	51.6	38.4	10.0	61.6	31.5	6.8	Assumption 3
35	50	$ 10	51.6	38.4	10.0	61.6	31.5	6.8	Assumption 3
36	250	$ 50	51.6	38.4	10.0	61.6	31.5	6.8	Assumption 4
37	500	$100	51.6	38.4	10.0	61.6	31.5	6.8	Assumption 4
38	1,000	$200	51.6	38.4	10.0	61.6	31.5	6.8	Assumption 4
39	125	$ 25	51.6	38.4	10.0	61.6	31.5	6.8	Assumption 4
40	50	$ 10	51.6	38.4	10.0	61.6	31.5	6.8	Assumption 4

Table A2-6 (ctd.)
Summary of Residential Calling Profiles

Profile	Total Minutes	Average Monthly Bill	Call Distribution (based on minutes) (%)			Call Distribution (based on calls) (%)			Mileage Distribution
			Day	Even.	NWE	Day	Even.	NWE	
41	250	$ 50	12.0	38.0	50.0	20.8	30.6	48.6	Assumption 1
42	500	$100	12.0	38.0	50.0	20.8	30.6	48.6	Assumption 1
43	1,000	$200	12.0	38.0	50.0	20.8	30.6	48.6	Assumption 1
44	125	$ 25	12.0	38.0	50.0	20.8	30.6	48.6	Assumption 1
45	50	$ 10	12.0	38.0	50.0	20.8	30.6	48.6	Assumption 1
46	250	$ 50	12.0	38.0	50.0	20.8	30.6	48.6	Assumption 2
47	500	$100	12.0	38.0	50.0	20.8	30.6	48.6	Assumption 2
48	1,000	$200	12.0	38.0	50.0	20.8	30.6	48.6	Assumption 2
49	125	$ 25	12.0	38.0	50.0	20.8	30.6	48.6	Assumption 2
50	50	$ 10	12.0	38.0	50.0	20.8	30.6	48.6	Assumption 2
51	250	$ 50	12.0	38.0	50.0	20.8	30.6	48.6	Assumption 3
52	500	$100	12.0	38.0	50.0	20.8	30.6	48.6	Assumption 3
53	1,000	$200	12.0	38.0	50.0	20.8	30.6	48.6	Assumption 3
54	125	$ 25	12.0	38.0	50.0	20.8	30.6	48.6	Assumption 3
55	50	$ 10	12.0	38.0	50.0	20.8	30.6	48.6	Assumption 3
56	250	$ 50	12.0	38.0	50.0	20.8	30.6	48.6	Assumption 4
57	500	$100	12.0	38.0	50.0	20.8	30.6	48.6	Assumption 4
58	1,000	$200	12.0	38.0	50.0	20.8	30.6	48.6	Assumption 4
59	125	$ 25	12.0	38.0	50.0	20.8	30.6	48.6	Assumption 4
60	50	$ 10	12.0	38.0	50.0	20.8	30.6	48.6	Assumption 4

TABLE A2-7
SUMMARY OF SMALL-BUSINESS CALLING PROFILES

Profile	Total Minutes	Average Monthly Bill	Call Distribution (based on minutes) (%)			Call Distribution (based on calls) (%)			Mileage Distribution
			Day	Even.	NWE	Day	Even.	NWE	
1	1,000	$200	85	10	5	90	8	2	Assumption 1
2	500	$100	85	10	5	90	8	2	Assumption 1
3	250	$ 50	85	10	5	90	8	2	Assumption 1
4	1,500	$300	85	10	5	90	8	2	Assumption 1
5	1,000	$200	75	10	15	86	8	6	Assumption 1
6	500	$100	75	10	15	86	8	6	Assumption 1
7	250	$ 50	75	10	15	86	8	6	Assumption 1
8	1,500	$300	75	10	15	86	8	6	Assumption 1
9	1,000	$200	95	5	0	96	4	0	Assumption 1
10	500	$100	95	5	0	96	4	0	Assumption 1
11	250	$ 50	95	5	0	96	4	0	Assumption 1
12	1,500	$300	95	5	0	96	4	0	Assumption 1
13	1,000	$200	85	10	5	90	8	2	Assumption 2
14	500	$100	85	10	5	90	8	2	Assumption 2
15	250	$ 50	85	10	5	90	8	2	Assumption 2
16	1,500	$300	85	10	5	90	8	2	Assumption 2
17	1,000	$200	75	10	15	86	8	6	Assumption 2
18	500	$100	75	10	15	86	8	6	Assumption 2
19	250	$ 50	75	10	15	86	8	6	Assumption 2
20	1,500	$300	75	10	15	86	8	6	Assumption 2

TABLE A2-7 (CTD.)
SUMMARY OF SMALL-BUSINESS CALLING PROFILES

Profile	Total Minutes	Average Monthly Bill	Call Distribution (based on minutes) (%)			Call Distribution (based on calls) (%)			Mileage Distribution
			Day	Even.	NWE	Day	Even.	NWE	
21	1,000	$200	95	5	0	96	4	0	Assumption 2
22	500	$100	95	5	0	96	4	0	Assumption 2
23	250	$ 50	95	5	0	96	4	0	Assumption 2
24	1,500	$300	95	5	0	96	4	0	Assumption 2
25	1,000	$200	85	10	5	90	8	2	Assumption 3
26	500	$100	85	10	5	90	8	2	Assumption 3
27	250	$ 50	85	10	5	90	8	2	Assumption 3
28	1,500	$300	85	10	5	90	8	2	Assumption 3
29	1,000	$200	75	10	15	86	8	6	Assumption 3
30	500	$100	75	10	15	86	8	6	Assumption 3
31	250	$ 50	75	10	15	86	8	6	Assumption 3
32	1,500	$300	75	10	15	86	8	6	Assumption 3
33	1,000	$200	95	5	0	96	4	0	Assumption 3
34	500	$100	95	5	0	96	4	0	Assumption 3
35	250	$ 50	95	5	0	96	4	0	Assumption 3
36	1,500	$300	95	5	0	96	4	0	Assumption 3
37	1,000	$200	85	10	5	90	8	2	Assumption 4
38	500	$100	85	10	5	90	8	2	Assumption 4
39	250	$ 50	85	10	5	90	8	2	Assumption 4
40	1,500	$300	85	10	5	90	8	2	Assumption 4

TABLE A2-7 (CTD.)

SUMMARY OF SMALL-BUSINESS CALLING PROFILES

Profile	Total Minutes	Average Monthly Bill	Call Distribution (based on minutes) (%)			Call Distribution (based on calls) (%)			Mileage Distribution
			Day	Even.	NWE	Day	Even.	NWE	
41	1,000	$200	75	10	15	86	8	6	Assumption 4
42	500	$100	75	10	15	86	8	6	Assumption 4
43	250	$ 50	75	10	15	86	8	6	Assumption 4
44	1,500	$300	75	10	15	86	8	6	Assumption 4
45	1,000	$200	95	5	0	96	4	0	Assumption 4
46	500	$100	95	5	0	96	4	0	Assumption 4
47	250	$ 50	95	5	0	96	4	0	Assumption 4
48	1,500	$300	95	5	0	96	4	0	Assumption 4

FIGURE A2–7
RESIDENTIAL INDEX PRICES FOR AT&T STANDARD
SERVICE AND THEORETICAL MINIMUM PRICE PLAN

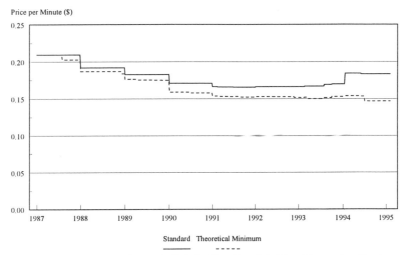

Notes: Prices from 60 residential profiles. Standard is basic MTS and theoretical minimum is lowest price calling plan.

FIGURE A2–8
SMALL-BUSINESS INDEX PRICES FOR AT&T STANDARD
SERVICE AND THEORETICAL MINIMUM PRICE PLAN

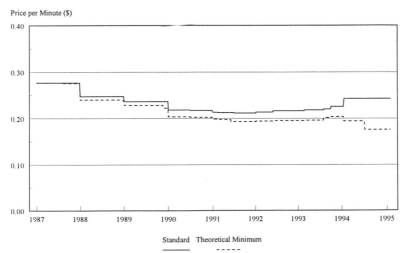

Notes: Prices from 40 small business profiles. Standard is Basic MTS and theoretical minimum is lowest price calling plan.

FIGURE A2–9

RESIDENTIAL INDEX PRICES FOR MCI STANDARD
SERVICE AND THEORETICAL MINIMUM PRICE PLAN

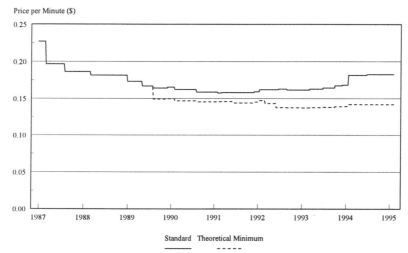

Notes: Prices from 60 residential profiles. Standard is basic MTS and theoretical minimum is lowest price calling plan.

FIGURE A2–10

SMALL-BUSINESS INDEX PRICES FOR MCI STANDARD
SERVICE AND THEORETICAL MINIMUM PRICE PLAN

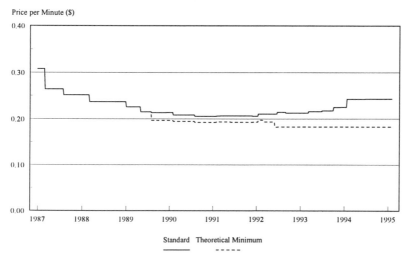

Notes: Prices from 40 small business profiles. Standard is basic MTS and theoretical minimum is lowest price calling plan.

FIGURE A2-11

RESIDENTIAL INDEX PRICES FOR SPRINT STANDARD
SERVICE AND THEORETICAL MINIMUM PRICE PLAN

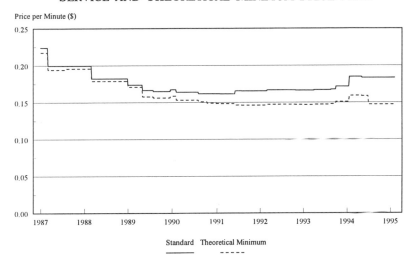

Notes: Prices from 60 residential profiles. Standard is basic MTS and theoretical minimum is lowest price calling plan.

FIGURE A2-12

SMALL-BUSINESS INDEX PRICES FOR SPRINT STANDARD
SERVICE AND THEORETICAL MINIMUM PRICE PLAN

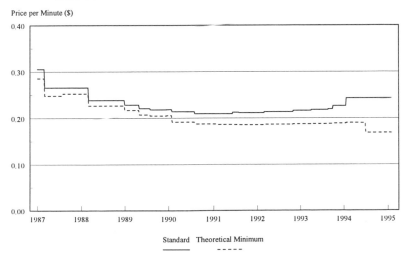

Notes: Prices from 40 small business profiles. Standard is basic MTS and theoretical minimum is lowest price calling plan.

FIGURE A2–13
RESIDENTIAL PRICE-COST MARGINS FOR AT&T STANDARD SERVICE AND THEORETICAL MINIMUM PRICE PLAN

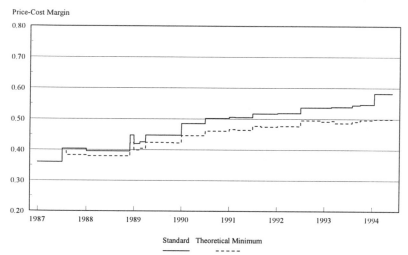

Notes: Prices from 60 residential profiles. Standard is basic MTS and theoretical minimum is lowest price calling plan.
Sources: Marginal costs from FCC and rates from HTL Telemanagement, Ltd.

FIGURE A2–14
SMALL-BUSINESS PRICE-COST MARGINS FOR AT&T STANDARD SERVICE AND THEORETICAL MINIMUM PRICE PLAN

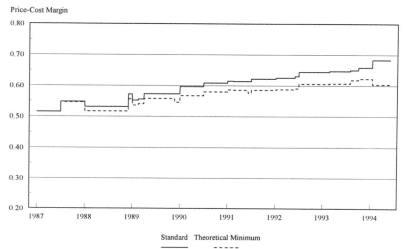

Notes: Prices from 48 small business profiles. Standard is basic MTS and theoretical minimum is lowest price calling plan.
Sources: Marginal costs from FCC and rates from HTL Telemanagement, Ltd.

FIGURE A2–15

RESIDENTIAL PRICE-COST MARGINS FOR MCI STANDARD
SERVICE AND THEORETICAL MINIMUM PRICE PLAN

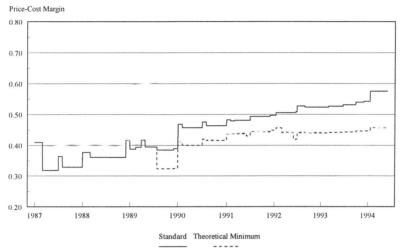

Notes: Prices from 60 residential profiles. Standard is Execunet and theoretical minimum is lowest price calling plan.
Sources: Marginal costs from FCC and rates from HTL Telemanagement, Ltd.

FIGURE A2–16

SMALL-BUSINESS PRICE-COST MARGINS FOR MCI STANDARD
SERVICE AND THEORETICAL MINIMUM PRICE PLAN

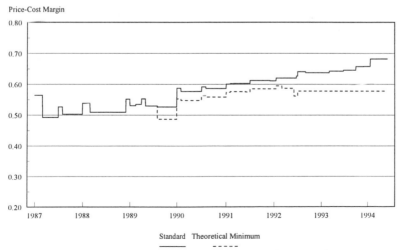

Notes: Prices from 48 small business profiles. Standard is Execunet and theoretical minimum is lowest price calling plan.
Sources: Marginal costs from FCC and rates from HTL Telemanagement, Ltd.

FIGURE A2–17

RESIDENTIAL PRICE-COST MARGINS FOR SPRINT STANDARD
SERVICE AND THEORETICAL MINIMUM PRICE PLAN

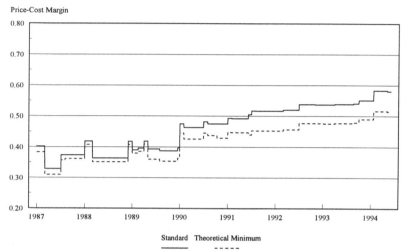

Notes: Prices from 60 residential profiles. Standard is Dial "1" and theoretical minimum is lowest price calling plan.
Sources: Marginal costs from FCC and rates from HTL Telemanagement, Ltd.

FIGURE A2–18

SMALL-BUSINESS PRICE-COST MARGINS FOR SPRINT STANDARD
SERVICE AND THEORETICAL MINIMUM PRICE PLAN

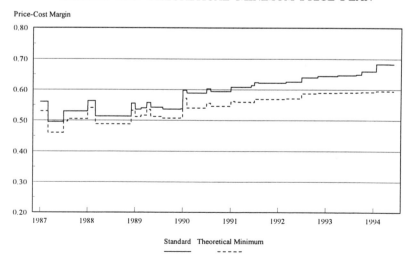

Notes: Prices from 48 small business profiles. Standard is Dial "1" and theoretical minimum is lowest price calling plan.
Sources: Marginal costs from FCC and rates from HTL Telemanagement, Ltd.

Appendix 3

Standard and Discount Prices
in International Markets

THE FOLLOWING TABLES SHOW index prices on long-distance calls from the United States to Canada, Mexico, the United Kingdom, Germany, France, Italy, Japan, and the Dominican Republic. Tables A3–1 and A3–2 show prices for standard and discount plan services in message toll markets. Table A3–3 shows prices for WATS services.

TABLE A3-1 STANDARD IMTS AND DISCOUNT IMTS CALLING PATTERN DISTRIBUTION			
Country Pair	Calling Distribution (%)		
	Standard	Discount	Economy
U.S. to Canada			
Base Case	40	30	30
Sensitivity Run 1	60	25	15
Sensitivity Run 2	20	30	50
U.S. to Mexico			
Base Case	40	30	30
Sensitivity Run 1	60	25	15
Sensitivity Run 2	20	30	50
U.S. to United Kingdom			
Base Case	30	50	20
Sensitivity Run 1	60	25	15
Sensitivity Run 1	20	30	50
U.S. to Germany			
Base Case	30	50	20
Sensitivity Run 1	60	25	15
Sensitivity Run 2	20	30	50
U.S. to Japan			
Base Case	30	50	20
Sensitivity Run 1	60	25	15
Sensitivity Run 2	20	30	50
U.S. to France			
Base Case	30	50	20
Sensitivity Run 1	60	25	15
Sensitivity Run 2	20	30	50
U.S. to Italy			
Base Case	30	50	20
Sensitivity Run 1	60	25	15
Sensitivity Run 2	20	30	50
U.S. to Dominican Republic			
Base Case	40	30	30
Sensitivity Run 1	60	25	15
Sensitivity Run 2	20	30	50

TABLE A3–2 IWATS CALLING PATTERN DISTRIBUTION			
Country Pair	Calling Distribution (%)		
	Standard	Discount	Economy
U.S. to Canada			
Base Case	85	10	5
Sensitivity Run 1	75	10	15
Sensitivity Run 2	95	5	0
U.S. to Mexico			
Base Case	85	10	5
Sensitivity Run 1	75	10	15
Sensitivity Run 2	95	5	0
U.S. to United Kingdom			
Base Case	60	20	20
Sensitivity Run 1	75	10	15
Sensitivity Run 2	50	30	20
U.S. to Germany			
Base Case	60	20	20
Sensitivity Run 1	75	10	15
Sensitivity Run 2	50	30	20
U.S. to Japan			
Base Case	75	25	0
Sensitivity Run 1	85	10	5
Sensitivity Run 2	60	20	20
U.S. to France			
Base Case	60	20	20
Sensitivity Run 1	75	10	15
Sensitivity Run 2	50	30	20
U.S. to Italy			
Base Case	60	20	20
Sensitivity Run 1	75	10	15
Sensitivity Run 2	50	30	20
U.S. to Dominican Republic			
Base Case	85	10	5
Sensitivity Run 1	75	10	15
Sensitivity Run 2	95	5	0

TABLE A3–3
STANDARD IMTS INDEX PRICES FOR LONG-DISTANCE CALLS—
BASE CASE (PRICE PER MINUTE ($))

Country Pairs	1990	1991	1992	1993	1994
U.S. to Canada					
AT&T	—	0.443	0.443	0.475	0.475
MCI	0.430	0.423	0.433	0.473	0.485
Sprint	0.443	0.443	0.443	0.475	0.496
U.S. to Mexico					
AT&T	1.300	1.208	1.208	1.208	1.268
MCI	1.206	1.206	1.206	1.215	1.258
Sprint	—	1.208	1.208	1.225	1.268
U.S. to United Kingdom					
AT&T	0.877	0.877	0.877	0.895	0.895
MCI	0.852	0.852	0.867	0.894	0.955
Sprint	—	—	0.877	0.895	0.895
U.S. to Germany					
AT&T	1.020	1.020	1.020	1.051	1.112
MCI	1.113	0.991	0.991	1.049	1.049
Sprint	—	1.020	1.020	1.051	1.112
U.S. to France					
AT&T	1.015	1.015	1.015	1.015	1.078
MCI	1.077	0.987	0.987	1.014	1.014
Sprint	—	0.997	0.987	1.015	1.078
U.S. to Italy					
AT&T	0.987	0.987	0.987	1.124	1.152
MCI	—	0.977	0.977	1.122	1.240
Sprint	—	0.987	0.987	1.124	1.241
U.S. to Japan					
AT&T	1.352	1.352	1.352	1.352	1.375
MCI	—	1.342	1.342	1.351	1.427
Sprint	—	1.352	1.352	1.352	1.375
U.S. to Dominican Republic					
AT&T	0.934	0.934	0.934	1.060	1.261
MCI	—	0.923	0.923	1.058	1.193
Sprint	—	0.934	0.934	1.060	1.261

Notes: For Canada, Mexico, and the Dominican Republic, the calling pattern distribution is 40% standard, 30% discount, and 30% economy. For the United Kingdom, Germany, France, Italy, and Japan, the calling pattern distribution is 30% standard, 50% discount, and 20% economy.

International calls billed in the United States are charged prices that depend on when the calls are made with respect to the U.S. Eastern Standard Time zone. Calls to each foreign country are billed under specified "standard," "discount," and "economy" rates. For example, standard rates are charged for calls from the United States to the United Kingdom for the period 7 A.M. to 1 P.M. EST, while rates for calls from the United States to Japan are charged for the period 2 P.M. to 8 P.M. EST.

To determine whether the price-cost margin calculations are sensitive to assumptions regarding the distribution of international calls across the three time-of-day periods, a sensitivity analysis has been conducted. For each country pair, two alternative time-of-day distributions were selected. Carriers' prices per minute for each country pair were calculated for standard IMTS, discount IMTS, and IWATS with those sensitivity distributions. Given those different time-of-day periods, tables A3–4 and A3–5 show the base-case assumptions regarding usage, as well as those regarding the two sensitivity runs for each of the country pairs.

TABLE A3–4

DISCOUNT IMTS INDEX PRICES FOR LONG-DISTANCE CALLS—
BASE CASE (PRICE PER MINUTE ($))

Country Pairs	1991	1992	1993	1994
U.S. to Canada				
AT&T	—	—	—	0.410
MCI	—	—	0.388	0.400
Sprint	0.394	0.394	0.416	0.425
U.S. to Mexico				
AT&T	—	—	—	1.204
MCI	—	—	—	1.166
Sprint	1.177	1.177	1.184	1.212
U.S. to United Kingdom				
AT&T	—	—	—	0.758
MCI	—	—	0.748	0.748
Sprint	—	0.758	0.846	0.846
U.S. to Germany				
AT&T	—	—	—	0.947
MCI	—	—	0.811	0.811
Sprint	0.809	0.809	0.809	0.809
U.S. to France				
AT&T	—	—	—	0.815
MCI	—	—	0.805	0.805
Sprint	0.799	0.820	0.825	0.825
U.S. to Italy				
AT&T	—	—	—	0.974
MCI	—	—	0.868	0.964
Sprint	0.802	0.823	0.878	0.950
U.S. to Japan				
AT&T	—	—	—	1.085
MCI	—	—	1.022	1.022
Sprint	1.038	1.038	1.038	1.070
U.S. to Dominican Republic				
AT&T	—	—	—	1.020
MCI	—	—	0.938	1.010
Sprint	—	—	—	—

Notes: For Canada, Mexico, and the Dominican Republic, the calling
pattern distribution is 40% standard, 30% discount, and 30% economy.
For the United Kingdom, Germany, France, Italy, and Japan, the calling
pattern distribution is 30% standard, 50% discount, and 20% economy.

TABLE A3–5 IWATS INDEX PRICES FOR LONG-DISTANCE CALLS— BASE CASE (PRICE PER MINUTE ($))				
Country Pairs	1991	1992	1993	1994
U.S. to Canada				
AT&T	0.520	0.520	0.541	0.549
MCI	0.494	0.500	0.546	0.590
Sprint	0.489	0.489	0.511	0.533
U.S. to Mexico				
AT&T	1.387	1.387	1.423	1.490
MCI	1.373	1.373	1.384	1.449
Sprint	1.389	1.389	1.408	1.424
U.S. to United Kingdom				
AT&T	0.877	0.877	0.912	0.953
MCI	0.833	0.841	0.939	1.015
Sprint	—	0.842	0.908	0.908
U.S. to Germany				
AT&T	1.023	1.023	1.062	1.147
MCI	0.971	0.980	1.094	1.182
Sprint	—	0.989	1.068	1.110
U.S. to France				
AT&T	0.996	0.996	1.035	1.118
MCI	0.947	0.956	1.066	1.152
Sprint	—	0.963	0.920	0.955
U.S. to Italy				
AT&T	1.003	1.003	1.041	1.126
MCI	0.953	0.962	1.074	1.160
Sprint	—	0.961	1.043	1.084
U.S. to Japan				
AT&T	1.410	1.410	1.464	1.582
MCI	1.339	1.353	1.509	1.631
Sprint	—	1.340	1.452	1.507
U.S. to Dominican Republic				
AT&T	1.029	1.029	1.069	1.155
MCI	0.998	0.998	1.101	1.190
Sprint	—	1.004	1.065	1.107

Notes: For Canada, Mexico, and the Dominican Republic, the calling pattern distribution is 85% standard, 10% discount, and 5% economy. For the United Kingdom, Germany, France, and Italy, the calling pattern distribution is 60% standard, 20% discount, and 20% economy. For Japan the calling pattern distribution is 75% standard and 25% discount.

In the case of standard IMTS, the first sensitivity run assumes that a customer makes 60 percent of calls during the standard period, 25 percent of calls during the discount period, and 15 percent of calls during the economy period. (See table A3-6.) As can be seen by comparing the results from that run with base-case prices, the alternative index price per minute across the country pairs exceeds the index price under the base case. That result is as expected, given that 60 percent of calls are assumed to be placed during the more expensive standard period, while the base case assumes that only 30 or 40 percent of calls are made during that period. The second sensitivity distribution assumes that only 20 percent of calls are made during the standard period, that 30 percent are made during the discount period, and that half of all calls are made during the less expensive economy period. (See table A3-7.) As such, the index price per minute is lower than under the base case. Notice that the changes in prices per minute under the base case and the two sensitivity runs move together over time. Therefore, the results in testing for price change/concentration relationships for standard IMTS are not sensitive to changes in calling pattern distributions.

Discount plan prices per minute were calculated under four alternative sensitivity distributions, two based on time-of-day calling patterns (identical to those mentioned above for standard IMTS) and two based on usage levels. The results from the first two sensitivity runs mirror the results for standard IMTS under the two sensitivity distributions. (See tables A3-8 and A3-9.) Again, the price per minute under the first sensitivity distribution is higher than the price per minute under the base-case assumption. That results from the fact that more calls are made during the more expensive standard period than under the base case. Similarly, because the second sensitivity distribution assumes that calls are highly concentrated in the less expensive discount and economy time periods, the prices per minute are lower than under the base case.

TABLE A3-6 STANDARD IMTS INDEX PRICES FOR LONG-DISTANCE CALLS— SENSITIVITY RUN 1 (PRICE PER MINUTE ($))					
Country Pairs	1990	1991	1992	1993	1994
U.S. to Canada					
AT&T	—	0.500	0.500	0.535	0.535
MCI	0.483	0.476	0.489	0.534	0.545
Sprint	0.500	0.500	0.500	0.535	0.555
U.S. to Mexico					
AT&T	1.417	1.314	1.314	1.314	1.374
MCI	1.313	1.313	1.313	1.322	1.364
Sprint	—	1.314	1.314	1.332	1.374
U.S. to United Kingdom					
AT&T	0.934	0.934	0.934	0.952	0.952
MCI	0.896	0.896	0.924	0.950	0.985
Sprint	—	—	0.934	0.952	0.952
U.S. to Germany					
AT&T	1.090	1.090	1.090	1.107	1.140
MCI	1.140	1.046	1.079	1.106	1.106
Sprint	—	1.090	1.090	1.107	1.140
U.S. to France					
AT&T	1.080	1.080	1.080	1.080	1.115
MCI	1.114	1.052	1.052	1.079	1.079
Sprint	—	1.063	1.063	1.080	1.115
U.S. to Italy					
AT&T	1.063	1.063	1.063	1.201	1.231
MCI	—	1.053	1.053	1.199	1.282
Sprint	—	1.063	1.063	1.201	1.283
U.S. to Japan					
AT&T	1.421	1.421	1.421	1.421	1.481
MCI	—	1.411	1.411	1.420	1.460
Sprint	—	1.421	1.421	1.421	1.481
U.S. to Dominican Republic					
AT&T	1.022	1.022	1.022	1.142	1.334
MCI	—	1.011	1.011	1.141	1.284
Sprint	—	1.022	1.022	1.142	1.334
Note: For all country pairs the calling pattern distribution is 60% standard, 25% discount, and 15% economy.					

TABLE A3–7 STANDARD IMTS INDEX PRICES FOR LONG-DISTANCE CALLS— SENSITIVITY RUN 2 (PRICE PER MINUTE ($))					
Country Pairs	1990	1991	1992	1993	1994
U.S. to Canada					
AT&T	—	0.397	0.397	0.425	0.425
MCI	0.386	0.380	0.386	0.424	0.436
Sprint	0.397	0.397	0.397	0.425	0.447
U.S. to Mexico					
AT&T	1.241	1.155	1.155	1.155	1.222
MCI	1.154	1.154	1.154	1.163	1.212
Sprint	—	1.155	1.155	1.173	1.222
U.S. to United Kingdom					
AT&T	0.814	0.814	0.814	0.832	0.832
MCI	0.793	0.793	0.803	0.830	0.902
Sprint	—	—	0.814	0.832	0.832
U.S. to Germany					
AT&T	0.929	0.929	0.929	0.961	1.013
MCI	1.014	0.906	0.919	0.959	0.959
Sprint	—	0.929	0.929	0.961	1.013
U.S. to France					
AT&T	0.934	0.934	0.934	0.934	0.996
MCI	0.996	0.905	0.905	0.932	0.932
Sprint	—	0.916	0.916	0.934	0.996
U.S. to Italy					
AT&T	0.911	0.911	0.911	1.037	1.061
MCI	—	0.900	0.900	1.035	1.175
Sprint	—	0.911	0.911	1.037	1.175
U.S. to Japan					
AT&T	1.251	1.251	1.251	1.251	1.242
MCI	—	1.241	1.241	1.250	1.309
Sprint	—	1.251	1.251	1.251	1.242
U.S. to Dominican Republic					
AT&T	0.875	0.875	0.875	1.020	1.249
MCI	—	0.864	0.864	1.018	1.153
Sprint	—	0.875	0.875	1.020	1.249
Note: For all country pairs the calling pattern distribution is 20% standard, 30% discount, and 50% economy.					

TABLE A3-8 DISCOUNT IMTS INDEX PRICES FOR LONG-DISTANCE CALLS— SENSITIVITY RUN 1 (PRICE PER MINUTE ($))				
Country Pairs	1991	1992	1993	1994
U.S. to Canada				
AT&T	—	—	—	0.480
MCI	—	—	0.462	0.470
Sprint	0.460	0.460	0.486	0.495
U.S. to Mexico				
AT&T	—	—	—	1.316
MCI	—	—	—	1.264
Sprint	1.254	1.254	1.263	1.290
U.S. to United Kingdom				
AT&T	—	—	—	0.866
MCI	—	—	0.856	0.856
Sprint	—	0.875	0.933	0.933
U.S. to Germany				
AT&T	—	—	—	1.034
MCI	—	—	0.952	0.952
Sprint	0.978	0.978	0.978	0.978
U.S. to France				
AT&T	—	—	—	0.950
MCI	—	—	0.940	0.940
Sprint	0.958	0.970	0.979	0.979
U.S. to Italy				
AT&T	—	—	—	1.118
MCI	—	—	1.006	1.108
Sprint	0.965	0.977	1.065	1.120
U.S. to Japan				
AT&T	—	—	—	1.280
MCI	—	—	1.214	1.214
Sprint	1.247	1.247	1.247	1.309
U.S. to Dominican Republic				
AT&T	—	—	—	1.080
MCI	—	—	0.982	1.070
Sprint	—	—	—	—
Note: For all country pairs the calling pattern distribution is 60% standard, 25% discount, and 15% economy.				

TABLE A3–9

DISCOUNT IMTS INDEX PRICES FOR LONG-DISTANCE CALLS—
SENSITIVITY RUN 2 (PRICE PER MINUTE ($))

Country Pairs	1991	1992	1993	1994
U.S. to Canada				
AT&T	—	—	—	0.340
MCI	—	—	0.314	0.330
Sprint	0.312	0.312	0.328	0.338
U.S. to Mexico				
AT&T	—	—	—	1.092
MCI	—	—	—	1.068
Sprint	1.064	1.064	1.067	1.091
U.S. to United Kingdom				
AT&T	—	—	—	0.722
MCI	—	—	0.712	0.712
Sprint	—	0.726	0.825	0.825
U.S. to Germany				
AT&T	—	—	—	0.918
MCI	—	—	0.764	0.764
Sprint	0.761	0.761	0.761	0.761
U.S. to France				
AT&T	—	—	—	0.770
MCI	—	—	0.760	0.760
Sprint	0.754	0.778	0.781	0.781
U.S. to Italy				
AT&T	—	—	—	0.926
MCI	—	—	0.822	0.916
Sprint	0.755	0.779	0.824	0.903
U.S. to Japan				
AT&T	—	—	—	1.020
MCI	—	—	0.958	0.958
Sprint	0.975	0.975	0.975	1.002
U.S. to Dominican Republic				
AT&T	—	—	—	0.960
MCI	—	—	0.894	0.950
Sprint	—	—	—	—

Note: For all country pairs the calling pattern distribution is 20% standard, 30% discount, and 50% economy.

In addition to the two time-of-day variations, a sensitivity analysis was conducted by assuming alternative usage levels. The assumed level of usage is potentially important, as discounts often vary with usage. The base-case calling distribution assumes that a customer averages fifty minutes of calls per month. The third sensitivity run conducted uses the base-case calling distribution but assumes only thirty minutes per month. (See table A3–10.) As would be expected, the discounts are not so large as under the standard usage level of fifty minutes, and therefore the price per minute across the country pairs is higher. The fourth sensitivity run assumes the base-case calling distribution and a usage per month of 100 minutes. (See table A3–11.) Notice that the prices are lower than those in the base case.

Those sensitivity runs show that although prices may change slightly as a result of alternative assumptions about time-of-day calling patterns and usage levels, the prices calculated under the sensitivity runs and under the base-case change in the same direction over time. Therefore, inferences about price-cost margins for discount prices, and their relationship with changes in concentration over time, are not sensitive to changes in the base-case assumptions.

The sensitivity analysis of IWATS prices per minute assumes three alternative sensitivity distributions: two based on time-of-day assumptions and one based on usage level. Tables A3–12 through A3–14 show the results of the sensitivity runs that assume alternative time-of-day distributions and those that detail prices from sensitivity and assume the same time-of-day distributions as in the base case and a usage level of 1,000 hours. The results are similar to those presented for standard and discount IMTS rates. For those sensitivity runs that assume more calls during the standard time, the prices per minute are higher than under the base case. Alternatively, for sensitivity runs assuming more calls made during discount or economy periods, the prices per minute are lower than under the base case. Finally, the price per minute calculated under the assumption that a customer makes on average 100 minutes of calls per month is lower than the price calculated under the base-case assumptions.

Thus, the index price per minute of IWATS service varies as the underlying calling distribution changes. But the index price moves over time with the prices per minute under the base-case assumptions. As such, an analysis of the movement of price-cost margins over time is robust to assumptions about the distribution of a customer's calls.

TABLE A3–10

DISCOUNT IMTS INDEX PRICES FOR LONG-DISTANCE CALLS—
THIRTY MINUTES' MONTHLY USAGE—
SENSITIVITY RUN 3
(PRICE PER MINUTE ($))

Country Pairs	1991	1992	1993	1994
U.S. to Canada				
AT&T	—	—	—	0.450
MCI	—	—	0.428	0.440
Sprint	0.434	0.434	0.456	0.465
U.S. to Mexico				
AT&T	—	—	—	1.244
MCI	—	—	—	1.206
Sprint	1.217	1.217	1.224	1.252
U.S. to United Kingdom				
AT&T	—	—	—	0.798
MCI	—	—	0.788	0.788
Sprint	—	0.798	0.886	0.886
U.S. to Germany				
AT&T	—	—	—	0.987
MCI	—	—	0.851	0.851
Sprint	0.849	0.849	0.849	0.849
U.S. to France				
AT&T	—	—	—	0.855
MCI	—	—	0.845	0.845
Sprint	0.839	0.860	0.865	0.865
U.S. to Italy				
AT&T	—	—	—	1.014
MCI	—	—	0.908	1.004
Sprint	0.842	0.863	0.918	0.990
U.S. to Japan				
AT&T	—	—	—	1.125
MCI	—	—	1.062	1.062
Sprint	1.078	1.078	1.078	1.110
U.S. to Dominican Republic				
AT&T	—	—	—	1.030
MCI	—	—	0.956	1.020
Sprint	—	—	—	—

Note: For all country pairs the calling pattern distribution is 40% standard, 30% discount, and 30% economy.

TABLE A3–11
DISCOUNT IMTS INDEX PRICES FOR LONG-DISTANCE CALLS—
100 MINUTES MONTHLY USAGE—
SENSITIVITY RUN 4
(PRICE PER MINUTE ($))

Country Pairs	1991	1992	1993	1994
U.S. to Canada				
AT&T	—	—	—	0.380
MCI	—	—	0.358	0.370
Sprint	0.364	0.364	0.386	0.395
U.S. to Mexico				
AT&T	—	—	—	1.174
MCI	—	—	—	1.136
Sprint	1.147	1.147	1.154	1.183
U.S. to United Kingdom				
AT&T	—	—	—	0.728
MCI	—	—	0.781	0.781
Sprint	—	0.728	0.816	0.816
U.S. to Germany				
AT&T	—	—	—	0.917
MCI	—	—	0.781	0.781
Sprint	0.779	0.779	0.779	0.779
U.S. to France				
AT&T	—	—	—	0.785
MCI	—	—	0.775	0.775
Sprint	0.769	0.790	0.795	0.795
U.S. to Italy				
AT&T	—	—	—	1.944
MCI	—	—	0.838	1.934
Sprint	0.772	0.793	0.848	0.920
U.S. to Japan				
AT&T	—	—	—	1.055
MCI	—	—	1.992	1.992
Sprint	1.008	1.008	1.008	1.040
U.S. to Dominican Republic				
AT&T	—	—	—	0.960
MCI	—	—	0.886	0.950
Sprint	—	—	—	—

Note: For all country pairs the calling pattern distribution is 40% standard, 30% discount, and 30% economy.

TABLE A3–12 IWATS INDEX PRICES FOR LONG-DISTANCE CALLS— SENSITIVITY RUN 1 (PRICE PER MINUTE ($))				
Country Pairs	1991	1992	1993	1994
U.S. to Canada				
AT&T	0.497	0.497	0.516	0.558
MCI	0.472	0.479	0.522	0.564
Sprint	0.471	0.471	0.492	0.513
U.S. to Mexico				
AT&T	1.342	1.342	1.378	1.443
MCI	1.329	1.329	1.340	1.403
Sprint	1.344	1.344	1.362	1.378
U.S. to United Kingdom				
AT&T	0.914	0.914	0.950	1.026
MCI	0.867	0.876	0.978	1.057
Sprint	—	0.874	0.945	0.945
U.S. to Germany				
AT&T	1.068	1.068	1.109	1.198
MCI	1.014	1.023	1.142	1.234
Sprint	—	1.028	1.113	1.156
U.S. to France				
AT&T	1.039	1.039	1.079	1.166
MCI	0.987	0.997	1.112	1.202
Sprint	—	0.999	0.948	0.985
U.S. to Italy				
AT&T	1.049	1.049	1.089	1.177
MCI	0.996	1.006	1.123	1.213
Sprint	—	1.003	1.090	1.132
U.S. to Japan				
AT&T	1.433	1.433	1.288	1.607
MCI	1.360	1.375	1.533	1.657
Sprint	—	1.367	1.483	1.540
U.S. to Dominican Republic				
AT&T	0.993	0.993	1.031	1.114
MCI	0.963	0.963	1.062	1.148
Sprint	—	0.979	1.038	1.078
Notes: For all country pairs except Japan, the calling pattern distribution is 75% standard, 10% discount, and 15% economy. For Japan the calling pattern distribution is 85% standard, 10% discount, and 5% economy.				

TABLE A3–13

IWATS INDEX PRICES FOR LONG-DISTANCE CALLS—
SENSITIVITY RUN 2 (PRICE PER MINUTE ($))

Country Pairs	1991	1992	1993	1994
U.S. to Canada				
AT&T	0.542	0.542	0.563	0.609
MCI	0.514	0.521	0.568	0.614
Sprint	0.506	0.506	0.530	0.552
U.S. to Mexico				
AT&T	1.432	1.432	1.457	1.525
MCI	1.416	1.416	1.428	1.495
Sprint	1.434	1.434	1.454	1.470
U.S. to United Kingdom				
AT&T	0.854	0.854	0.888	0.960
MCI	0.811	0.819	0.914	0.988
Sprint	—	0.820	0.883	0.883
U.S. to Germany				
AT&T	0.996	0.996	1.034	1.117
MCI	0.945	0.954	1.065	1.151
Sprint	—	0.963	1.038	1.079
U.S. to France				
AT&T	0.970	0.970	1.008	1.089
MCI	0.922	0.931	1.039	1.123
Sprint	—	0.938	0.901	0.936
U.S. to Italy				
AT&T	0.963	0.963	1.000	1.081
MCI	0.915	0.924	1.032	1.114
Sprint	—	0.923	1.003	1.042
U.S. to Japan				
AT&T	1.348	1.348	1.399	1.512
MCI	1.279	1.293	1.442	1.558
Sprint	—	1.301	1.405	1.458
U.S. to Dominican Republic				
AT&T	1.059	1.059	1.100	1.189
MCI	1.028	1.028	1.133	1.225
Sprint	—	1.028	1.093	1.136

Notes: For Canada, Mexico, and the Dominican Republic, the calling pattern distribution is 95% standard and 5% discount. For the United Kingdom, Germany, France, and Italy, the calling pattern distribution is 50% standard, 30% discount, and 20% economy. For Japan the calling pattern distribution is 60% standard, 20% discount, and 20% economy.

TABLE A3–14

IWATS INDEX PRICES FOR LONG-DISTANCE CALLS—

1,000 HOURS MONTHLY USAGE

(PRICE PER MINUTE ($))

Country Pairs	1991	1992	1993	1994
U.S. to Canada				
AT&T	0.520	0.520	0.541	0.585
MCI	0.494	0.500	0.546	0.590
Sprint	0.489	0.489	0.511	0.533
U.S. to Mexico				
AT&T	1.387	1.387	1.423	1.490
MCI	1.373	1.373	1.384	1.449
Sprint	1.389	1.389	1.408	1.424
U.S. to United Kingdom				
AT&T	0.877	0.877	0.912	0.985
MCI	0.833	0.841	0.939	1.015
Sprint	—	0.842	0.908	0.908
U.S. to Germany				
AT&T	1.023	1.023	1.062	1.147
MCI	0.971	0.980	1.094	1.182
Sprint	—	0.989	1.068	1.110
U.S. to France				
AT&T	0.996	0.996	1.035	1.118
MCI	0.947	0.956	1.066	1.152
Sprint	—	0.963	0.920	0.955
U.S. to Italy				
AT&T	1.003	1.003	1.041	1.126
MCI	0.953	0.962	1.074	1.160
Sprint	—	0.961	1.043	1.104
U.S. to Japan				
AT&T	1.410	1.029	1.069	1.155
MCI	0.998	0.998	1.101	1.190
Sprint	—	1.004	1.065	1.107
U.S. to Dominican Republic				
AT&T	1.059	1.059	1.100	1.189
MCI	1.028	1.028	1.133	1.225
Sprint	—	1.028	1.093	1.136

Notes: For Canada, Mexico, and the Dominican Republic, the calling pattern distribution is 85% standard, 10% discount, and 5% economy. For the United Kingdom, Germany, France, and Italy, the calling pattern distribution is 60% standard, 20% discount, and 20% economy. For Japan the calling pattern distribution is 75% standard and 25% discount.

Appendix 4

Price-Cost Margins and Market Concentration in International Markets

THE FOLLOWING FIGURES show price-cost margins and the Herfindahl-Hirschman indexes for outbound U.S. message toll and WATS services to eight foreign countries: Canada, Mexico, the United Kingdom, Germany, France, Italy, Japan, and the Dominican Republic. Figures A4–1 through A4–8 present the data for standard international message toll service. Figures A4–9 through A4–16 show the data for discount international message toll service. Finally, figures A4–17 through A4–24 present the data for international WATS calls.

FIGURE A4–1

PRICE-COST MARGIN AND MARKET CONCENTRATION FOR
STANDARD IMTS CALLS FROM THE UNITED STATES TO CANADA

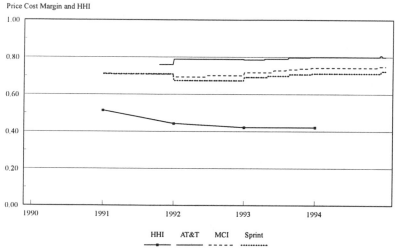

Notes: Marginal costs based on net settlement payments. Time of day based on 40% standard, 30% discount, and 30% economy.
Sources: Marginal costs from FCC and WEFA, rates from HTL Telemanagement, Ltd., and market concentration from FCC.

FIGURE A4–2

PRICE-COST MARGIN AND MARKET CONCENTRATION FOR
STANDARD IMTS CALLS FROM THE UNITED STATES TO MEXICO

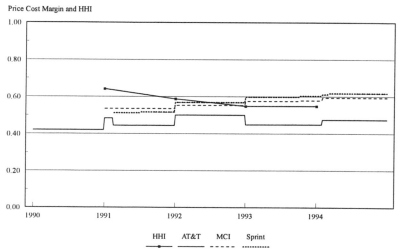

Notes: Marginal costs based on net settlement payments. Time of day based on 40% standard, 30% discount, and 30% economy.
Sources: Marginal costs from FCC and WEFA, rates from HTL Telemanagement, Ltd., and market concentration from FCC.

FIGURE A4–3

PRICE-COST MARGIN AND MARKET CONCENTRATION FOR STANDARD
IMTS CALLS FROM THE UNITED STATES TO THE UNITED KINGDOM

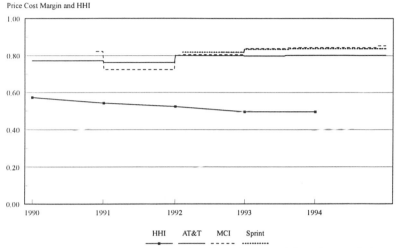

Notes: Marginal costs based on net settlement payments. Time of day based on 30% standard, 50% discount, and 20% economy.
Sources: Marginal costs from FCC and WEFA, rates from HTL Telemanagement, Ltd., and market concentration from FCC.

FIGURE A4–4

PRICE-COST MARGIN AND MARKET CONCENTRATION FOR
STANDARD IMTS CALLS FROM THE UNITED STATES TO GERMANY

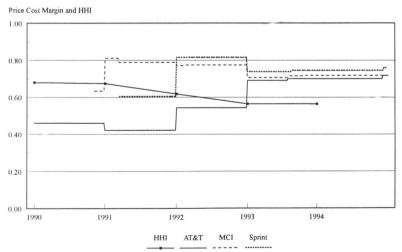

Notes: Marginal costs based on net settlement payments. Time of day based on 30% standard, 50% discount, and 20% economy.
Sources: Marginal costs from FCC and WEFA, rates from HTL Telemanagement, Ltd., and market concentration from FCC.

FIGURE A4–5
PRICE-COST MARGIN AND MARKET CONCENTRATION FOR STANDARD IMTS CALLS FROM THE UNITED STATES TO FRANCE

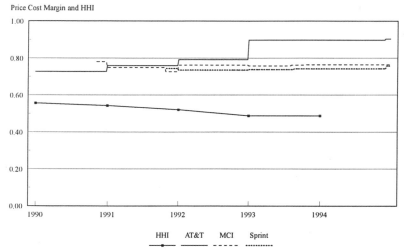

Notes: Marginal costs based on net settlement payments. Time of day based on 30% standard, 50% discount, and 20% economy.
Sources: Marginal costs from FCC and WEFA, rates from HTL Telemanagement, Ltd., and market concentration from FCC.

FIGURE A4–6
PRICE-COST MARGIN AND MARKET CONCENTRATION FOR STANDARD IMTS CALLS FROM THE UNITED STATES TO ITALY

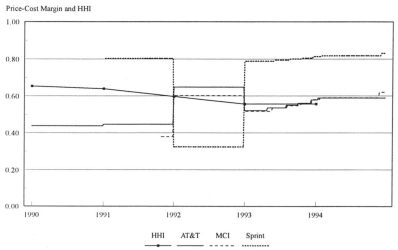

Notes: Marginal costs based on net settlement payments. Time of day based on 30% standard, 50% discount, and 20% economy.
Sources: Marginal costs from FCC and WEFA, rates from HTL Telemanagement, Ltd., and market concentration from FCC.

FIGURE A4-7

PRICE-COST MARGIN AND MARKET CONCENTRATION FOR
STANDARD IMTS CALLS FROM THE UNITED STATES TO JAPAN

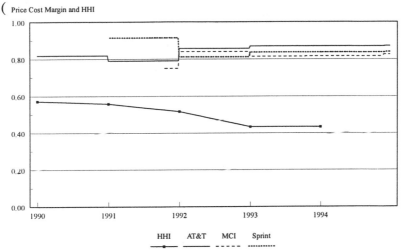

HHI   AT&T   MCI   Sprint

Notes: Marginal costs based on net settlement payments. Time of day based on 30% standard, 50% discount, and 20% economy.
Sources: Marginal costs from FCC and WEFA, rates from HTL Telemanagement, Ltd., and market concentration from FCC.

FIGURE A4-8

PRICE-COST MARGIN AND MARKET CONCENTRATION FOR STANDARD
IMTS CALLS FROM THE UNITED STATES TO THE DOMINICAN REPUBLIC

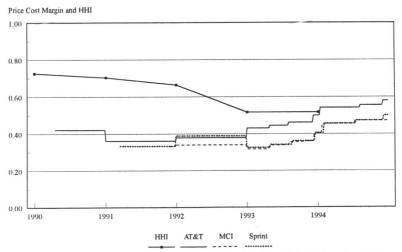

HHI   AT&T   MCI   Sprint

Notes: Marginal costs based on net settlement payments. Time of day based on 40% standard, 30% discount, and 30% economy.
Sources: Marginal costs from FCC and WEFA, rates from HTL Telemanagement, Ltd., and market concentration from FCC.

FIGURE A4–9
PRICE-COST MARGIN AND MARKET CONCENTRATION FOR DISCOUNT IMTS CALLS FROM THE UNITED STATES TO CANADA

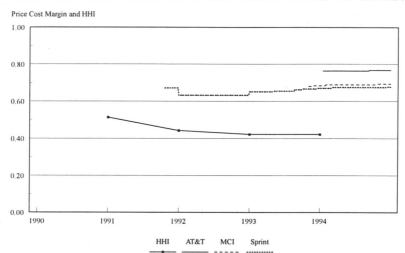

Notes: Marginal costs based on net settlement payments. Prices based on 50 minutes per month. Time of day based on 40% standard, 30% discount, and 30% economy.
Sources: Marginal costs from FCC and WEFA, rates from HTL Telemanagement, Ltd., and market concentration from FCC.

FIGURE A4–10
PRICE-COST MARGIN AND MARKET CONCENTRATION FOR DISCOUNT IMTS CALLS FROM THE UNITED STATES TO MEXICO

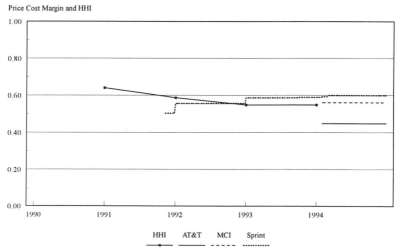

Notes: Marginal costs based on net settlement payments. Prices based on 50 minutes per month. Time of day based on 40% standard, 30% discount, and 30% economy.
Sources: Marginal costs from FCC and WEFA, rates from HTL Telemanagement, Ltd., and market concentration from FCC.

FIGURE A4–11

PRICE-COST MARGIN AND MARKET CONCENTRATION FOR DISCOUNT
IMTS CALLS FROM THE UNITED STATES TO THE UNITED KINGDOM

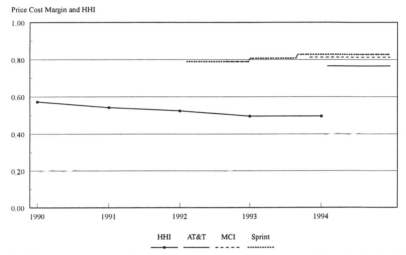

Notes: Marginal costs based on net settlement payments. Prices based on 50 minutes per month. Time of day based on 30%
standard, 50% discount, and 20% economy.
Sources: Marginal costs from FCC and WEFA, rates from HTL Telemanagement, Ltd., and market concentration from FCC.

FIGURE A4–12

PRICE-COST MARGIN AND MARKET CONCENTRATION FOR
DISCOUNT IMTS CALLS FROM THE UNITED STATES TO GERMANY

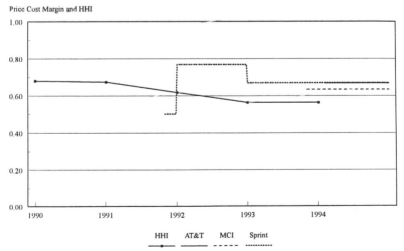

Notes: Marginal costs based on net settlement payments. Prices based on 50 minutes per month. Time of day based on 30%
standard, 50% discount, and 20% economy.
Sources: Marginal costs from FCC and WEFA, rates from HTL Telemanagement, Ltd., and market concentration from FCC.

FIGURE A4–13
PRICE-COST MARGIN AND MARKET CONCENTRATION FOR
DISCOUNT IMTS CALLS FROM THE UNITED STATES TO FRANCE

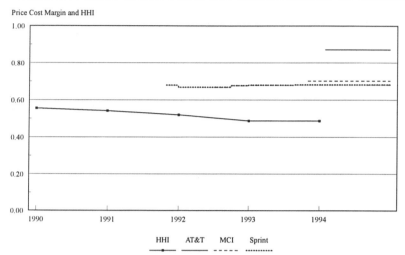

Notes: Marginal costs based on net settlement payments. Prices based on 50 minutes per month. Time of day based on 30% standard, 50% discount, and 20% economy.

Sources: Marginal costs from FCC and WEFA, rates from HTL Telemanagement, Ltd., and market concentration from FCC.

FIGURE A4–14
PRICE-COST MARGIN AND MARKET CONCENTRATION FOR
DISCOUNT IMTS CALLS FROM THE UNITED STATES TO ITALY

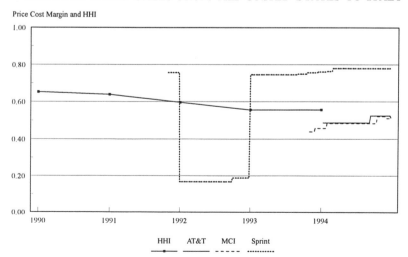

Notes: Marginal costs based on net settlement payments. Prices based on 50 minutes per month. Time of day based on 30% standard, 50% discount, and 20% economy.

Sources: Marginal costs from FCC and WEFA, rates from HTL Telemanagement, Ltd., and market concentration from FCC.

FIGURE A4-15
PRICE-COST MARGIN AND MARKET CONCENTRATION FOR DISCOUNT IMTS CALLS FROM THE UNITED STATES TO JAPAN

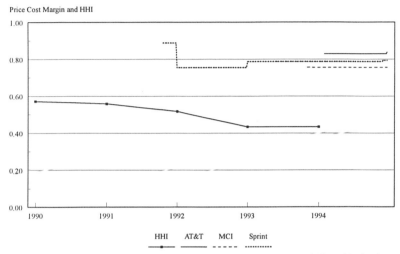

Notes: Marginal costs based on net settlement payments. Prices based on 50 minutes per month. Time of day based on 30% standard, 50% discount, and 20% economy.
Sources: Marginal costs from FCC and WEFA, rates from HTL Telemanagement, Ltd., and market concentration from FCC.

FIGURE A4-16
PRICE-COST MARGIN AND MARKET CONCENTRATION FOR DISCOUNT IMTS CALLS FROM THE UNITED STATES TO THE DOMINICAN REPUBLIC

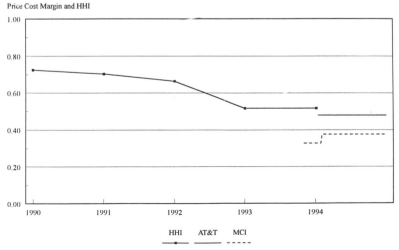

Notes: Marginal costs based on net settlement payments. Prices based on 50 minutes per month. Time of day based on 40% standard, 30% discount, and 30% economy.
Sources: Marginal costs from FCC and WEFA, rates from HTL Telemanagement, Ltd., and market concentration from FCC.

FIGURE A4-17
PRICE-COST MARGIN AND MARKET CONCENTRATION FOR
IWATS CALLS FROM THE UNITED STATES TO CANADA

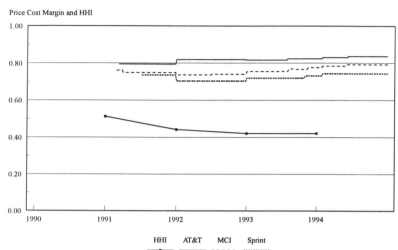

Notes: Marginal costs based on net settlement payments. Prices based on 200 hours per month. Time of day based on 85% standard, 10% discount, and 5% economy.

Sources: Marginal costs from FCC and WEFA, rates from HTL Telemanagement, Ltd., and market concentration from FCC.

FIGURE A4-18
PRICE-COST MARGIN AND MARKET CONCENTRATION FOR
IWATS CALLS FROM THE UNITED STATES TO MEXICO

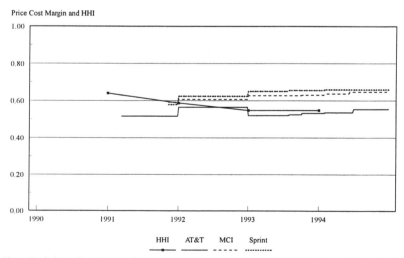

Notes: Marginal costs based on net settlement payments. Prices based on 200 hours per month. Time of day based on 85% standard, 10% discount, and 5% economy.

Sources: Marginal costs from FCC and WEFA, rates from HTL Telemanagement, Ltd., and market concentration from FCC.

FIGURE A4–19
PRICE-COST MARGIN AND MARKET CONCENTRATION FOR IWATS CALLS FROM THE UNITED STATES TO THE UNITED KINGDOM

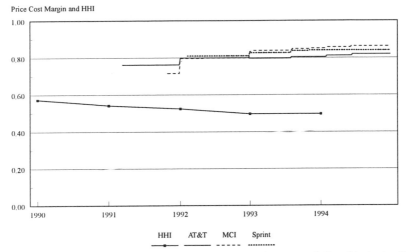

Notes: Marginal costs based on net settlement payments. Prices based on 200 hours per month. Time of day based on 60% standard, 20% discount, and 20% economy.
Sources: Marginal costs from FCC and WEFA, rates from HTL Telemanagement, Ltd., and market concentration from FCC.

FIGURE A4–20
PRICE-COST MARGIN AND MARKET CONCENTRATION FOR IWATS CALLS FROM THE UNITED STATES TO GERMANY

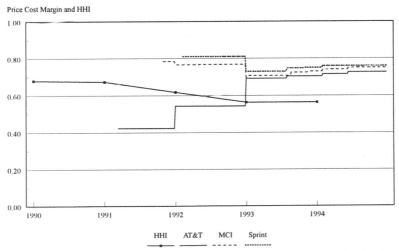

Notes: Marginal costs based on net settlement payments. Prices based on 200 hours per month. Time of day based on 60% standard, 20% discount, and 20% economy.
Sources: Marginal costs from FCC and WEFA, rates from HTL Telemanagement, Ltd., and market concentration from FCC.

FIGURE A4–21

PRICE-COST MARGIN AND MARKET CONCENTRATION FOR IWATS CALLS FROM THE UNITED STATES TO FRANCE

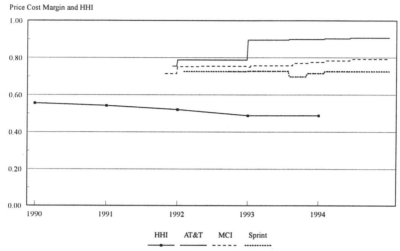

Notes: Marginal costs based on net settlement payments. Prices based on 200 hours per month. Time of day based on 60% standard, 20% discount, and 20% economy.

Sources: Marginal costs from FCC and WEFA, rates from HTL Telemanagement, Ltd., and market concentration from FCC.

FIGURE A4–22

PRICE-COST MARGIN AND MARKET CONCENTRATION FOR IWATS CALLS FROM THE UNITED STATES TO ITALY

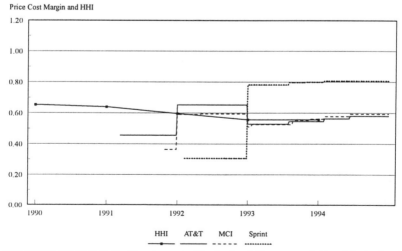

Notes: Marginal costs based on net settlement payments. Prices based on 200 hours per month. Time of day based on 60% standard, 20% discount, and 20% economy.

Sources: Marginal costs from FCC and WEFA, rates from HTL Telemanagement, Ltd., and market concentration from FCC.

FIGURE A4–23

PRICE-COST MARGIN AND MARKET CONCENTRATION FOR
IWATS CALLS FROM THE UNITED STATES TO JAPAN

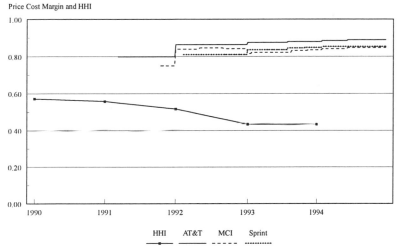

Notes: Marginal costs based on net settlement payments. Prices based on 200 hours per month. Time of day based on 75% standard and 25% discount.
Sources: Marginal costs from FCC and WEFA, rates from HTL Telemanagement, Ltd., and market concentration from FCC.

FIGURE A4–24

PRICE-COST MARGIN AND MARKET CONCENTRATION FOR IWATS
CALLS FROM THE UNITED STATES TO THE DOMINICAN REPUBLIC

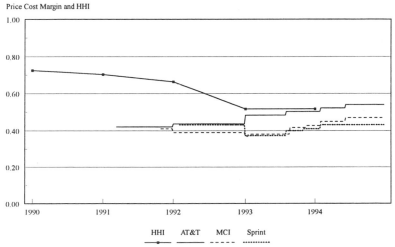

Notes: Marginal costs based on net settlement payments. Prices based on 200 hours per month. Time of day based on 85% standard, 10% discount, and 5% economy.
Sources: Marginal costs from FCC and WEFA, rates from HTL Telemanagement, Ltd., and market concentration from FCC.

References

AirTouch Communications, Inc., *1994 SEC Form 10-K* (1995).

AirTouch Communications, Inc., *1994 Annual Report* (1995).

American Telephone and Telegraph Company, *1983 Annual Report* (1984).

Ameritech Corporation, *1993 SEC Form 10-K* (1994).

"Ameritech Open Market Plan Attacked by Other RHCs," *Common Carrier Week,* May 8, 1995.

"Ameritech Seeks Entry into Long Distance," *Illinois Legal Times*, Apr. 1994, at 1.

Areeda, Phillip, and Donald F. Turner, "Predatory Pricing & Related Practices Under Section Two of the Sherman Act," 88 *Harvard Law Review* 697 (1975).

Arrow, Kenneth J., Dennis W. Carlton, and Hal S. Sider, "The Competitive Effects of Line-of-Business Restrictions in Telecommunications," 16 *Managerial & Decision Economics* 301 (1995).

"AT&T 'More Vulnerable' Than BOC's; AT&T Chairman Brown

Charges Bias by FCC, Congress & Courts," *Communications Daily*, Sept. 11, 1984, at 3.

Averch, Harvey, and Leland L. Johnson, "Behavior of the Firm under Regulatory Constraint," 52 *American Economic Review* 1052 (1962).

"Baby Bell Seeks Help on Waiver," *New York Times*, Feb. 1, 1995, at D4.

Baumol, William J., and David F. Bradford, "Optimal Departures from Marginal Cost Pricing," 60 *American Economic Review* 265 (1970).

Baumol, William J., and Janusz A. Ordover, "Use of Antitrust to Subvert Competition," 28 *Journal of Law and Economics* 247 (1985).

Baumol, William J., and J. Gregory Sidak, "The Pricing of Inputs Sold to Competitors," 14 *Yale Journal on Regulation* 171 (1994).

Baumol, William J., and J. Gregory Sidak, *Toward Competition in Local Telephony* (AEI Press & MIT Press 1994).

Baxter, William, Charles L. Brown, Stanley M. Besen, and Henry Geller, "Questions and Answers with the Three Major Figures of Divestiture," in *After the Breakup: Assessing the New Post-AT&T Divestiture Era* (Barry G. Cole ed., Columbia University Press 1991).

"Bell Companies Ask Court to Vacate Decree in AT&T Case," 67 *Antitrust and Trade Regulation Report* (BNA) (No. 1672) 62 (July 14, 1994).

Bell Communications Research, "BOC Notes on the LEC Networks, 1994" (Bell Communications Research 1994).

Bork, Robert H., *The Antitrust Paradox: A Policy at War with Itself* 347 (Basic Books 1978; Free Press rev. ed. 1993).

Brander, James A., and A. Zhang, "Market Conduct in the Airline

Industry: An Empirical Investigation," 21 *RAND Journal of Economics* 569 (1990).

Brandon, Paul S., and Richard L. Schmalensee, "The Benefits of Releasing the Bell Companies from the Interexchange Restrictions," 16 *Managerial and Decision Economics* 349 (1995).

Bresnahan, Timpthy J., "Sutton's Sunk Costs and Market Structure: Price Competition, Advertising, and the Evolution of Concentration," 23 *RAND Journal of Economics* 137 (1992).

Breyer, Stephen G., *Regulation and Its Reform* (Harvard University Press 1982).

British Telecommunications Union Committee, *The American Experience: A Report on the Dilemma of Telecommunications in the U.S.A.* (1983).

Brock, Gerald W., *Telecommunication Policy for the Information Age: From Monopoly to Competition* (Harvard University Press 1994).

Brown, Charles L., "A Personal Introduction," in *Disconnecting Bell: The Impact of the AT&T Divestiture* (H. Shooshan ed., Pergamon Press 1984).

Brown Brothers Harriman & Co., *AT&T Basic Report* (Mar. 31, 1992).

Cole, Barry G., ed., *After the Breakup: Assessing the New Post-AT&T Divestiture Era* (Columbia University Press 1991).

"Commerce Department Considers Universal Service Proposals," *Washington Telecommunications News*, Dec. 26, 1994.

Congressional Budget Office, *The Changing Telephone Industry: Access Charges, Universal Service and Local Rates* (1984).

Crandall, Robert W., *After the Breakup: U.S. Telecommunications in a More Competitive Era* (Brookings Institution 1991).

Davis, Blaine E., Gerald J. Caccappolo, and Muhammed Ali Chaudry, "An Econometric Planning Model for American Telephone and Telegraph Company," 4 *Bell Journal of Economics and Management Science* 29 (1973).

DeSurvire, Emmanuel, "Lightwave Communications: The Fifth Generation," *Scientific American*, Jan. 1992, at 114.

Domowitz, I., R. Hubbard, and B. Petersen, "Business Cycles and the Relationship between Concentration and Price-Cost Margins," 17 *RAND Journal of Economics* 1 (1986).

Donovan, Karen, "Move Over, Ms. Bingaman, New Trustbuster Is in DC," *National Law Journal*, Apr. 24, 1995, at B1.

Dorfman, Robert, and Peter O. Steiner, "Optimal Advertising and Optimal Quality," 44 *American Economic Review* 835 (1954).

Easterbrook, Frank H., "Predatory Strategies and Counterstrategies," 48 *University of Chicago Law Review* 263 (1981).

Federal Communications Commission, *Fiber Deployment Update—End of Year 1994* (July 1995).

Federal Communications Commission, *International Telecommunications Data Report* § 43.61 (various years).

Federal Communiations Commission, *Long-Distance Market Shares, Fourth Quarter* (1993).

Federal Communiations Commission, *Long-Distance Market Shares, Second Quarter* (1994).

Federal Communications Commission, *Statistics of Communications Common Carriers* (1994).

Federal Communications Commission, "What Makes the Dominant

Firm Dominant?" OPP Working Paper No. 25 (Apr. 1989).

"Five Bell Companies Seeking Permission to Offer DBS Service," *Daily Report for Executives*, Mar. 1, 1995, at A40.

Gates, Susan, Paul Milgrom, and John Roberts, "Deterring Predation in Telecommunications: Are Line-of-Business Restraints Needed?" 16 *Managerial and Decision Economics* 427 (1995).

Ginn, Sam, "Restructuring the Wireless Industry and the Information Skyway," 4 *Journal Economics and Management Strategy* 139 (1995).

Gordon, K., and John R. Haring, "The Effects of Higher Telephone Prices on Universal Service," FCC Office of Plans and Policy Working Paper (1984).

Griffen, James M., and Bruce L. Egan, "Demand System Estimation in the Presence of Multi-Block Tariffs: A Telecommunications Example," 67 *Review of Economics and Statistics* 520 (1985).

Gross, J., "Local Telephone Competition," Donaldson Lufkin & Jenrette Report No. 1226863 (May 18, 1992).

Gruley, Bryan, and Albert Karr, "Passage Reflects Bipartisan Push," *Wall Street Journal* (Feb. 2, 1996), at B1.

Hausman, Jerry A., "Competition in Long-Distance and Telecommunications Equipment Markets: Effects of the MFJ," 16 *Managerial and Decision Economics* 365 (1995).

Heckart, Christine, "SONET Strategies: Sprint Has Ring Fling," *Network World*, May 16, 1994, at 45.

Holsendolph, Ernest, "U.S. Settles Phone Suit, Drops IBM Case; AT&T to Split Up, Transforming Industry," *New York Times*, Jan. 9, 1982, at A1.

Huber, Peter W., Michael K. Kellogg, and John Thorne, *The*

Geodesic Network II: Report on Competition in the Telephone Industry (The Geodesic Co. 1992).

Joskow, Paul L., and Alvin K. Klevorick, "A Framework for Analyzing Predatory Pricing Policy," 89 *Yale Law Journal* 213 (1979).

"Justice Approves Plan to Allow Bell Company into Long-Distance," *Daily Report for Executives*, Apr. 4, 1995, at A64.

"Justice Settles AT&T Case; Bell System Agrees to Divest Local Operating Companies," 42 *Antitrust and Trade Regulation Report* (BNA) (No. 1047) 82 (Jan. 14, 1982).

"Justice Department Publishes Competitive Impact Statement on Settlement with AT&T," 42 *Antitrust and Trade Regulation Report* (BNA) (No. 1052) 371 (Feb. 18, 1982).

"Justice Department Seeks Limits on AirTouch," *New York Times*, Mar. 14, 1995, at D10.

Kellogg, Michael K., John Thorne, and Peter W. Huber, *Federal Telecommunications Law* (Little, Brown & Co. 1992).

Knieps, Gunter, and Pablo T. Spiller, "Regulation by Partial Deregulation: The Case of Telecommunications," 35 *Administrative Law Review* 391 (1983).

Kraushaar, J., *Fiber Deployment Update, 1991* (Federal Communications Commission March 1992).

"The Little Guys of Long-Distance Are Mighty Nervous," *Business Week*, June 3, 1991, at 29.

MacAvoy, Paul W., "Deregulation by Means of Antitrust Divestiture: How Well Has It Worked?" 15 *Regulation* 88 (Winter 1992).

MacAvoy, Paul W., "The Failure of Antitrust and Regulation to Establish Competition in Markets for Long-Distance Telephone

Services," Yale School of Management Working Paper (1995).

MacAvoy, Paul W., "Prices after Deregulation: The United States Experience," 1 *Hume Papers on Public Policy* 42 (1993).

MacAvoy, Paul W., and Kenneth Robinson, "Losing by Judicial Policymaking: The First Year of the AT&T Divestiture," 2 *Yale Journal on Regulation* 225 (1985).

MacAvoy, Paul W., and Kenneth Robinson, "Winning by Losing: The AT&T Settlement and Its Impact on Telecommunications," 1 *Yale Journal on Regulation* 1 (1983).

MacAvoy, Paul W., Michael Doane, and Michael Williams, "Policy vs. Reality in Establishing Competition in California Long-Distance Telephone Service Markets," Yale School of Management Working Paper (1995).

Martin, S., *Advanced Industrial Economics* (Blackwell 1993).

MCI Communications Corp., "MCI Deploys Technology Capable of Increasing Capacity by Fifty Percent without New Fiber," MCI Press Release (Aug. 30, 1995).

"MCI Hopes to Boost Network Capacity 50% through New Method," *Wall Street Journal*, Aug. 31, 1995, at B5.

Merrill Lynch, "United States Telecom Services: Long Distance Second-Tier: Pump up the Volume" (Oct. 13, 1993).

Mulqueen, John T., "Ten Years of Change," *Communications Week*, Jan. 3, 1994, at 8.

Noll, Roger, and Susan Smart, "Pricing of Telephone Services," in *After the Breakup: Assessing the New Post-AT&T Divestiture Era* (Barry G. Cole ed., Columbia University Press 1991).

"On Regulatory Front, Smaller Carriers See Major Battles in 1992," *Long Distance Outlook*, Mar. 1992, at 3.

Ordover, Janusz A., and Garth Saloner, "Predation, Monopolization, and Antitrust," in 1 *Handbook of Industrial Organization* 537 (Richard Schmalensee and Robert D. Willig eds., North-Holland 1989).

Orr, Daniel, and Paul W. MacAvoy, "Price Strategies to Promote Cartel Stability," 32 *Economica* 186 (1965).

O'Shea, Dan, "AT&T Forges Ahead with Network Upgrades," *Telephony*, June 12, 1995, at 12.

Pacific Telesis Group, *1993 Annual Report* (1994).

Pacific Telesis Group, *1992 SEC Form 10-K* (1993).

Paine Webber Inc., "Long-Distance Industry," Industry Report No. 1105870 (Feb. 25, 1991).

Patrick, Dennis, "On the Road to Telephone Deregulation," *Public Utilities Fortnightly*, Dec. 6, 1984, at 19.

Ravenscraft, David J., "Structure-Profit Relationships at the Line of Business and Industry Level," 65 *Review of Economics and Statistics* 22 (1983).

Raymond James & Assocs., Inc., *Telecommunications Industry Report: Outlook for the Interstate Access Charge* 3 (Feb. 10, 1992).

Rubenstein, David, "Ameritech Seeks Entry into Long Distance," *Illinois Legal Times*, Apr. 1994, at 1.

Rubin, Paul H., and Hashem Dezhbakhsh, "Costs of Delay and Rent-Seeking under the Modification of Final Judgment," 16 *Managerial and Decision Economics* 385 (1995).

Sappington, David E. M., and Dennis L. Weisman, *Designing Incentive Regulation for the Telecommunications Industry* 31 (MIT Press and AEI Press 1996).

Schmalensee, Richard L., "On the Use of Economic Models in Antitrust: The *ReaLemon* Case," 127 *University of Pennsylvania Law Review* 994 (1979).

Schwartz, Louis B., "Stacked Competition and Phony Deregulation for AT&T: The Proposed Telecommunications Competition and Deregulation Act of 1981," 3 *Communication/Entertainment* 411 (1981).

Sibley, David S., and Dennis L. Weisman, "Competitive Incentives of Vertically Integrated Local Exchange Carriers," University of Texas Working Paper (Aug. 9, 1995).

Sibley, David S., and Simon J. Wilkie, "A Repeated Game of Price Cap Regulation," University of Texas Working Paper (revised: Jan. 1996).

Sidak, J. Gregory, "Debunking Predatory Innovation," 83 *Columbia Law Review* 1121 (1983).

Spulber, Daniel F., "Deregulating Telecommunications," 12 *Yale Journal on Regulation* 25 (1995).

Taylor, Lester D., *Telecommunications Demand in Theory and Practice* (Kluwer Academic Publishers 1994).

Taylor, William, *Effects of Competitive Entry in the U.S. Interstate Toll Markets: An Update* (National Economic Research Associates May 28, 1992).

Thelen, Jennifer, "Dialing Direct," *Recorder*, July 22, 1994, at 1.

Tirole, Jean, *The Theory of Industrial Organization* (MIT Press 1988).

Trienens, Howard J., "Deregulation in the Telecommunications Industry: A Status Report," 50 *Antitrust Law Journal* 409 (1982).

Vogelsang, Ingo, and Bridger M. Mitchell, *Telecommunications*

Competition: The Last Ten Miles (MIT Press and AEI Press 1996).

Weichselbaum, Paul, "MCI's Broadband Telecommunications Solutions for Demanding Imaging Apps; MCI Communications Corp.," *Advanced Imaging*, June 1994, at 42.

Wiley, Richard E., "The End of Monopoly: Regulatory Change and the Promotion of Competition," in *Disconnecting Bell: The Impact of the AT&T Divestiture* (H. Shooshan ed., Pergamon Press 1984).

Williams, Tom, "Carriers Pick Up Speed on SONET Deployment; Synchronous Optical Network Transport Architecture," *Telephony*, May 15, 1995, at 32.

Wharton Econometric Forecasting Associates, *Economic Impact of Eliminating the Line-of-Business Restrictions on the Bell Companies* (1993).

Case and Regulatory Proceeding Index

Name Index

Subject Index